s for the Real Estate Investment Network's Investment Programs

"An excellent step-by-step real estate investment business to give you the confidence to become an active, successful investor."

—Cheryl Shaw

"The system has given me a proven means to buy Canadian real estate. Without this support, I would be left clueless and left without valuable mentorship!"

—Jamelle Alexander

"Good to understand the 12 Economic Fundamentals and what drives markets."

—Daniel Goff

"The system has allowed me to understand my role as a real estate investor and landlord and to decrease and/or minimize my risk."

—Dan LeBlanc

"It gave me more focus, directions, and tools to move my business of investing in real estate forward."

—Lance Bisson

"Amazing the amount of clarity I gained in a sometimes confusing industry."
—Jason Malmquist

"Absolutely essential in getting my investing jump-started. A few months in, it's keeping me on track and helping me adjust my strategy to keep the cash flow going. Thank you!"

—Marianne Malo Chenard

"Good to get me organized and systemized."

—Leonard Kolstad

"More information than I have been given in the past and I have spent thousands of dollars."

—Terry Kaiser

"To compare this system to other real estate investing educators is like comparing day to night. I get all the information on a proven system I need. I don't have to pay thousands of extra dollars to get the "next level" of training."
—Michael Colson

"Amazing, I have received so much insight on so many things that I thought I knew but didn't. A great program!"
—Bryan Nickel

"Excellent advice on making profitable business decisions and how to recognize the red flags."
—Kimberly Pashak

"The system gave me the foundation for running a successful business in real estate investing. It also gave me the impetus and confidence to pursue my goal."
—Editha Payumo

"Great. It gave me perspective, knowledge and assurance that what we are doing is right. It also gave me a kick in the pants. Thank you!"
—Chris Schulz

"Wow, like finding the goose that can lay the golden eggs—if I feed and care for it! Can't believe I found REIN! Finally."
—Mark Yates

"Way above my expectations. I can't wait to start investing. Very inspiring and motivating to have such sound information."
—Tanya Lachance

"The system is so simple and straightforward; step-by-step. It would be ridiculous of me to not do this."
—James Lawson

"It has clarified a lot of information I had already learned but had not had the chance to digest. The simplicity of the system has given me hope that even I could do this business."
—Raynah Hur

"The system provided me with an absolutely 100% proven process as well as many like-minded people who are already achieving success using it."

—Nick Davis

"Authentic—lots of Canadian and local data. Unexpected, reasonably priced and full of tips. I've now finished my window shopping of three years (Trump, Rich Dad, Poor Dad Ozzie Jurock, CANREIG, Don Campbell), books, free two-hour info nights and seminars. I have now committed to REIN and will not second-guess them."

—Joanne Smith

"It has given me a higher level of confidence in knowing it is possible for me to explore the option of investing in multi-family in the future. It has created in me more hunger and thirst for more information."

—Vee Catabay

"Incredibly useful, practical, eye-opening. I learned so many brilliant strategies to improve our business 100-fold and apply to our first apartment building, which we just purchased, and next time we buy, I have such a massive support system to back me up. Thank you so much for doing all you do to make this happen. Invaluable, impressive, professional."

—Marnie Griffiths

97 TIPS FOR THE CANADIAN REAL ESTATE INVESTOR

2nd Edition

97 TIPS FOR THE CANADIAN REAL ESTATE INVESTOR

2nd Edition

DON R. CAMPBELL

PETER KINCH | BARRY MCGUIRE | RUSSELL WESTCOTT

John Wiley & Sons Canada, Ltd.

Library and Archives Canada Cataloguing in Publication

97 tips for Canadian real estate investors / Don R. Campbell . . . [et al.]. — 2nd ed.

Issued also in electronic formats.
ISBN 978-0-470-96363-0

1. Real estate investment—Canada. I. Campbell, Don R II. Title:
Ninety-seven tips for Canadian real estate investors.

HD316.N56 2011   332.63'240971   C2010-906144-6

ISBN 978-0-470-96363-0 (print); 978-0-470-96418-7 (ePDF);
978-0-470-96420-0 (eMobi); 978-0-470-96419-4 (ePub)

Production Credits
Cover design: Ian Koo
Interior text design: Adrian So
Interior layout: Thomson Digital
Printer: Printcrafters

Editorial Credits
Executive Editor: Don Loney
Production Editor: Pauline Ricablanca

John Wiley & Sons Canada, Ltd.
6045 Freemont Blvd.
Mississauga, Ontario
L5R 4J3

Printed in Canada

1 2 3 4 5 PC 15 14 13 12 11

CONTENTS

INTRODUCTION

WHY A NEW EDITION?

The first version of *97 Tips for Canadian Real Estate Investors* drove home the fundamental truth that sophisticated real estate investors follow proven investment systems. Learn those systems and you can replicate investment success again and again and again!

We also spoke about how important it is to keep current and to adapt to shifting business conditions. This updated edition provides information to help you quickly adapt to marketplace changes. In addition to updated tips, you will also find additional financing and marketing strategies designed to enhance your investing system.

WARNING: NEVER INVEST BASED ON TIPS!

This statement may seem to be a rather odd way to begin a book titled *97 Tips for Canadian Real Estate Investors*. However, if you have read *Real Estate Investing in Canada*, by Don R. Campbell, you know that real estate investing is all about following a proven system that dramatically reduces risk and helps you cut through all the hype and misinformation that characterizes the industry.

NOW, THE GOOD NEWS ABOUT TIPS.

There are really two types of tips in the investment world. The first ones are the "hot tips" you hear from your neighbour, co-worker or family member. They're not really tips but rumours inspired by the hope of getting rich quickly. For instance, "This stock is going to go through the roof, and my friend knows someone who has insider information. You better buy now!" We've all heard dozens of these kinds of tips—and we're sure you know where most of these lead. *Nowhere*. We promise you that you won't find any of these dead-end tips in this book.

The second (and best) type of tips that exist are honed from the insights and observations of veterans who have detailed experience in the subject matter of which they speak. Most importantly, these tips do not come from people who profit if you take action on their tips. No hype, no baloney, just a lot of invaluable experience. The tips shared in this book are designed to give you advantages and strategies that make your current investments perform even better. Throughout this book, pay particular attention to each tip's **What do you need to do?** section. This is where real-world experience delivers real-world investment advice that will provide short-term results and create long-term wealth.

WHAT'S IN THIS BOOK?

What you're going to discover in the second edition of *97 Tips* is the wisdom and experience of four Canadian real estate experts all of whom are investors and, each with their own area of expertise: Barry McGuire, a legal expert; Peter Kinch, a mortgage and financing expert; Russell Westcott, one of Canada's leading real estate researchers and educators; and Don R. Campbell, an active investor with a large Canadian property portfolio of more than 150 properties, who is also president of the Real Estate Investment Network (www.donrcampbell.com) and a best-selling author.

Each of the authors has dug deeply into our decades of experience to uncover tips and secrets with the sole purpose of giving you, the reader, an advantage in the real estate market. You'll learn about mortgage secrets your banker may not even know. You'll discover legal land mines you can avoid, even if your lawyer doesn't know they exist, plus closing and buying tips that can each save you thousands of dollars on *every* property you purchase!

In addition to these *97 Tips*, you will also hear from additional experts in their field who will talk about on-line advertising secrets for real estate investors; little-known GST/HST rebate opportunities for investors; and powerful negotiation secrets. Plus, you'll discover the Critical Success Event in real estate—and how this knowledge will change your investment focus.

Each and every one of the 97 tips you'll find in this book has the potential to make your real estate investments run more easily and become more profitable. Veteran real estate investors understand how one simple tip can quickly save them thousands of dollars on their next transaction or refinance, and there are 97 of these key money- and time-saving tips at your fingertips in this easy-to-read guide.

Veteran and beginning real estate investors alike can instantly access these informative ideas and strategies anytime, anyplace—expert insights that can make or break your next deal. In other words, this book will become the real estate reference guide you'll refer to over and over again. We highly recommend you read it with a highlighter and pen, as it will spark many ideas and change how you invest, lowering risk and increasing results. It is a perfect companion to the Authentic Canadian Real Estate investment system found in the book *Real Estate Investing in Canada*.

Remember, successful real estate investing is all about focusing on the fundamentals and following a system that forces you to ask the tough questions. Use these 97 tips to help make your investment system even more fun and profitable.

The authors wish to acknowledge the extensive effort of Joy Gregory in the preparation of the manuscript this book. Wrangling so many authors and contributors was a feat of magic.

PART 1

Stop Thinking . . . Start Knowing! The Foundation on Which All Is Built

Tip #1: Go on Facts—Not on Hype.

Forget guessing or hoping. Ask the tough questions of everyone involved— vendor, realtor and banker. If you are informed, you're investing. If you are uninformed (or guessing), you are speculating.

Right up front in this book, we must be frank. We've all heard the stories about instant real estate riches, and there's a certain thrill in thinking the deal-of-a-lifetime is just around the corner. But in order to be a long-term, wealth-creating investor (instead of a speculator), you need to be realistic. Real estate, like any investment vehicle, needs to have a system, a system that forces you to ask the tough questions . . . and removes any guesswork.

To be successful in real estate investing is to build long-term wealth. The quest for the "right" property, the thrill of the negotiation and the adrenaline rush of the offer are all kind of exciting. They also complicate the process, and firmly underline the need to develop an *emotion-free* approach to decision-making.

When experienced real estate investors talk about removing the emotion from their investment decisions, they're not talking about conducting business from behind an emotional wall. They're talking about making business decisions based on solid business information and what sophisticated investors call "market fundamentals."

What do you need to do?

Commit to the facts

To make a decision based on fundamentals, always do your homework—all of it. Your homework will be complete once you can substitute the word "know" in the following sentences (where you may now be using the word "think"). For example:

"I know (not think) these renters will stay after the property changes hands."

"I know (not think) the economics of the region and the neighbourhood are primed for long-term growth."

"I know (not think) this property can be rezoned to accommodate my plans."

"I know (not think) the income this investment generates will cover *all* of the expenses of the property."

"I know (not think) that I am working with legitimate real estate investors and that any documents I sign are above board because I will not participate in a fraudulent deal."

Adopt a proven investment system

You'll learn more about what it means to "know, not think" as you move through this book. For now, it's important to get a good handle on the idea that a real estate investment system means operating on *fact-based* decision-making.

To be successful, a system must do several things:

1. Be proven to work in your country, town and neighbourhood, thus not leading you down the wrong path.
2. Force you to ask the tough questions and not allow you to buy until *all* the homework is done (thus removing emotion).
3. Leave very little to chance, thus giving you a distinct advantage buying in any market that meets the criteria.

Ⓢ SOPHISTICATED INVESTOR TIP

Remember: "Fundamentals, not emotions!" Make this your business mantra. Never lose sight of the fact that when it comes to investing money, you need cold, hard facts, not just hopes and dreams.

❶ KEY INSIGHT

In the beginning, investing with a system may proceed at a slower pace than you expect. However, with time and experience, you will learn to interpret critical information more quickly. A system-based approach means you'll never miss a critical piece of information and never get caught in a bad deal. That makes the extra effort worthwhile!

NOTES:_____

_____

_____

_____

_____

Tip #2: Fear: The Greatest Motivator and the Greatest De-Motivator. Deal with It.

Analysis paralysis is an investment killer. You get over it if you have a proven system you can trust.

Too much of the wrong kind of information can hold you back from making investment decisions. Even though you may feel like you are moving forward by collecting lots of information (some of which is useful and some of which is not), you will find that in the real world you will not make any money until you actually take the step and purchase a property.

We've all heard the "if only" stories from would-be investors. They're the offspring of those who never took any action because fear held them back. As with all things in life, action fuels success.

Novice investors need to face the fact that, when it comes to the business of learning to be a successful investor, there comes a time when just listening will hold you back. Indeed, the ability to take action is the number one difference between successful real estate investors and wannabes.

What do you need to do?

Use fear as a tool—make it work in your favour

Fear is an instinct designed to keep us alive, not control us. Use it as a motivator by turning the fear of action into the fear of missing out and you'll never have to tell those future grandkids about the time fear made you miss out on a real estate investment opportunity!

This step demands honesty. Ask yourself how often you've allowed fear to hold you back from making important decisions. Now ask yourself if that choice served you well financially. Recognize how the fear of stepping into real estate investment can keep us from earning long-term wealth.

Mind your W, S & Qs

Use the Write–Scratch–Question approach to fear management and you will find yourself answering your toughest questions.

Write: Don't let yourself stew over a new excuse. Stop what you're doing and write the excuse down on a piece of paper.

Scratch: Now cross it out with your pen.

Question: Turn that excuse into a "positive-spin question." Even if X is true, what can I do about it? Get the answers you need to eliminate the fear.

Here's what that looks like in action:

Write the excuse: "I heard that as a landlord you can get stuck with a bad tenant."

Now, **scratch out** the excuse.

Formulate the **positive-spin question**: What system can I follow to ensure I provide great tenants with a great place to live?

Answer: Check credit and references. Set the standards by which you'll accept a tenant, and set them high. Remember, you're looking for an equity-building tenant—someone who wants to treat your property as if it were his own.

Use a lease agreement that gives you a proactive way to deal with any eventuality. (Include late penalties, non-sufficient-funds (NSF) cheques, move-out notices, pets, noise, etc.)

Know your local tenancy laws and do a move-in inspection (take your digital camera along) *before* the tenant moves in. Get postdated cheques where allowed.

Write the excuse: "I don't have time to invest."

Now, **scratch out** the excuse.

Formulate the **positive-spin question**: What can I do to prioritize my time to find a couple of hours a week to focus on my real estate investment business?

Answer: Talk to your spouse/family. Look at the demands of your family life; where is extra time available?

Seek out joint-venture partners to share the time and capital investment. Explore creative but less time-intensive investment opportunities using joint ventures or registered retirement savings funds. Surround yourself with like-minded people who understand long-term investing; they will gladly teach you their tricks.

Write the excuse: "I missed the market boom."

Now, **scratch out** the excuse.

Formulate the **positive-spin question**: If real estate investment is about long-term wealth development, it must be about more than the "boom." Where can I find a trusted system to help me see the advantages of the current market?

Answer: You're in the real estate business to make money. Build a team of professionals that is designed to give you a market edge, not hold you back. Refer to the next tip for more on how to choose your team.

ⓢ SOPHISTICATED INVESTOR TIP

Practise the win-win approach to team building. Don't waste your team's time and they'll learn not to waste yours.

Never (ever!) build your team based on a discount price for services rendered.

Discount Team Members = Potential for Disaster!

ⓘ KEY INSIGHT

Learn to channel healthy fear into positive investment decisions. If the answers to your due diligence questions aren't leading you toward actual investment action, keep following the proven system until they do! Fear keeps you sharp—just don't let it hold you back. If anyone gives you advice or an opinion, always look at the source to see if they really and truly know what they're talking about. There are a lot of instant real estate "experts" popping up across the country; don't let these fly-by-nighters steal your dreams or cost you your business and your reputation.

Your 3 Biggest Investment Fears:_____

_____

_____

_____

_____

_____

_____

_____

_____

_____

_____

_____

_____

_____

Tip #3: You're the Captain, So Lead Like One!

You can invest in an island . . . you can't be the island.

You now know that sophisticated real estate investors surround themselves with experienced professionals they come to view as part of their team. *If you focus on relationships instead of money, you will optimize your business results and avoid chasing deals that prove to be time-wasters.*

To surround yourself with experience that benefits your business, you want to make sure you are getting advice based on real-life expertise and knowledge. *You want advice based on business experience, not theory. You want action takers, not action talkers!*

What do you need to do?

Go "pro" (or go home)

Surround yourself with the best of the best experts and learn to use their talent and experience as much as possible. If you surround yourself with pretenders, you may become one!

Focus on your system

Find a *real estate agent* for your system. When choosing your realtor, don't select the one you just happen to know from down the street or one you found on-line. Finding investment real estate for clients is a unique talent, so you want a realtor who has a few years of experience and who knows how to choose investment properties that fit your investment system. (See the book *Real Estate Investing in Canada* by Don R. Campbell for such a system.) These agents work for you. When you give them the parameters you're looking for and ask them not to waste your time with properties that don't even come close to fitting your system, they become valuable members of your team.

Be prepared to work with several before you find the right match, and then be prepared to listen to their advice. They may have inside information about what kind of renovations best increase value in a particular neighbour-hood. They may know about problems that landlords are experiencing in the area, or the reasons particular vendors are "highly motivated" to sell a particular property.

Find a *mortgage broker*. Once again, you're probably not going to go with the guy down the street or your local banker. Because you are now in the business of investment real estate, you need the services of a broker whose experience lies in getting mortgages for investment properties. There are bankers and brokers out there who do not fully understand the nuances of investment real estate. Don't use them. Remember, specific experience for what you need is critical. Instead, find one with extensive knowledge about mortgages for investments. Find out why they will get you the absolute best rates and the absolute best terms. The good news is, your mortgage broker gets paid by the banks—not by you.

Your *accountant* must, and we mean *must*, have a complete grasp of all the tax laws and strategies that surround real estate investing. Many accountants specialize in working with real estate investors. They have studied this aspect of Canadian tax law and know the best structures and best systems to use. An accountant with this specialized knowledge is worth his or her weight in gold. A good accountant will save you a lot of money over the years, and help you to structure your real estate so as to minimize taxes upon sale.

Work with a *lawyer* who has at least 10 years of real estate investment experience. A real estate legal specialist is critical to building wealth. A general-purpose lawyer can easily close the deal on your first home and will probably do an okay job on all your real estate purchases, but a lawyer who specializes in real estate investment can give you much more counsel. He or she will have the knowledge and strategies to save you a ton of money, protect you from liability and help you gain the confidence to keep moving your business forward.

🕐 KEY INSIGHT

Make sure each of the professionals on your team has investment experience specific to the residential real estate market. You also want them to have extensive experience in working with investors. A case in point: A real estate agent who knows you want undervalued homes to renovate and resell won't waste your time with homes already fetching market value.

Interview potential team members

Look for a real estate agent, banker, broker, lawyer and accountant who owns or has owned residential investment real estate. Experienced investors will understand why you're asking questions about their own portfolio.

Build your circle of support

Find appraisers, home inspectors and property managers that other investors know and respect.

Develop a win-win approach to business opportunities. If one lender gets all of your business, your relationship will mean more to him than if he recognizes you as a "constant shopper." If one lawyer or home inspector gets all your business, he may be more willing to help out with a tight deadline.

⚑ RED FLAG

Never choose a lawyer, accountant or any other professional based on price! This may well be the ultimate false economy, as a deal could cost you thousands of dollars if things go awry. Real estate deals are complicated. Experienced lawyers and accountants look for the critical pieces hidden within a real estate deal and they protect you from the pitfalls.

NOTES:_____
_____
_____
_____
_____
_____
_____
_____
_____
_____
_____
_____
_____
_____
_____
_____
_____
_____

TIP #4: CHOOSE YOUR JOINT-VENTURE PARTNERS CAREFULLY.

You are the captain of your own investments. Joint-venture relationships, however, can make your money go further, faster.

We've all heard the old maxim that it's not what you know, but whom you know. In real estate it is very similar: It's whom you know—and who knows what.

The opportunity to be part of joint-venture (JV) partnerships is a side benefit to building a strong real estate investment team. These partnerships help you and your like-minded partners pool money and expertise to buy more properties.

In parts 2 and 9 of this book, we will cover a number of tips about what you need to do to make these partnerships work. Here, we want to focus on the most basic elements of the successful joint-venture relationship.

Choose your partners wisely. A JV is most effective when two or more parties join together and each party brings something different to the relationship. It is quite easy to "partner" with someone in the same situation as yourself, but that will get you nowhere. For instance, if you have money but need expertise, don't partner with someone who has money but is lacking in expertise. If you are well versed in real estate and require investment funds, don't partner with someone who has the same strengths and weaknesses as you.

Build a partnership that is stronger than the two parties separately. You may have time and expertise; your partners may have investment capital and relationships with key professionals. Together, you have the potential makings of a huge winner!

WHAT DO YOU NEED TO DO?

Take control

Even if it's not your deal, it is your money. There is never a valid excuse for not doing your full due diligence. Do rely upon your JV partner's expertise, but always take responsibility for the end result. Make sure your relationship is detailed in a written agreement that has been reviewed by all partners' lawyers. Design the divorce (or exit strategy) in advance!

Get a criminal and credit background check on all partners. (It's best to know in advance just whom you're dealing with.)

Ask the tough questions

If your partner will find and manage the property in return for your investing cash or credit, make sure she has the experience and expertise to fulfil that role. Check her references; learn what other joint-venture partners have experienced when working with her. Ask about her management experience with the specific kind of property you're about to invest in and visit some of the properties she is managing. Find out if her experience includes managing property through times of high and low vacancy rates.

Make sure you ask yourself the tough questions as well: Am I doing this joint venture because I have been "sold" on it? Is it the exact relationship I need to get my investments moving forward? After doing a background check, what is my instinct telling me about this person? Can I trust her to be a partner who lives up to her obligations? And the bottom line: Does what I know about the partner fit my investment system?

Check out the deal yourself

Take a close look at the basic details. Even if your partner is the one who finds the deals, it is still your responsibility to make sure all the due diligence is completed so that you are happy with the deal.

JV deals are often bigger than those financed individually and that *will* be reflected in your financial responsibility. Sometimes a deal sounds too good to be true—because it is. Be realistic about rates of return and payback periods. Never assume your partners have done as much due diligence as you demand from yourself as a sophisticated investor. Tour every part of the property yourself some time before closing.

Never accept the basic facts at face value. Ask real estate agents familiar with the neighbourhood about current market prices. Better yet, have an accredited appraiser review the property. If renovations are required, make sure the cost estimates are accurate and protect your investment by building in a 20% overrun factor.

If the JV involves a condominium unit purchase, get a copy of the deferred reserve plan study. Look at how maintenance issues are dealt with.

 **KEY INSIGHT**

Always follow a proven system when creating a joint venture. You can find one titled, "Joint Venture Secrets" at www.reincanada.com .

 RED FLAG

Don't be a silent partner unless the deal is going well. If something seems to be going off the rails, take immediate action. Make sure you request regular updates on how the property is performing so there are no surprises.

KEY INSIGHT

If the investment property is a distance away from your core market, it is even more important that you do your homework. This *must* include price comparisons and neighbourhood analysis. And you must visit the property yourself! No exceptions!

NOTES:_____

_____

_____

_____

_____

_____

_____

_____

_____

_____

_____

_____

_____

_____

_____

_____

_____

_____

_____

Tip #5: The Critical Success Event (CSE) in Real Estate: Ask for What You Want.

Written by Alan Jacques, founder of REIN.

A few years ago, I was interviewed for a program on success. A couple of days before the interview, the interviewer was kind enough to give me a list of all the questions he was going to ask, so I had time to prepare my answers. The interview went really well until we came to the last question—it wasn't on the list.

"Before we close," he said, "I have one last question for you, Alan. With all your success in developing and identifying systems in real estate, stocks, marketing and business, what is the single most important, multi-million-dollar idea you've learned that, if you could only keep one, if you could only teach one, if you could only use one, this would be the one?"

There was a slight pause while I recovered from the surprise of getting a question that wasn't on the list. Then, without thinking, I said, "The critical success event."

There was another pause before the interviewer asked me to explain what the critical success event was. As I thought of ways to explore the critical success event concept, there was something in the way the interviewer asked me his question that caused me to reflect on my answer and deal with the concept at a much deeper level. As you will see, it has an immediate and very important application to real estate, but it applies to any area of your life.

If we stand back and observe human behaviour, we notice that most people spend most of their time working towards something. It could be completing a task at work, reading a book or making dinner. Most human activity has some sort of desired result attached to it—there is something we want to achieve. And generally humans are pretty good at doing this, especially with day-to-day tasks.

If we look more closely, we see that most things we accomplish are the result of completing a series of steps in a particular order. When this series of steps can be repeated over and over again, by different people, and still produce the same result, we call this a system.

Thus, if we want to grow a vegetable garden or buy an investment property or coach a team to victory, there are a series of steps we must take to complete the task. That's all rather obvious.

What's not so obvious is that in most processes or systems there is one critical step that, if done, virtually guarantees a result. If that same step is left undone, nothing happens. The key to being a success at anything, the key to producing the results you want, is *identifying this single "pivotal" event that leads to success*. This is the "critical success event" or "CSE." Once you identify this critical event, *all you have to do is keep doing it*! Sounds simple, doesn't it?

Let's look at a few examples. If you want to grow vegetables, the "critical success event" is planting the seeds. If you want to get in shape, the CSE is doing a physical activity, even just walking. Pretty obvious stuff.

To win a football game, the CSE is getting touchdowns. In hockey, it's shots on goal that beat the goaltender.

In business, many people get trapped by all of the distractions that go along with starting and running a business. Financial statements, business plans, financing, hiring staff, inventory control—the list goes on and on. But none of these is the CSE. How about making a profit? No, that's a goal, not an action step. The "critical success event" in business is selling something! In business, until something is sold, nothing happens.

Now, to real estate. The "critical success event" in real estate investing is *not* looking at properties, talking to realtors, doing renovations or finding investors. It's *not* getting good tenants, going through the MLS book, getting financing or even closing on a property.

No, it's none of these things. While many of these things may be important, they are really just the "extra stuff" that you may have to do. None of them are critical to your success as a real estate investor.

You see, many investors get caught up in this "extra stuff" and forget about their *real job*.

Your real job as a real estate investor, the key to wealth in real estate, the "critical success event," is . . . **submitting offers**!

If you don't submit offers, you'll never own any real estate. If you don't submit offers, all you'll have is a bunch of ideas and dreams. They're a dime a dozen. Everybody has "great ideas" (and notice how many of these people are broke!). Until you actually submit an offer, you've done nothing!

How you structure your offer and how you make the deal will affect every aspect of owning that property—what resources you need now, how much cash flow will be generated while you own the property and ultimately how much money you'll make when you sell the property.

There's an old adage about real estate that is so true: "You make your money when you buy, not when you sell." If you buy properly, your profit will be built in from day one. Donald Trump's first book wasn't called *The Art of Property Analysis*. It was called *Trump: The Art of the Deal*. I'm not saying property analysis isn't important—it is. But until you make an offer in writing, you'll never own any real estate.

"But I'm broke, I have no cash!" If this is the case, then make offers that require no cash.

"But I can't qualify for any financing!" Then make offers that do not require you to qualify for financing.

"But I'm really broke, I need cash flow!" Then make offers that produce a positive cash flow.

Whatever your barrier is, submit an offer that deals with that barrier. The worst that can happen is the vendor says no. If a vendor declines your offer, so what? Move on to the next motivated vendor.

Look at this from the vendor's side for a moment. Once a property is listed for sale, what is the one thing the vendor, and indeed the vendor's realtor, is waiting for? Written offers. Believe me, they understand that no offer means no sale!

There's an extra bonus here that may not be immediately apparent. You will learn as much from offers that are *not* accepted as from the ones that are! You'll learn how to negotiate. You'll learn about the things that motivate vendors. You'll learn about realtors. You'll learn how to analyze a property. You'll learn about yourself. You'll learn "the art of the deal."

Remember the most important rule of negotiating: Ask for what you want.

NOTES:_____

_____

_____

_____

_____

_____

_____

_____

TIP #6: PATIENCE IS AN INVESTMENT VIRTUE. "GET RICH QUICK = GET POOR QUICK."

If you focus on what you think will be "fast money," you'll waste time and resources chasing the next deal. Real estate success does not come from a "day trade" mentality.

Real estate markets are in constant flux, moving up and down as the months and years progress. You've probably met some real estate investors who chase the "fast money." As a matter of fact, we guarantee you have. They talk about each deal as if it's the *only* deal, that it is the one that will make them fabulously rich. When you see them a year later, they're often no better off financially, and still talking about the next deal that will make them fabulously rich. You'll notice they often appear anxious and exhausted. They're really up—or really down.

Worse yet, they often burn the relationship bridges that are meant to sustain their investment systems—they use people until they are done with them and then move on. Recreating their investment systems and relationships as they go along, they never ride the momentum of market fundamentals. Instead, these get-rich-quick artists become very good salespeople, with great stories about how you can join them and become fabulously wealthy. Their stories can be very compelling, even hard to resist. But resist you must if you truly want to make a long-term financial difference in your life and your family's. These short-term investors give real estate a bad name.

At the other end of the spectrum are investors who learn to practise the art of patience. Focusing on fundamentals, not emotions, will soon lead to a much more enjoyable and profitable way of investing. *Veteran real estate investors will tell you that it will take at least three years of real estate investing before you start to see the real fruits of your labour. Make sure you are emotionally prepared for this investment timeline.* Also make sure your other partners, including your spouse, share your commitment to long-term wealth.

In an average market, it takes three years for a property to really start outperforming the market. In a hot market, your results will come more quickly. But the bottom line is simple: Don't quit your day job thinking you'll be dining off your real estate profits in the first few years.

During these first three years of owning a property, you are building a foundation for your investment business. As you build that foundation, based on systems, relationships and follow-through, you will learn what it really means to make real estate investment decisions based on emotion-free *market fundamentals.*

⊘ SOPHISTICATED INVESTOR TIP

Real estate investing should not be exciting; it should be boring. Indeed, a lack of excitement is one way to know your system is working well. Feel free to look for excitement elsewhere in your life, but not in your investments!

WHAT DO YOU NEED TO DO?

Develop your research strategy

Sophisticated investors must be committed to researching the latest market information and data. Use that information to look at your target market and identify the direction the long-term real estate market is poised to take. In an average Canadian real estate market, properties will go up in some regions and down in others. Not every region is a good investment all the time. Follow the proven system outlined in the book *Real Estate Investing in Canada* and you will be sure to look at the long-term fundamentals of your market. Don't get caught by a slick salesperson—do your own research.

Use accurate and trustworthy information

Visit www.reincanada.com and sign up for the free *Canadian Real Estate Insider* newsletter. It discusses the latest trends and economic shifts and will help you keep apprised of where the markets are moving. You can also log onto www.donrcampbell.com and follow the authors on Twitter and their blogs. Remember, once you start investing in real estate, you become a business owner. That means it's your job to stay informed about market trends, market shifts and opportunities. Read the business pages, look for opportunities, speak to experts in your target market and find out the inside information.

Learn your way around websites with good economic statistics. Use the Internet to look for Canada-specific economic analysis. Find local data and local contacts you can call to ask for more information.

Read economic analysis reports released by credible sources like the economics departments of the major banks and Statistics Canada. Make sure the source is unbiased.

🚩 RED FLAG

Avoid taking direction from a company with something to sell you. If a company delivers information about why a certain town offers a great investment opportunity, look behind the curtain. Does that company have properties to sell in that region?

NOTES:_____

Tip #7: Be Prepared for the Ups and Downs: Know When to Hang On and When to Cut Your Losses.

All investment systems require some financial commitment. You also need to be committed emotionally.

Sophisticated investors learn to focus on economic fundamentals instead of the emotional aspects of investment deals. Still, there are times when emotions will creep into your investment decisions. In many cases, those emotions will be positive ones, like the good feeling that comes when you've completed a deal with lots of upside. Negative emotions can also impact decision-making, although such emotions should be kept in check because you are following a system. An example may be the worry and exasperation you feel when a property is vacant and you have to carry it without rental income.

Negative emotions can lead to poor decision-making. In the case of an untenanted property, for instance, the two worst things you could do are:

1. *Sell the property out of frustration, leaving profits on the table.* A sophisticated investor will gladly scoop the property from you—and will know your decision is based on emotions.
2. *Accept any tenant you can find.* This always backfires and ends up costing you more in the long run. Sophisticated investors follow a clear and unwavering system to choose their tenants because they know a good tenant is worth waiting for—and that compromises are detrimental.

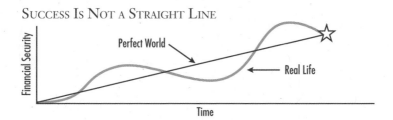

Investors who take the time to develop a good investment system know they will need to be prepared for financial contingencies. That is why it is critical that you have a Staying Power Fund for all your properties. This fund should equal a minimum of two months' worth of mortgage, condo and tax payments. Think of this money as being on stand-by. It's ready when you need it!

Once you own several properties, the fund could hold a lot of money. An emotional investor may want to use that that money elsewhere. A wise, system-savvy investor will know that money needs to stay put in case it's ever needed to cover a contingency. These reserves level out the emotional highs and lows. It is much easier to sleep at night if these funds are sitting there.

The emotional impact of financial decisions can be tricky to handle. A healthy Staying Power Fund lets you manage the highs and lows without emotion impacting decisions.

WHAT DO YOU NEED TO DO?

Develop a game plan for before and after you purchase the property

Before you buy, follow your system and take an informed look at the deal, including the creation of your Staying Power Fund. Remove the emotions— *never* fall in love with an investment property!

After you own it, run it like a business. Use tested marketing strategies to make sure it is performing at or above your projections. If the property begins to underperform, do not panic or become an emotionally motivated vendor. If the property truly fit the system when you bought it, it probably still does. But do take immediate action to solve the problem. Address why the property is vacant. Look at why it's not generating positive cash flow. Talk to your network of real estate investors and get their advice. Use sound information to avoid making decisions based on desperation.

Be honest with yourself

Remember that your system is designed to help you understand how the numbers really work. If you make the emotional decision to sell too early, you will miss the eventual payoff. As long as you bought the property without emotion and the numbers worked, all you need to do is understand that this is a business and it is your job to make it work.

Some investments simply do take much longer to pay off. Do you have what it takes emotionally to stick with an investment for five to eight years or more?

Need to know if it is time to sell? Check out the following tip.

TIP #8: KNOW WHEN TO SELL: THERE COMES A TIME WHEN CASHING IN IS THE BEST DECISION.

There are two costs to every investment: a financial cost and an emotional cost. Learn to balance the two to make it easier on you.

Most real estate investors will eventually find themselves holding a property that hasn't performed the way they wanted it to. In fact, if you haven't yet experienced this, you haven't owned enough properties. This is not like school where you get a big red "X" and are kept after school to write an essay about your mistakes. No, this is real life, where everyone makes mistakes. You need to deal with the mistake head-on, then learn from the experience and move forward.

This is true in all investments, from stocks to mutual funds to real estate. Not all investments will turn out exactly as planned. The difference between a successful investor and an unsuccessful investor lies in how they deal with these underperforming assets. Sadly, the majority of below-average real estate investors use one bad deal as an excuse to never invest in real estate again, thus killing their opportunity to create long-term wealth. Legendary investor Sir John Templeton was happy and wealthy when he was right 60% of the time.

So, be prepared. Every once in a while, a poor performer will sneak into your portfolio. Let's deal with what to do if that happens. As soon as you find yourself *worrying* about whether you should sell a property, take a step back and recognize the obvious: *You are letting emotions cloud an investment decision. It is time to eliminate the emotions and look at just the facts.*

WHAT DO YOU NEED TO DO?

Ask the obvious question

Ask yourself, "Would I buy this investment right now?"

If the answer is yes, then your job as a sophisticated investor is to look for unique ways in which to make the property work again. You may need a creative marketing strategy to attract the right type of tenant, or a few small renovations to change the income level of the property. It may even be time to fire your property management company and get one that performs to the level you need, with no excuses.

Is the bad: tenant experience making it seem like the property's not worth owning? If so, find a way to get rid of that tenant and find a new one. Each province has clear rules and regulations regarding eviction. Is vacancy an issue? Maybe you need to change your marketing strategy to attract a good tenant. Frustration over tenants—or a lack of tenants—can turn investors into the kind of emotionally motivated vendor that sophisticated investors look for! Recognize the financial drawbacks of selling based on an emotional response to a situation, then focus on fixing the frustration.

Be honest with yourself. Were your revenue projections based in reality or did you push the numbers to make them fit? Investors often find that underperforming properties didn't really fit the system and were bought based on assumptions that lacked hard and true facts. Learn from this for next time. Don't force a property to fit. It either fits the system, or it doesn't.

If the answer is no, then you need to analyze whether selling it would be the best choice. You need to look at the numbers, without emotion, and, at the same time, identify any emotional attachment you may have to that property. Maybe property values haven't increased as you expected them to. Maybe they've actually dropped, or the property's cash flow is negative, or development plans fell through that would have made the investment boom. Regardless of the specifics, it is sometimes best to take your losses, sell the property and move on to getting a positive cash flow property in your portfolio.

Ⓢ SOPHISTICATED INVESTOR TIP

Look for solutions, not problems.

Do not wait. Once the decision is made, do it

Talk to your accountant about the best tax strategies for taking a loss. Then sell the property, take your cash and immediately get back on the horse and buy a property that fits a proven investment system. Do learn from the previous deal and tighten up your investment system. Also remember to stay focused; you need to cut your losses and look for a property that will outperform your projections.

❶ KEY INSIGHT

The payoff associated with selling an underperforming property is not always easy to see. Once it's gone, however, you will experience a major decrease in your stress level. That alone will help you make better decisions and find a property you'll be proud to own.

TIP #9: LEARN FROM YOUR MISTAKES—AND THE MISTAKES OF OTHERS.

Everyone makes mistakes; the key is to make these lessons count.

You must take full responsibility for your mistakes before you can take full responsibility for your wins. If you blame everything and everyone but yourself, you must then share the spotlight every time you do well.

Taking responsibility for investments that go well is easy. Sophisticated investors know they also have to take responsibility for the investments that don't meet performance expectations. More importantly, they know that every investment-gone-bad offers a valuable lesson about what they need to do better!

These mistakes make you aware that you are moving forward, not just sitting still. If you are not making mistakes, you are not being aggressive enough. Of course, don't go out with a plan to make a mistake just so you feel you're moving forward—that would be ridiculous. Just make sure that when you make mistakes (large and small), you learn from them.

Talk with like-minded real estate investors and learn from *their* mistakes as well as your own. Members of the Real Estate Investment Network (www. reincanada.com) share their mistakes and successes so that everyone can learn from the ups and downs. Find a place where you can do the same, so you are continually learning.

What's the biggest mistake you could make? You could keep repeating the same mistake over and over. According to Albert Einstein, the definition of insanity is doing the same thing over and over—and expecting different results!

WHAT DO YOU NEED TO DO?

Base each hold/sell decision on the facts

If you buy a property that initially "fit your system" and it isn't working out, decide if it is worth selling or fixing. Creating wealth takes some courage—courage to act and courage to wait. Follow a system so you know when to move and when to sit still.

Never let a mistake hold you back from taking future action. That's what unsuccessful investors do. And never let anyone in your life ridicule you for making a mistake; in most cases they are just jealous that you are moving forward and they don't understand that *all* great investors make mistakes.

Take responsibility

Learn to acknowledge that you made a mistake, then learn from it. The insights you gain from experience will far outweigh what anyone else can ever teach you. What you know now probably would have influenced your decision to buy. That moves your personal knowledge of due diligence up a notch!

Keep your system intact; just tighten it up so you don't repeat your mistake, then move on to the next deal.

Duplicate success

The power of a proven investment system rests in its ability to consistently create results that can be duplicated. This is how you achieve what you really want—having financially consistent results over time. Practise your system and your tough decisions will become simple.

 **KEY INSIGHT**

Recognize the three components of a successful system based on duplication:

1. If it works, keep doing it.
2. If it doesn't work, stop doing it.
3. If it works, but you can't do it again, then it doesn't really work and it's not really a system!

Suppose, for example, that you get lucky and the city buys a property from you because it needs to build a new highway. Or maybe you get a hot tip on a golf-course development coming to town and buy a key part of land the developers will need. These aren't duplicatable investments. If it can't be duplicated, it's not part of a system.

NOTES:_____

_____

_____

_____

_____

_____

TIP #10: BEWARE THE REAL ESTATE PRETENDER: THEY COME OUT OF THE WOODWORK WHENEVER THE REAL ESTATE MARKET GETS HOT.

Hype sells. Your job as a sophisticated real estate investor is to pull back the curtain to see what's behind the hype.

Sadly, the real estate market is often manipulated by two key emotions: hype and fear. These two emotions are commonly used to get investors to take action. Free seminars, late-night TV infomercials and syndicated shows that try to convince you that a certain city or development is *the* place to buy into are all good examples of bad real estate hype. The seminars are free only until the pitch is made to you to buy their products. The infomercials you see on television are typically based on the market realities in the United States.

In fairness, some of the pitches might be good investments. But you'll only know if you do your *complete* due diligence. Similarly, some of the packages sold at so-called free seminars may be helpful. Just don't get caught up in the "there are only nine packages available" baloney. There are always more where they came from, but the promoters are capitalizing on the fear of missing out.

These are just a few of the many, many ways hucksters take advantage of your emotions in the real estate market. Your job is to cut through the hype and see what's real.

Just do your homework and make sure that the product you are about to buy is fact-based and proven for at least 10 years of market ups and downs—and actually works in your target geographic area! Real estate investing is not about getting rich quick, so don't buy into anyone who tells you it is.

Research can show you why the $5,000 investment in a seminar might be better spent investing in the actual real estate market. It will also help you understand that because the real estate market is constantly changing, the strategies that worked a few years ago might not work today. Similarly, the people you meet may have investment systems that truly do work for them, but won't work for you.

That's why it is so important to approach this business with a healthy perspective on what it is you plan to accomplish, served up alongside an equally healthy dose of skepticism.

What do you need to do?

You need to buy real estate

Always remember that your goal is to take action and buy real estate that fits *your* system. In real estate investment, submitting an offer and closing a deal represents the peak of your Critical Success Event.

Keep it real

The tips outlined in this book and in the book *Real Estate Investing in Canada* will help you practise the real-world application of the old adage that information is power.

Never forget that you're responsible for the decisions you make based on the information you've gathered. Make sure the information you use is dependable and comes from dependable sources. You don't want to spend money needlessly and you certainly do not want to lose money. Avoid those who decide to call themselves real estate experts because they've done well in a hot market. Look for a long-term track record.

Keep it relevant

You need to learn to make business decisions based on data that are relevant to your specific market. You'll discover that a national average price means *nothing* to you, although it is discussed frequently in the media and on the Internet.

 RED FLAG

> Positive market statistics that are nationally based may have little or no relevance to the region in which you invest. Likewise, the positive investment economics of one city won't apply to every neighbourhood in that city, and not every property in the neighbourhood will perform the same as the neighbourhood as a whole. Do your homework: Use the Property Goldmine Score Card in the Appendix to ensure you are asking the key questions.

Ask "what's behind the curtain?"

Apply the same "what's behind the curtain?" rationale to every deal you encounter. This is also true of every joint-venture partner, every mortgage broker, every "real estate guru" and every advisor you listen to. Find out what the truth is and uncover their *real* motivation. You may be disappointed.

 RED FLAG

> As a novice investor, you're an obvious target for "experts" who want your money! They will try to sell you systems. They will try to talk you into deals. They will want cash up front—reducing their risk, but increasing yours.

Learn the "What's behind the curtain?" questions!
Ask yourself:

1. What's in it for them?
2. Do they have a financial incentive to get me to take a particular action based on the information they're giving me?
3. Do they have experience in the market or are they part of the cult of opinion? (These guys know someone who knows someone who did something somewhere. That's not good enough for you!)
4. Are they currently investing in real estate and using the strategies they're teaching?
5. Do they have a bare minimum of 20 real estate transactions to their name, thereby giving them the experience of dealing with different buying and selling situations?
6. Have they been investing for at least five years, preferably 10 years, giving them experience in different market conditions? It's even better if they've been through a full up and down real estate cycle, which often takes a decade or more.

"General rules of thumb" are for those who don't really want to create long-term success. Be aware, don't get caught up in the hype of the market and, most importantly, do your own homework. It is easier to sit back and listen to someone tell you what to do, but that puts your future in someone else's hands—someone who may not have your best interests at heart. Ask yourself, Are you truly ready to do that? Are you ready to take control?

KEY INSIGHT

Coulda. Woulda. Shoulda. These are the real estate investment world's three most depressing words! They also imply a lack of due diligence. If it's information that could make a difference tomorrow, you need to have it today.

KEY INSIGHT

This book will help you investigate every deal and every person that comes your way. Don't invest on basic rules of thumb. And definitely don't invest based on a list of 97 tips! Use the tips to enhance an investment system like the REIN Quickstart system, a system used by REIN members to accumulate over $3.3 billion of real estate.

FURTHER ACTION

Join the local chapter of the Real Estate Investment Network (see www. reincanada.com). There, you'll build a network of experienced, knowledgeable team members and access unbiased research to help you reduce the fear factor.

NOTES:_____
_____
_____
_____
_____
_____
_____
_____
_____
_____
_____
_____
_____
_____
_____

PART 2

MONEY MATTERS: MORTGAGE AND FINANCING TIPS

Tip #11: Beware the New Investment Mood: Let Caution Reign.

Make sure your mortgage and financing plan shows that you're serious about being a sophisticated investor.

This tip underscores the fact that the Canadian real estate market has changed significantly since this book was first published in 2006. But if you think that market adjustments and interest rate creep are the biggest issues on the sophisticated investor's mind, you're dead wrong.

The principles of sophisticated real estate investment hold true regardless of market shifts, including those triggered by an international economic recession. What has changed post-2008 is the investment climate, a point-of-fact that's most easily recognized in the new mood of bankers and other lenders. In simplest terms: Caution reigns.

To counter market wariness of investment fraud and mortgage default, wise investors are shoring up their efforts to secure mortgages and financing by approaching lenders with a financing plan that reflects their real-world commitment to making payments and avoiding illegal activity. This strategy follows a rash of U.S. media stories about mortgage defaults and a number of high-profile mortgage fraud cases in the Canadian media. It is a shining example of how honest investors must respond to situations well outside of their control!

What do you need to do?

Be clear about your plan

Sophisticated real estate investors know that real estate investment deals cannot be approached the same way as they might approach the financing of a principal residence. Canadian banks look at mortgages for real estate investments in a dramatically different light than a residential mortgage for a principal residence.

Understand the bank's perspective

The vast majority of Canadian real estate investors conduct their businesses with honesty and integrity. That's a fact. Unfortunately, it's a fact with a complicated history.

If you've attended a real estate seminar since the latest recession started to rock the Canadian market in late 2008, you may think that *everyone* is still buying real estate. Look behind the curtain and you'll realize that that perception is clouded by the fact that you've been spending time in rooms with hundreds of informed, enthusiastic and active investors and investor-wannabes. Novice and veteran investors do need to surround themselves with people who are doing what they want to do—but don't lose sight of the bigger picture because, when it comes to securing financing, the truth will set you free!

And the truth of the matter is that real estate investors represent less than 5% of the overall mortgage business in Canada. That means that 95% of all of the mortgages originated in Canada are for homeowners—people who intend to live in the property they are buying. And here's where the story gets nasty. According to industry insiders, up to 70% of all of the fraud, foreclosures and defaults that occur within the Canadian mortgage market come from within the investment market. With numbers like that, it's no wonder lenders shine a brighter spotlight on that small group of less than 5%.

This does not mean that 70% of all investors commit fraud, or that 70% of those who invest in real estate will default. But it is true that the majority of mortgage frauds and defaults occur within a small percentage of investors that represents only 5% of the whole mortgage universe in Canada.

🛈 KEY INSIGHT

The number of Canadian homeowners who default on their principal residence mortgages is shockingly and pleasantly low (unlike their counterparts down south). Indeed, Canadians go to great (and legal) lengths to protect the roofs over their family's heads. The stats tend to tell a shockingly different story when it comes to mortgages for investment properties.

Take action on the bias

The bottom line here is that Canadian banks have a bias. They are well aware of the statistics about fraud and mortgage defaults, and you ignore those statistics at your peril. Lenders have good reason to doubt that investors will do what they say they'll do, even if you would *never* default. By the same token, that apprehension is mitigated to a certain extent when investors can show lenders that they have a plan to successfully invest in real estate with honesty and integrity. But even more important is the need for the investor to be aware of the new "mood" and rules so you can learn to work with them, not fight against them.

Update that financing game plan

Step number one in your updated financing plan requires you to understand that there are five categories of lenders in the marketplace:

1. The chartered banks
2. Credit unions
3. Mortgage-backed securities (MBS) lenders (also known as non-bank lenders)
4. Subprime lenders
5. Private lenders

Your goal as a real estate investor is to develop a game plan that will allow you to maximize your mortgage options. This will require a strategic approach that may involve all five of the above-mentioned lending options. A sophisticated investor knows that the order in which they align their lenders is more important in the long run than simply seeking out the best rate.

NOTES:_____

TIP #12: MANAGE YOUR CAP SPACE.

You will need more than one lender, so be prepared.

Chartered banks, credit unions and mortgage-backed securities lenders will be where you will want to start. But, depending on how aggressive your investment goals are, don't think you will be able to finance all of your mortgages with one lender, or even one type of lender.

ⓢ SOPHISTICATED INVESTOR TIP

Since the majority of lenders does not work with investors on a regular basis, and those that do will often only be exposed to one or two purchases per client, don't be surprised if you are not asked about your long-term plan. However, smart investors will offer this plan to their lender (or broker) so the lender can get an idea about the number of properties you intend to buy. This gives the lender an opportunity to see the potential in you as a client, and you get the opportunity to see what the lender's appetite is for working with you. You will soon learn that this is a critical step in the process, as it will help you determine the order in which you choose to do business with your lenders.

The reason you will need to finance mortgages with more than one lender is that every lender has what insiders call a "cap" space. It is the maximum amount of mortgages or dollar amount the lender will advance to you. This amount varies from one institution to another and the number is not posted, or written in stone. Indeed, because few individual clients ever encounter this cap, it is not unusual for a sophisticated real estate investor to find herself dealing with a loans officer who does not know his institution even has a cap!

That can be a big problem for investors and loan officers who encounter the cap space rule during a particular deal. But don't be alarmed. Because you are a sophisticated investor, you have already anticipated this outcome and are ready to take your portfolio to another lender and build a new relationship. This underlines why it is extra important in today's lending atmosphere to work with a mortgage broker who understands investment-specific lending.

WHAT DO YOU NEED TO DO?

Plan ahead

The number-one rule with cap space is to be proactive so that you never get caught off-guard, declined by a bank and without any back-up plan or options. As a basic rule of thumb, investors who plan to buy two to five properties over the next five years will not have to deal with cap space. If this describes your plan, focus on getting the best mortgage available in the marketplace and don't worry about who the lender should be, as it's not likely to matter.

If you plan to build a portfolio of more than 10 properties, you need to be more strategic in terms of which lenders you choose and the order in which you choose them.

Play it like a chess game

If your strategic plan includes buying 10 or more properties, approach your financing strategy as if you're playing high-stakes chess. That is, look at the chessboard from above. Those who study a chessboard at eye level only see the open space in front of them. Those who examine the board from above will see the cause and effect of each move.

From a real estate perspective, that means that you never make a move without knowing what your next move will be. Better yet, aim to think at least three moves in advance. If you're on your second property and plan to buy three more, recognize how that might impact your cap space and make sure you have a financing strategy that will move your investment game forward.

NOTES:_____

_____

_____

_____

_____

_____

_____

_____

_____

Tip #13: Know the New CMHC Rules.

The new CMHC rules can impact an investor's financing strategy.

The new CMHC rules did eliminate the "high-ratio" option, meaning the CMHC no longer insures a mortgage on an investment property without at least 20% for the down payment. But the real impact of the rule changes occurred with the underwriting rules and guidelines.

Prior to April 2010, CMHC-insured mortgages used an 80% rental offset policy. Quite simply, they took 80% of the rent and offset it against the mortgage payments. The new rules apply a 50% rental add-back policy, whereby 50% of the rent can be added to the income and only 40% of that can be used to service the applicant's personal consumer debt (which now includes their rental property expenses). Investors who do the math will realize that under the new rules, you can only use 40% of 50% (which equals 20%) of the actual rental income.

 RED FLAG

The new 50% rental add-back is a major shift from what used to be allowed under an 80% rental offset. This is a fundamental change for investors using mortgage-backed securities lenders and substantially reduces the number of investment loans that will be approved.

WHAT DO YOU NEED TO DO?

Understand the connection to CMHC

A lot of investors think the change doesn't impact them because they're putting 20% down and are not using CMHC. That's true, to a point. What many investors don't realize is that once they move into the third category of preferred lenders mentioned—the mortgage-backed securities (MBS) lenders—their link to CMHC changes. That's because MBS lenders (such as Street Capital, Dominion Lending Mortgages and Merix Financial) use institutional investors as their source of capital (as opposed to deposits from customers, upon which the chartered banks and credit unions rely). These institutional investors will make monies available to the MBS lenders on the condition that their portfolio of mortgages is bulk-insured on the back end. That means their mortgages are insured, often by CMHC (or a private insurer like Genworth Financial).

Recognize the MBS connection

Naïve investors may think they can ignore the potential link to CMHC by avoiding MBS lenders. And that may be possible if you plan to buy five or fewer properties over the next five years. If that's really your plan, you probably will be able to work with a chartered bank or credit union.

Realistically, those institutions will eventually cap your financing program, making MBS financing a critical component of your overall strategy. Investors whose strategies employ MBS lenders will obviously find themselves with more options.

Keep in mind, too, that many MBS lenders will now use Genworth for their insurance, as well as or in addition to CMHC. Even with the private insurance option, however, they will not take on a mortgage for any client who has more than four rental properties and one principal residence. Moreover, MBS lenders often have access to rates that are equal to or lower than a chartered bank at any given time, so investors who want to maintain valuable cap space at chartered banks for future deals will want to take advantage of MBS lender deals for their first four purchases.

Avoid the most common mistake

Novice investors often want to work with a loans officer at a bank or credit union where they already have a good relationship. Perhaps it's where they arranged their first home mortgage and they've already had pre-approval discussions about their new rental business.

What's typically missing from this scenario is a straightforward conversation about the new investor's long-term plan. Since neither brings up the topic of how many properties the investor plans to buy over the next five years, they never talk about cap space.

🅢 SOPHISTICATED INVESTOR TIP

Actively manage your cap space. While the bank or credit union restricts how many mortgages you can have with them, MBS lenders restrict how many you have in total. If you plan to build a larger portfolio, utilize the MBS lenders first.

RED FLAG

> Cap space decisions are further compounded when an investor involves joint-venture partners who also have a portfolio.

Never say never

Sophisticated investors know there are times when they will need to consider the last two mortgage options, the subprime and private money categories. Here's what you need to know before you enter these markets.

Subprime lenders

The subprime market has some potential for investors who've exhausted the banker, credit union and MBS options. Virtually every subprime lender in the Canadian market has lost their backing and stepped out of the market since the subprime crisis in the United States. This and the fact that conventional lenders have tightened up their lending guidelines have left a void in the marketplace that has yet to be filled.

Sophisticated investors should keep an eye on this market, as it's likely to re-emerge in the coming years. There is a market for investors who have capped out at the conventional markets and it is just a matter of time before a subprime lender steps into the void with funding that is not tied to a "securitization/insured" condition.

Private money

Other investors are challenging the idea that private money is the "option of last resort." A private lending option usually takes the form of a Mortgage Investment Corporation (MIC). This is a company that pools monies from individuals who have invested in the MIC (usually as part of their RSP contribution), then lends that money out in the marketplace on a variety of first or second mortgages. The MIC is willing to take a slightly higher (although carefully calculated) risk, in exchange for a higher rate, which they then pass on to their investors. Because MICs are usually run by a small number of directors, they can often make decisions that would otherwise not fit into a bank's parameters. As such, they will lend based on the cash flow of the property and are often not concerned with the total number of mortgages the client already owns. MICs should not be misconstrued as a zero-down option. Most private lenders will go to 80% maximum Loan to Value (LTV). Some will go as high as 85%, but they will want to see a strong borrower.

KEY INSIGHT

Private money is more expensive than a conventional loan. But borrowers must ask themselves two questions:

1. If I can avoid having a JV partner by using private money, is that a cheaper alternative than giving away up to 50% of the deal?
2. If it means the difference between actually getting the property or not, is the cash flow from the property sufficient enough to still make it a "good deal" despite the higher rates?

NOTES:_____

Tip #14: Recognize that Credit Counts.

Boost your investment options with a good credit rating.

Having a good credit rating is one of the most important factors in qualifying for a mortgage. But did you know that your credit rating is based on a "scoring" system that can make—or break—your investment opportunities? (Your credit score is a computer algorithm that computes a personal score or number based on past activity, not future promise.) Before you even visit your broker, you can (make that *should*!) use the contact information at the end of this tip to get your credit score via the country's two major credit bureaus, Equifax and TransUnion. These bureaus use scoring systems called the Beacon and Empirica. The systems generate a score derived from data based on the five categories listed below. Study them. Then look for ways to use the information to improve or strengthen your credit rating. The percentages listed with each section outline the weight they are given when determining your overall score.

Past payment performance: 35%
This is as straightforward as it gets. The fewer late payments, judgments, liens or collections against you, the better. More weight is given to recent history versus payment issues two years or older.

Credit utilization: 30%
Low balances on a few cards are better than high balances on just one or two! So review your credit card needs. Be aware that access to too many cards (and frequent use) can be deemed detrimental.

Credit history: 15%
Your record speaks for itself: the longer accounts have been open and are in good standing, the better.

Types of credit in use: 10%
Finance company accounts score lower than traditional banking or retail accounts. In other words, too many buy-now-pay-later accounts may be interpreted as a potential for future risk.

Inquiries: 10%

Promotional or administrative inquiries (including credit grant or updates) will show on your report, but won't affect your score. Shopping for credit, however, can indicate a higher risk.

WHAT DO YOU NEED TO DO?

Be honest

Problems happen. Be ready to explain any past issues. Hide nothing.

If you do have a problem with your credit history, make sure you provide a detailed reason to your mortgage broker. The more information you provide, the better they will be able to package your deal.

Watch your credit-card balances

Keep credit-card balances at or below 30% of the available credit. If you exceed 80% of the available credit on these cards, your score will dive.

Avoid credit surfing

Opening new accounts to pay down old accounts will earn you a red flag—fast.

When shopping for a mortgage, let your mortgage broker do the work. If you shop your deal from bank to bank, each bank will pull a credit report on you, thus lowering your credit score (see Inquiries, above). Brokers pull one credit history and use it for all the financial institutions.

> **🛈 KEY INSIGHT**
>
> The rise in fraudulent use of technology means many banks now insist on pulling their own "verified" credit bureau report in addition to one provided by the broker. Similarly, expect banks to pull their own report even after you provide them with one. This may have a temporary impact on your score but it will be very minor. If your score has dropped significantly in recent months, that's likely a different issue.

Use credit wisely

Always remember: someone *is* watching. Every time you apply for a credit card or loan, your score is affected, so having too many credit cards in your name is *not* a great idea. If you need a credit card, get a couple at higher limits instead of a number of different ones.

Consolidate your consumer credit in a low-interest loan or a secured line of credit. Keep your credit-card balances as low as possible. Using loans and mortgages wisely provides you with the leverage all investors need.

Keep the big picture in mind

Sound credit choices generate a sound credit history. Poor choices may come back to haunt you.

Check your history every six months

This step is really important. Contact the two main credit-history providers at least twice a year to review your credit history. You may find inaccurate information in your file, which needs to be immediately removed. All it takes is one wrong keystroke to give you a bad credit rating based on someone else's record. Make sure your rating is based on accurate data.

RED FLAG

The frequency of fraud and identity theft is increasing, so it's even more important today to keep an eye on your credit file. Simple identity theft could leave you with a mortgage, loan or credit card that you never applied for. Imagine your shock when you get a call from a bank saying you've missed the last three payments on a mortgage you didn't even know you had! One key way to protect against this is to continually monitor your credit history. In fact, for a small fee, you can be advised electronically every time something changes on your credit file. It's a great investment and you can contact the credit bureaus to sign up! And remember to never listen to someone who offers to pay you a fee to "use" your credit. As crazy as it seems, this scam is all too common.

KEY INSIGHT

Mistakes happen. If your credit history has a few flaws, highlight them when talking to your broker. Provide them with the information they need to recognize that your borrowing strategies are back on track and what you're prepared to do to maintain a positive credit rating. Honesty is always the best policy.

To request a copy of your report and more information:

Equifax
1-800-465-7166
www.equifax.ca

TransUnion Canada
1-800-663-9980
Quebec only: 1-877-713-3393 or 514-335-0374
www.transunion.ca

Get a copy of the report "Understanding Your Credit History and Credit Score" by registering as a buyer of this book at www.realestateinvest ingincanada.com . This 16-page guide, produced by the federal government and available at no charge, clearly outlines how to read and fix your credit history and credit score. Register your book today to receive it!

NOTES:_____

_____

_____

_____

_____

_____

_____

_____

_____

_____

_____

_____

_____

_____

_____

_____

_____

_____

_____

TIP #15: GET PRE-POSITIONED, NOT PRE-APPROVED.

Start your property hunting expedition with a visit to your banker or mortgage broker.

Your relationship with your mortgage broker is going to be critical as you move forward as an investor. (Start building that relationship early; use the strategies outlined in *Real Estate Investing in Canada* to ensure you are maximizing the relationship.)

A good mortgage broker will do more than source a mortgage for you. He or she will help you design a long-term plan so that the types and terms of mortgages correlate with that plan. Any mortgage broker can get you a mortgage, but one with expertise and vision will make sure it fits into your plan. Be selective.

The best way to know if the person you are dealing with is an expert in investment financing is to ask them to help you with your "plan." If they do not show interest in where you want to be five years from now and how many properties you plan to buy, you will be in danger of not structuring your portfolio in the best way. Also beware of brokers or bankers who tell you that you will be "pre-approved" for a mortgage. Technically speaking, since you are buying a rental property, the key to qualifying (in most cases) will be the cash flow from the property. Since you will not know this before shopping for a property, a broker or banker cannot "pre-approve" you for a certain amount.

What they should do is "pre-position" you for your next purchase. Pre-positioning a client takes into consideration his current and long-term needs/goals and positions the client to qualify for his next purchase based on certain assumptions. This is referred to as taking a "portfolio approach" to lending as opposed to a "transactional approach." A portfolio approach looks at the best way to structure your mortgage portfolio based on your long-term goals so that you do not run into cap space issues or, as many investors refer to it, "the brick wall." A transactional lender/broker will only look at the deal in front of him or her and ignore or be unaware of the long-term implications of the wrong advice today. That is why it is critical to be pre-positioned with a rate-hold for your next property.

WHAT DO YOU NEED TO DO?

Understand what pre-positioning means

A pre-positioning consultation is not a licence to buy! The lender still needs to approve the property in terms of value, location, type and condition.

Beware what are estimates only

You cannot get a formal pre-approved mortgage over the Internet. Know that and act accordingly. Internet mortgage calculators do not give you permission to borrow funds from a specific lender, nor do they provide any kind of "guarantee" regarding how much money a certain lender will be prepared to let you borrow. **They are just estimates.**

Mortgage-calculator tools available on various websites will help you determine how much you *may* be able to borrow. This can provide a useful starting point to help you apply for a mortgage. These tools can also help you forecast what your monthly mortgage and interest costs will be.

 **KEY INSIGHT**

When using online calculators and mortgage loan analysis tools, make sure you use Canadian sites. Mortgages are calculated differently in Canada than in the United States and you'll want to do your analysis based on Canadian calculations!

Ask for a rate-hold

If you're still not committed to a particular property, ask for a "rate-hold," especially if interest rates are rising. This sets an interest rate for your future use, without committing you to that lender. If interest rates rise during the term of the rate-hold, you're protected. If rates go down or you find a better deal with another lender, you're under no obligation to use the rate-hold.

While the interest rate are a key factor in finances, you must always confirm the numbers with your broker after you find a property to ensure you are properly pre-positioned for making an offer and know exactly how much is required for the down payment.

RED FLAG

Never, ever remove your financing conditions before getting confirmation that all of your conditions have been met. Just because your banker or broker says you are approved doesn't mean it is a done deal. Only after you receive an official written confirmation from the lending institution that all of your conditions and subjects have been met can you feel comfortable about removing financing conditions. *Don't get caught short by acting too hastily!*

NOTES:_____

Tip #16: Use Facts to Tackle the Mortgage Qualifying Obstacle.

Banks want to know you can make your payments.

Qualifying for a mortgage is the first obstacle faced by real estate investors. Sophisticated investors know it's possible to overcome this hurdle even if they have a fixed income. All you need to do is clarify your personal financial situation and show you can make payments.

What do you need to do?

Verify your debt and income

Before you qualify for a mortgage, you'll need to verify your debt and income. Banks want to know you're not spending more than 40% of your total verifiable income on your monthly debt commitments. They do this via the Total Debt Service Ratio (TDSR). It shows your total verifiable income versus your monthly mortgage payments (P&I), property taxes, condo/strata fees (if applicable) and any other monthly consumer debt that shows up on your credit bureau report.

Mortgage insiders call this ratio your Debt Service Limit (DSL). It's calculated by multiplying your verifiable income × 40%. *Verifiable* is key. If you are an employee, verifiable income is the amount that shows up on your T-4, pay stub or T-1 General. If you are self-employed, your verifiable income is a two- to three-year average of line 150 of your tax return (which is the "net" income, not your gross earnings).

Separate personal and portfolio

To buy multiple properties with a fixed income, separate your debt into two categories: personal and portfolio. Draw a line down the middle of a page and write Personal and Portfolio on either side of the line. On the personal side of the divide, add up the amount of your monthly Personal Consumer Debts (PCDs). Then calculate your DSL (verifiable income × 40%). The rule is simple: Your PCDs cannot be higher than your DSL.

Look for positive cash flow

If 40% of your verifiable income covers your personal monthly debt commitments, look at your portfolio/investment mortgages. If the real estate you are buying is generating a positive cash flow, work with a bank or broker who will offset at least 70% of the rent. That should ensure that you end up with a surplus of cash flow every month.

Most investor-friendly banks will either add the surplus income to your verifiable income or, at the very least, use it to neutralize the expenses of your rental portfolio. Once the mortgage debt on the right side of the page is neutralized (in other words, the portfolio services itself), then all we need to do is to ensure that we can service your monthly PCDs with 40% of your verifiable income on the left side and you should be able to continue purchasing real estate until you hit the cap space at each lender.

🔑 KEY INSIGHT

Lenders use your personal debt data to calculate mortgage eligibility and how much they're prepared to lend you. Lenders won't give you money based on fictitious numbers or a financial picture based on wishes. This is another important reason to keep track of your consumer (non-investment) debt and to check your credit history often.

NOTES:_____

_____

_____

_____

_____

_____

_____

_____

_____

_____

_____

_____

_____

_____

_____

_____

_____

_____

TIP #17: OPTIMIZE YOUR DOWN-PAYMENT OPTIONS.

Learn to make a limited amount of investment capital cover a maximum number of investment properties.

Once you know you can qualify for a mortgage, the second obstacle is the down payment. While many late-night TV real estate "gurus" talk about low-down or zero-down options, smart investors know that positive cash flow is critical to overcoming the obstacles associated with qualifying for a mortgage. They put down 20% or more because it boosts cash flow. Those in tune with recent changes to government-backed insurance through CMHC also know that high-ratio mortgages for investment properties are no longer available to Canadian consumers. Ultimately, the burning question becomes: "How do I make the amount of money I have stretch to be able to purchase as many properties as possible?" There is no magic answer. But there are a variety of strategies and options with which you need to be familiar.

 RED FLAG

Review these strategies with care. While there are ways to borrow money with less than 20% down, always analyze how putting less money down will impact your cash flow and impede your ability to qualify for the next mortgage.

WHAT DO YOU NEED TO DO?

Know your 7 options for down payments

1. Liquid Assets

Liquid assets comprise any money you have that is readily available in cash form, or an investment that could be liquidated on short notice. Having 20% of your own capital is ultimately the strongest position to be in, if only because it's money you won't have to borrow or be required to take on a partner to access. Since you don't pay interest on your own money, this helps you maximize your cash flow and make a profit.

2. Equity from Real Estate

This is an area that can create some confusion for market neophytes. Generally speaking, a percentage of money that you have as equity in your principal residence or another rental property may be used to form part or all of your down payment on an investment property. It is important to note that they will not allow you to use borrowed money in the form of an unsecured line of credit as part of the down payment on a rental property. However, you may take money from a secured line of credit on your home or other property and use it to create the 20% required to buy an investment property.

But isn't money borrowed from home equity the same as financing 100% of your purchase? Yes and no. Canadian banks see home equity as your own capital (as opposed to an unsecured line of credit). As such, you can use it to formulate your down payment.

🔇 SOPHISTICATED INVESTOR TIP

Sophisticated investors calculate the accessible equity in their homes with the following equation:

(Market Value of Home × 80%*) − Existing Mortgage and/or Line of Credit = Potential Accessible Equity

*80% is the conventional limit before the mortgage is considered "high ratio" and requires insurance.

3. Subprime Mortgages

Prior to 2008, there were many subprime mortgage options on both sides of the border. Although the U.S. subprime-market boom and bust is well-documented, few people realize that until 2008, the number of subprime mortgage options in Canada was also growing, with some brokers offering zero-down options for Canadian real estate investors. After 2008, many of these subprime options were no longer available. Others, like XCEED Mortgage, applied for "bank status" and became "A" lenders backed by CMHC. By 2010, this segment of the market was virtually eliminated, with the exception of a few subprime lenders such as Optimum Mortgages and Home Trust.

Today's subprime lenders offer the flexibility of "stated-income" or relaxed rules on income verification. They are not likely to allow high-ratio mortgages and may even require down payments as high as 35%. With higher rates and sometimes fees, these are not considered a "first choice" lender.

🕐 KEY INSIGHT

Markets change. Tighter rules by CMHC do open new opportunities for a different kind of subprime lender. Look for more subprime options in years to come.

4. Private Money: Second Mortgages

Frequently maligned as a "last resort" alternative for those who cannot qualify at the bank, private money is a legitimate alternative for some investors. It's definitely more expensive, with interest rates on first mortgages ranging between 7% and 10% and second mortgage interest rates between 12% and 14%, plus fees. But private lenders are not governed by bank rules and can apply a more "common-sense" approach to doing business. This may mean more flexibility in terms of income verification for self-employed individuals and allows loans based on the equity in the property as much as the strength of the borrower.

Do not construe private money as a "zero-down" option. Many private lenders are willing to lend up to 85% if the cash flow from the property warrants it. None is likely to lend above 90% of the property's value.

🅢 SOPHISTICATED INVESTOR TIP

Always do the math when working with any higher-priced alternative. If the property that you are buying is a great deal (i.e., in terms of cash flow and equity appreciation) and you need private money to close it, figure out if the cost of financing is worth it. Also, consider the duration of the loan. Savvy investors may use private money to close a deal knowing they can refinance within six months to a year. This strategy assumes that one of the following three things change:

1. Your personal financial situation (i.e., verifiable income)
2. An increase in rents (cash flow of the property)
3. An increase in equity (by way of the market or a cash infusion)

Again, does the math make sense?

RED FLAG

Private money may be used as a second mortgage to help with the down payment, but many banks will not allow a second mortgage to be placed behind their first for a rental property. Don't get caught short! Always confirm that the first mortgage holder will allow this strategy before you proceed with the second.

SOPHISTICATED INVESTOR STRATEGIES

Interalia Mortgages

An interalia mortgage is a blanket charge over two or more properties. This is a favourite tool for private lenders as it allows them to use more than one property as collateral security. Most banks will allow an interalia over two properties, but seldom will apply this type of mortgage to more than two properties. A private lender may elect four or five properties to "cross-collateralize."

This may allow an investor to effectively purchase a rental property with zero down, assuming the cumulative loan-to-value ratio of the five properties combined did not exceed 80%.

5. Vendor Take-Back

A vendor take-back (VTB) is a second mortgage provided by the vendor. Let's say a borrower arranges a first mortgage for up to 75% of the value of the home, but does not have the entire 25% in cash for the down payment. He could negotiate with the vendor to provide up to 10% of the down payment in the form of a second mortgage registered against the property. The vendor will receive monthly cash flow on the money they lent (and at a higher return than they could get at a bank). Better still, their loan is secured against their former home. Investors win because they can secure the purchase with a lower cash down payment.

Two key points to consider are

a. Because it's a second mortgage, not all banks will allow it. Check with the first mortgage holder before proceeding.
b. In light of the stricter credit guidelines since 2009, banks that do allow VTB mortgages will want the borrower to have at least 10% to 15% of his own money in the game. This is more than a guideline, it's a rule.

VTBs are more popular in a "buyer's market" because they typically require a motivated vendor. As many current homeowners are not happy with their investment options, this is an alternative they may well be open to if it's properly explained. Sophisticated investors make it their job to educate vendors about the benefits!

🔵 KEY INSIGHT

All high-ratio mortgages (including the VTB) give investors a chance to put less money down. Be honest about what that means. The less money you put down, the higher the cost of borrowing and the lower the cash flow. Make sure increased costs in your portfolio do not negatively impact your personal finances.

6. Joint-Venture Partnerships

The many forms a joint-venture (JV) partnership can take are discussed elsewhere in this book. In its simplest form, it generally means the investor does all of the work to find a property and finds another party willing to invest in that property. The outside party usually provides the down payment and closing costs, with the investor taking care of everything else. Both parties go on title and are 50/50 partners, with everything fully disclosed to the lender.

Sophisticated investors see JV partnerships as the best solution for real estate investors who want to acquire enough properties to accomplish their goals, but have a limited amount of capital to make it happen. It is far better to find two dollars than to try and stretch one dollar into two with various high-ratio options. If properly used, this strategy can provide unlimited opportunities for investors to grow their portfolios.

🚩 RED FLAG

When you approach a bank with a JV partner, the bank lumps together each party's assets and liabilities. So choose your partners carefully. They may have the down payment available, but could disqualify you based on debt or other issues. Remember the DSL and PCD equation from Tip #16? With a JV deal, the two are combined to form a joint DSL and PCD.

7. Property Flips

Flipping property in itself is not a down payment option. Indeed, many sophisticated investors discount any connection between the real estate flip/quick buy-and-sell deal and longer-term real estate investment.

With proper due diligence in the right market, however, this strategy can be a great way to increase your capital base so you can afford the down payment on a long-term buy-and-hold property.

RED FLAG

Banks are flip averse! Most will not provide a first mortgage on a property that will be resold within six months of purchase. Private lenders are more than happy to lend on this type of purchase. And why not? Since they charge fees on each transaction, they are happy to get their money back sooner than later so they can re-lend those funds back into the market (and charge another transaction fee).

KEY INSIGHT

"It's not illegal unless you get caught!" These are killer words from very poor advisors. No matter how desperate you are to get a property or a mortgage, *never ever* sign a document that outlines something you are not going to do. Some questionable mortgage brokers will ask investors to sign a document that states they are moving into the property, even though it is obvious they are not. This is not only lazy, it is bank fraud! Remember, brokers, real estate agents, accountants and lawyers work for you, not the other way around. Don't put yourself in a fraudulent situation just because you're told others are doing it. Remember, it will fall back into your lap when it gets discovered, and your advisors can claim innocence, leaving you to suffer the consequences of committing a fraudulent act.

NOTES:_____

_____

_____

_____

_____

_____

TIP #18: LET YOUR LONG-TERM PLAN SET YOUR FIXED VS. VARIABLE RATE OPTION.

To float or not to float? It's not as black and white as sink or swim!

The Canadian real estate investment market may no longer be characterized by low (and falling) interest rates. But the debate over opting for a fixed-versus variable-interest rate remains complicated, and part of the confusion is caused by a basic lack of understanding about how interest rates work, coupled with media stories that promote fear in all the wrong places!

Here's what you need to know. First, there are two kinds of interest rates in Canada and they are governed by different factors. The "prime" interest rate is controlled by the Bank of Canada (BOC) and dictates variable-rate mortgages. This rate is meant to either stimulate the economy or to maintain inflation at or near 2%.

"Long" or "fixed-term" interest rates are governed by the bond markets. Fluctuation in bond yields impact the profitability of fixed-rate mortgages for banks. Bond yields can experience daily fluctuations, but react to the *anticipation* of an event more than to an actual event itself.

Let's look at what that means. Before April 2010, markets were so confident the BOC was not going to change the prime lending rate that there was little change in bond yields and little change in long-term mortgage rates. That changed in April when talk of economic recovery prompted speculation the BOC would start to increase prime interest rates (largely to manage inflation). In anticipation of that move, the bond market reacted by "pricing in" an anticipated increase. That led to a sudden rise in long-term rates. When the BOC did not raise rates in April, the bond market settled down, this time anticipating prime rate stability. Subsequently, the long-term rates fell back to lower levels.

The same scenario erupted again in late May 2010 as we approached the BOC's June 1 rate announcement. This time the BOC raised its prime rate one-quarter of a point (to 2.50% from 2.25%). That was less than the bond market anticipated, so by the time the BOC announcement was made, long-term rates had already been pushed higher. Again, bond markets settled down after the BOC announcement. This is an example of how long-term interest rates can fluctuate on a consistent basis.

All of the hype that surrounds the *anticipation* of a BOC rate-change announcement feeds the emotional angst of investors. Many novice investors believe that the hype implies that it's better to lock in a rate than float. But is that advice correct? Not necessarily.

WHAT DO YOU NEED TO DO?

Avoid speculation

Interest rates matter, but sophisticated investors do not let the fixed- versus variable-rate decision keep them up at night! They recognize that efforts to predict rate changes are steeped in speculation, so wisely choose to make their rate choices based on their own situation.

Look at the facts

The prime rate will go up eventually. For this to happen, the economy will need to continue a steady recovery and the Canadian dollar will need to remain below its U.S. counterpart.

Crunch the numbers

Let's look at a $300,000 mortgage with a 35-year amortization. The buyer can take a variable-rate mortgage (VRM) at prime minus 0.50% or go with the prevailing five-year rate of 4.5%. Prior to June 1, 2010, the buyer's introductory interest rate would have been 1.75% (2.25% − 0.50%). This was obviously much less expensive than the existing five-year rate at the time. If prime increases to 6% over five years, the up-front savings will not last. But what's better: prime minus 0.5% today, but rising to 6% over the next five years, or the 4.5% fixed rate that builds in stability?

To make the comparison as real as possible, we decided to choose the VRM, but increased monthly payments to match what you would pay if you took the five-year fixed rate. This meant payments of $1,412.05 versus the $954.78 payments the buyer could have made under the VRM. The net result was the VRM mortgagor who made the higher payments ($457.27 extra per month) accelerated the principal paydown. The net result over a five-year period was that the buyer who took prime minus 0.5% but made the exact same payments as the consumer who chose a fixed rate of 4.5% paid an additional $16,608.17 off the principal balance by the end of their five-year term—even though the prime rate was as high as 6% (which arguably is not likely).

The real key to this argument is deciding what you believe. If you believe the prime rate is not likely to rise above 6% over the next five years, then float today but increase your monthly payments by as much as your budget can afford so that you reduce your debt exposure over those five years. If, however, you believe that our economy is vulnerable to a housing bubble and significant rate hikes, then simply take advantage of today's historically low interest rates and lock in now for five, seven, or even 10 years and sleep well at night.

Devise a game plan

The example cited above does not provide a definitive answer regarding an individual investor's decision to float or lock in. To make that choice, crunch your own numbers and then ask yourself the following:

• Can I adjust my investment budget and avoid payment shock when rates increase? (Always assume they will increase.)
• Can I accelerate the rate at which I reduce the principal balance so that when rates rise and my mortgage is renewed, I will renew with a lower principal balance in a higher-rate environment?

Be prepared to change your mind later

There is no harm in changing your mind and moving from a VRM to a fixed rate.

 **KEY INSIGHT**

A bad investment is one that keeps you up at night! If your late-night fears make you think the float-versus-fixed-rate decision is really sink or swim, swim to the edge and lock in a rate. Most VRMs feature a lock-in option that lets you convert your floating rate to a fixed rate. It is very helpful if interest rates begin to rise and you want a rate you can count on.

KEY INSIGHT

Keep the real facts in mind and don't get caught up in the hype. A quarter-point increase adds $10.41 a month for every $50,000 of mortgage. It's obvious there's no need to make a panic decision when rates move. Stay real. Avoid the hype!

ⓈSOPHISTICATED INVESTOR ACTION STEP

Statistically speaking, the variable-rate mortgage has outperformed a fixed-rate mortgage more than 80% of the time over the past 30 years. But the real key for real estate investors is to determine if they are at a point where they wish to accelerate their debt reduction or maximize their cash flow. If you are maximizing cash flow, then a variable-rate mortgage is the lowest-cost alternative in the short run, as long as you can live with the fact that it might go up. However, if your focus is to debt reduction and you want to accelerate the speed in which you pay off your mortgage, then the best option is still to take the variable rate today, but make your monthly payments based on the existing five-year rate. Doing so will accomplish two things:

1. The extra payment will go straight off your mortgage and accelerate your mortgage paydown.
2. When your mortgage comes up for renewal, you may be renewing into a higher-rate environment, but you will be doing so with a lower-principal balance.

NOTES:_____

_____

_____

_____

_____

_____

_____

_____

_____

_____

_____

_____

_____

_____

_____

_____

_____

_____

Tip #19: Shave Money Off that Mortgage.

Keep your eye on the prize: Learn how prepayment options let you pay off your mortgage or accumulate equity sooner.

The property is yours. Now what?

Real estate investors buy and sell property to generate long-term wealth. Sophisticated investors never lose sight of the fact they're working with borrowed money to create this wealth, and that by maximizing this financial leverage they will create wealth more quickly.

Ⓢ SOPHISTICATED INVESTOR TIP

Good debt vs. bad debt: Is there really a difference? The mainstream discussion regarding debt is that it is bad, so the more debt you have, the worse it is. That is true, but only in one sense. Debt is bad only if it is consumer debt or non-deductible debt. If the debt is used to create wealth through investing, then the debt is what we call good debt and it provides investors with the leverage they need. Make sure you analyze your debts, get rid of non-deductible and consumer debt and put deductible investment debt to good use.

So what's the bottom line? Mortgage prepayment options let you have a direct impact on your principal balance. Prepayment options let you pay off your mortgage sooner and can reduce your interest costs by thousands of dollars, while at the same time creating equity with no additional effort on your part. *That means more money in the bank—or more money to invest in future projects.*

Not all investors focus on paying down their investment mortgages, and some consider it a waste of good capital. However, if you can pay it down with no additional impact on your cash flow, then why not?

What do you need to do?

Review your prepayment options

Learn how your mortgage prepayment options work, then use any opportunity you can to pay off that principal. Interest-rate creep aside, today's low-rate environment provides an excellent opportunity to accelerate your debt reduction and pay down your mortgages or other high-interest debt. This is bullet-proof advice against future market uncertainties.

Virtually every mortgage has the option to prepay up to 20% of your mortgage balance in a given year. Most mortgages allow you to double your payments with no penalty.

🔵 SOPHISTICATED INVESTOR TIP

A lack of excess cash at the end of the year is the reason many investors don't prepay more of the mortgage. But why wait to the end of the year to make a lump sum payment? Determine how much extra you can allocate towards the mortgage every month, then increase your monthly payments to match that amount and enjoy watching your principal balance fall.

Every dollar you pay above the minimum payment is a dollar you never pay interest on!

Make bi-weekly payments

The simple switch from monthly to bi-weekly payments lets you make 26 payments a year. That equals two extra payments every year. The extra cash is taken straight off the principal balance and you really haven't dramatically increased the amount you've paid every year.

Round up that number

A penny saved is a penny earned and that same principle applies when you round up your mortgage payments. Every additional dollar you pay is taken directly off the principal. If rounding up your payment won't dramatically affect your cash flow, or put you into a negative situation, then speak with your bank. The math can really pay off.

This is what it looks like when you round up a bi-weekly payment of $1,150: Round up from $1,150 to $1,200 $50 × 26 payments = $1,300

That's $1,300 a year that goes straight off your principal.

Investors will always encounter people who are fearful of housing bubbles and rising rates. The truth is, no one knows for sure what the future holds. But one thing is certain: you will never regret having more equity in the future. If you take advantage of a low-interest-rate environment to accelerate your debt reduction while maintaining a positive cash flow, you will insulate yourself from whatever the future holds.

🌑 KEY INSIGHT

Wise investing demands keen attention to what sophisticated investors might call "sweating the details." Never treat this as a sideline hobby, even if it is something you are doing very part time. Take this business seriously; explore all the options that can reduce your expenses. Ask yourself, "If I saw a $100 bill lying on the sidewalk, would I pick it up?" If the answer is yes, think the same about every $100 you can save in expenses. It is all the same $100!

NOTES:_____

_____

_____

_____

_____

_____

_____

_____

_____

_____

_____

_____

_____

_____

_____

_____

_____

_____

_____

_____

_____

_____

_____

_____

_____

_____

_____

TIP #20: CHECK THE PAYOUT STATEMENT.

Whether replacing the current mortgage with a new one, or paying it out completely, you are responsible for what you don't know.

If making additional payments on a mortgage is a good policy, an outright payout must be better. Right? Maybe. It comes down to the math once again.

All mortgages have a payout penalty, and one will be applied if you want to pay out a mortgage before its term ends. A typical penalty is three months' interest on variable-rate mortgages and an interest-rate differential (IRD) on fixed-rate mortgages, which can be significantly higher. If you are going to pay out a mortgage for whatever reason, there is one strategy that will save you money. Most mortgages contain a provision that says you can pay out part of your mortgage without penalty. A 10% paydown used to be pretty standard, but some agreements go as high as 20%.

Here's how you take advantage of this strategy to save you money. Before you pay out the whole mortgage, you should make the maximum no-penalty principal paydown, thus reducing the remaining balance. When the lender calculates the interest penalty on the mortgage you want to pay out, the penalty will be calculated on this reduced balance.

WHAT DO YOU NEED TO DO?

Get your payout statement

Get a copy of the payout statement from the bank. If the rules regarding payout aren't clear, ask for clarification.

Make sure you know how your "penalty-free paydown" works. If you don't follow the right process, you may have to pay interest on the whole amount. You will likely need to provide *separate cheques*: one cheque is for the "free paydown" and the second is for the balance of the mortgage, including the three months' interest on the portion left after the free paydown.

NOTES:_____

_____

_____

_____

TIP #21: BEWARE THE CASH-BACK MORTGAGE.

An early payout of a cash-back mortgage means you pay the normal payout penalty—and a cash-back penalty.

Not all mortgages are created equal, and the cash-back mortgage is a great example of a mortgage that is a double-edged sword. One edge hands you money at closing. The other edge can take a big bite out of your bottom line!

A cash-back mortgage is a mortgage you take out with a lender who gives you a cash incentive to sign on the dotted line in exchange for a higher interest rate. Some investors will pay the higher rate if the property still cash flows in exchange for receiving a cash-back to offset closing costs or renovation costs. It's like getting a signing bonus for taking out the mortgage. These cash-back mortgages don't have the best market-interest rates (if they did they wouldn't have to give you a cash incentive to sign on). This interest rate can be as much as one full percentage point above the best non-cash-back rates. Before you take one of these mortgages, make sure you figure out what that money really costs you over the term of the mortgage!

The hitches continue. If, in the future, you want to renegotiate the mortgage, pay it out or refinance, you must be prepared to return a portion of that cash-back cheque to the bank. Remember, the lender provided funds for the full term of the mortgage, so if you're not going to full term, it will demand part of your signing bonus back.

🔘 KEY INSIGHT

If you are assuming an existing mortgage and have plans of not running it to the full term, make sure you know whether it is a cash-back mortgage. Even though you didn't receive the initial cash-back from the bank, you will be the one responsible to pay it back. OUCH!

Due diligence should identify the cash-back provisions. But it's better to be safe than sorry, and that means you *absolutely have to ask* if it's a cash-back mortgage. Believe it or not, many investors forget to cover this critical detail when assuming a mortgage, with or without qualification.

WHAT DO YOU NEED TO DO?

Get good advice

Get a real estate–savvy lawyer on your team. There are a lot of deals out there, and while the documents may add up to the same number of pages, they don't necessarily read the same way! Ask your lawyer to check to see if the mortgage you are assuming has a cash-back provision.

 RED FLAG

Not knowing whether the mortgage you're assuming or arranging has a cash-back provision, and the penalties that may be involved, can make the difference between profit and loss.

Ask now, save later

Always ask the lender if the mortgage is a cash-back mortgage, regardless of whether it's a new or assumed mortgage. Also, when assuming financing with or without pre-qualifications, insist that your realtor obtain a "Mortgage Verification" form, completed by the lender, from the listing realtor.

KEY INSIGHT

Nothing in life is free. You shouldn't assume anyone is out to cheat you, or to conceal information that could cost you later on. But you *must* make sure you are doing all that you can to be fully informed. Due diligence means asking the right questions—*all* the right questions, *all* the time.

NOTES:_____

_____

_____

_____

_____

_____

_____

_____

_____

_____

_____

Tip #22: Get the Goods on Mortgage Assumption.

The mortgage assumption picture is changing. Don't presume to assume.

Alberta is currently the only province that allows buyers to assume a previous mortgage without qualification, and even that scenario is changing. Lenders in that province are tightening up on mortgage assumptions. The end result is that many lenders are turning down attempts to assume a mortgage at the last minute—and catching investors by surprise and without adequate financing!

Other provinces and territories allow assumption of mortgages in certain cases, as long as the new buyer qualifies under their guidelines. This is often done to help the seller avoid massive interest-payout penalties.

Lenders across the county, including those in Alberta, have dramatically tightened mortgage assumptions by requiring specific documentation and loan agreements. This is in response to mortgage fraud that has been perpetrated on them by unscrupulous brokers and borrowers. Any previously held beliefs you may have had about assuming an existing mortgage may no longer hold true. In the very near future, no one will assume a mortgage until he's gone through the full mortgage qualification process.

What do you need to do?

Get your lender onside

A lender will be more interested in your deal, including a mortgage assumption, if she trusts your strategy and knows your business history. Use a Sophisticated Investment Binder (see Tip #27) to ensure full disclosure of information to your lender. Make it easy for them to say yes!

🛈 KEY INSIGHT

Sophisticated investors know they can make money with legitimate transactions. They also know there is no long-term advantage to having a dishonest relationship with a lender or broker. These are the people who loan you money, or call those loans in. There is never any harm in asking a lender for what you want. But the relationship must have mutual benefits. You get a good deal. Your lender gets a reliable client. Remember, it is all about long-term trusting relationships with everyone on your team.

TIP #23: DON'T REFINANCE YOUR HOUSE: USE A SECURED LINE OF CREDIT WHEN APPROPRIATE.

Not all line of credit arrangements are created equal. Secure a line of credit that takes your investments where you want them to go.

It's good to know lenders are offering more creative options for real estate investment financing. As you move through the investment process, however, you also need to understand how a secured line of credit (LOC) works and why it can be a very powerful financing tool for real estate investors. It is often a much less expensive and more flexible way to access the equity from your current residence to use for investing.

A LOC is like a bank loan, but it operates like a reverse bank account. You get approved to borrow a certain amount of money (the LOC limit), against which you can write cheques for any purpose you wish. You pay interest (and in some cases a small portion of the principal) only on the outstanding balance each month. If you are approved for $100,000, and you only use $15,000, you only make payments on the $15,000. This is a much more effective way to take out equity from a property. In the re-mortgage scenario, you start paying interest and principal payments on the full $100,000, even if you aren't using it. With the LOC strategy, you only pay for money you actually use! LOCs are very flexible. You can pay them off anytime you wish without penalty.

There are two kinds of credit lines, secured and unsecured. An **unsecured** personal line of credit (PLC) is more difficult to get and has no specific collateral to back up the loan. As with any loan, you must meet the lender's income and credit-rating criteria. For an unsecured LOC, you typically have to pay interest and principal payments every month. The unsecured PLC has a higher interest rate than a secured line, typically prime plus 1% to 4%, and cannot be used to formulate part of a down payment for future purchases. A PLC is considered personal consumer debt and the interest is not typically tax deductible.

A **secured** LOC is backed by some type of secure collateral, like the equity in your home or rental property, cash on deposit at the bank, or government bonds. The minimum monthly payment is often the monthly interest due that month (no principal payment required). The interest rate floats and is calculated every month. These lines are usually offered at around the prime lending rate plus 1%.

With a secured home equity line of credit (HELOC), you use your home as security and the bank effectively registers a second mortgage against your home.

WHAT DO YOU NEED TO DO?

Be ready to convert

Watch the interest rate! Convert the LOC to a fixed-rate loan if you believe interest rates are about to skyrocket. You may have to pay a higher rate for a fixed-rate loan, but leaving it to float could equal cash-flow trouble.

$ SOPHISTICATED INVESTOR STRATEGIES

If you are a homeowner and a real estate investor, then it is imperative that you structure your principal residence mortgage in the most cost-effective and strategic way possible for you to accomplish your goals. As an investor, you know that one of your future obstacles will be coming up with money for down payments. One of your down-payment options will be the equity in your home (as covered in Tip #17). The most valuable tool to use for this purpose is a re-advanceable mortgage/line of credit combination.

A re-advanceable mortgage/LOC will be set up initially with both a mortgage and a line of credit. In the beginning, the entire amount could be in the form of a mortgage and the LOC could be set at zero. The key is that every time you make a mortgage payment, the amount of equity that is paid off gets re-advanced to the line of credit. Over time, as your mortgage balance is reduced on one side, the equity starts to build in the line of credit on the other side. This built-up equity can then be used as a down payment on future investments.

Add up those tax savings

What makes the re-advanceable strategy even better is that when money is used from your line of credit for an investment that has the intention of making money, then the interest on the money borrowed is tax deductible.

Lenders have different names and variations of this product so make sure you ask your broker for a re-advanceable mortgage/line of credit combination on your principal residence. In the authors' opinion, every real estate investor should have their principal residence mortgage structured this way.

KEY INSIGHT

Never assume a lender has drafted the documents it wants you to sign for your benefit. These papers protect the lender's interest. Always review the complete agreement to ensure it meets your needs as well.

NOTES:_____

_____

_____

_____

_____

_____

_____

_____

_____

_____

_____

_____

_____

_____

_____

_____

_____

_____

_____

_____

_____

_____

_____

_____

_____

_____

_____

_____

TIP #24: KEEP FINANCING UP FRONT.

Keep your lender in the loop and make disclosure of secondary financing a priority.

Secondary financing is a blanket term that covers any additional funds (over and above the first mortgage) that are borrowed to make the deal work. This can include vendor take-back mortgages (as discussed in Tip #17), lines of credit, joint-venture or silent-partner funds, second and third mortgages and the like.

The bank will want to know the origin of the funds you are using to close the deal. In other words, it will be looking for a confirmation of funds that make up the difference between the purchase price and the first mortgage amount. Expect your lender to ask for at least three months of bank statements to confirm there were no "lump sum" deposits into your bank account over the past three months. Again, it is always better to be up front with exactly where your money is coming from.

Secondary financing isn't as straightforward as it sounds. For one thing, some mortgage contracts disallow the practice. Where secondary financing is allowed, the total amount will be limited.

WHAT DO YOU NEED TO DO?

Find out if secondary financing is allowed

Before you sign a mortgage agreement, understand the mortgage terms as to the permissibility of second mortgage financing. Also review such terms with your lawyer.

Always provide full disclosure with your lenders. When you put secondary financing in place, the banks in some provinces will automatically be informed through the land registry of your province, so don't even think that you are sneaking it in after the fact. They are watching for this exact transaction.

If necessary, let the person who negotiated the mortgage (your broker) sort out any difficulties with second-mortgage financing if it is required as part of your down payment.

 **KEY INSIGHT**

If you are ever told not to disclose secondary financing, run from that advisor as fast as you can. Surround yourself with professionals who conduct business legitimately!

Tip #25: Seek Joint-Venture Deals: Nothing Ventured, Nothing Gained.

Let the situation dictate the type of deal you make.

Joint ventures (JV) are business relationships that are especially effective in real estate investments. JVs are designed to put partners together to build on each other's strengths and they are likely to be more popular with investors now that CMHC rule changes mean investors need to come up with more money for down payments.

JV partnerships are the single most reliable and mutually beneficial way to find more money for down payments. But a strong joint-venture partnership must be structured to be stronger than the sum of its parts. In other words, two weaknesses don't add up to one strength. Make sure you only enter a JV relationship with someone you can trust and someone who bolsters one of your weaknesses. (See Bonus Tip #102.)

JV deals can be profitable, and if fairness rules each partner's actions, a solid partnership can result.

There are countless ways in which to set up the financials for a joint-venture relationship. The key is to ensure that it is fair for both parties. Here are four examples of joint ventures the authors of this book have been involved with. Use them only as idea generators! There is no right or wrong way to structure the deal. What's important is that you structure the deal so all parties agree—and you make sure it enables each party to bring individual strengths to the table.

🄺 Key Insight

Make sure *all* aspects of the joint-venture relationship are detailed in a joint-venture agreement. This agreement must be written by an experienced lawyer and be confirmed by each party's lawyers. It must cover all the contingencies that can be thought of in advance, including the goal of the JV, the financial arrangements, the performance requirements of all partners, what happens if a partner doesn't perform his or her duties, and the steps to dissolving the partnership. Make sure you talk about all the potential negative situations in advance, so there is less emotion should the situation ever arise!

WHAT DO YOU NEED TO DO?

Attract JV partners

Talking to people about potential JV partnerships is a skill you can perfect. Remember: Nothing ventured, nothing gained. So act with confidence, credibility and integrity—and learn to see each "rejection" for what it really is: a chance to fine-tune your JV presentation as you move towards the right partner and the right deal! (They are not rejecting you, they are rejecting your business proposal.)

Look for ways to show potential partners why they should trust you with their money. Become a student of the process by studying the Joint Venture Secrets Program at www.reincanada.com . As you progress, ask yourself these questions:

- What do they need to know about me and my deal?
- What do I know about a potential partner that makes this deal right for them?
- What would you want to see in someone else if you were giving them your money?

Put yourself in their shoes: would your presentation attract you to invest in the project?

Structure the right deal

JV deals are as unique as the partnerships that define them. Some investors develop a niche, others work in several areas. Remember: "Joint venture" is a catch-all phrase used to cover many different structures. Work with your lawyer and accountant to ensure you are structuring the deal to fit the partners' needs.

Structure the right JV for your circumstances

The classic 50/50 deal

This is the most traditional real estate deal. Here, both parties are registered as owners and have combined to arrange the mortgage financing. The deal is 50/50, with Investor A finding the property and Investor B putting up the cash down payment.

Positive cash flow is either split 50/50 or is put back into the Staying Power Fund. Upon sale of the property, Investor B gets her cash first. The remaining balance is then split 50/50.

The guaranteed mortgage deal

In this case, Investor A (30%) guarantees the mortgage, puts up 30% of the cash down payment and has good credit, but not a lot of real estate expertise or additional time. Investor B finds the property and makes the rest of the cash down payment.

Upon sale of the property, Investor A and Investor B receive their initial cash investments back, and the remaining profit balance is split 30% to A and 70% to B.

The renovation deal

The reno deal is a 50/50 arrangement, although each partner may contribute a different amount of cash. One may make the cash down payment; the other, cover renovation costs.

Upon sale of the property, Investors A and B receive all their cash outlay. The balance is then split 50/50.

Covering negative cash flow

In this deal, the partners share cash investment according to their own expertise and investment goals, with Investor A covering negative cash flow and co-signing the mortgage with his partner.

Upon sale of the property, Investors A and B receive their initial cash investment. Investor A receives a cheque to cover all of the negative cash flow he covered and the balance is then split 30% to A and 70% to B.

NOTES:_____
_____
_____
_____
_____
_____
_____
_____

Tip #26: Know that Multi-Family and Commercial Lenders Use Different Rules.

The rules change when you move from a typical house or condo to a multi-family building. It may even get easier for you!

When you enter into the world of six-plexes and above, right through to massive apartment blocks, you are working with what are called "commercial lenders and brokers." Expect different rules. With a residential mortgage, the borrower is the main focus. With a commercial mortgage, the property is primary.

🄀 Key Insight

The commercial deal's focus on property may be good news for self-employed investors who are not able to qualify for a residential mortgage. With a quality building, a self-employed investor has an easier time qualifying for a commercial mortgage. But beware: the down payment for a commercial property can be as high as 35% or more, depending on the building's cash flow.

Real estate investors learn the value in trading up when they move from buying a single-family home with a single tenant to buying a suited residence or a multi-family unit. The commercial mortgage market is one more step up the investment ladder. In fact, many investors find that it is easier to own one 20-unit apartment building rather than 20 single-family units. There are "economies of scale" when buying multi-family buildings that can make being a landlord easier. (Tip #58 looks at this aspect of a multi-family purchase in more detail.)

Earlier, in Tip #12, we talked about the obstacle of qualifying for a mortgage, the need to ensure that your verifiable income can service your personal consumer debts and the issue of cap space. The good news is that commercial lenders will put more focus on the cash flow of the building than they will your personal ability to service the debt. Better yet, there is no such thing as cap space with commercial lending. This is not to say that the borrower is not important and it is certainly not an avenue for those who are unemployed. The key with all commercial real estate is the quality, cash flow and location of the building.

The commercial mortgage

There are three components to a commercial mortgage and these vary from deal to deal. They are

1. **Loan to value:** A first mortgage can be as high as 85% if it is CMHC insured. It can also be as low as 50% if the cash flow is poor.
2. **Lender's fee:** Commercial lenders charge borrowers a fee to lend them money. This is often a surprise to borrowers. As the lender does not pay a referral fee to a mortgage broker for bringing them the business, the broker will charge a fee as well. Commercial mortgages also have more legal and environmental-study expenses associated with their deals.
3. **The interest rate:** This can vary greatly depending on whether the deal is CMHC insured or not. A CMHC-insured building may qualify for a mortgage rate that's lower than a residential rate. If the mortgage is not insured, however, the rate will be 1% to 2% higher than a residential mortgage.

When lenders do look at these deals, four areas get most of their attention and these four areas will determine the three above: 1. Cash flow; 2. Building quality; 3. The vacancy rate; and 4. The covenant. Let's take a closer look at what's happening.

- **Cash flow:** Lenders want to ensure the building can carry its own debt. Instead of paying attention to your personal income, they want proof of the income the building produces. The higher the income the property generates, the higher the mortgage amount you can receive. It's just that simple. The banker will still want to see your complete Sophisticated Investor Binder (see Tip #27) to check up on you and your partners. But it won't hold as much weight as the building itself. To qualify for a CMHC loan, you will need a debt-coverage ratio (DCR) of at least 1.25%, if not 1.35%. (That's $1.25 of income for every $1 of expense.)

RED FLAG

The lender will want to do a detailed analysis of the building's operating expenses. Don't be surprised if the lender challenges the numbers you give it (even if they are accurate). Each lender has its own ratios for determining expenses versus income. These operating expenses will have to fit its criteria to be approved.

- **Building quality:** The lender will focus on the age, quality and location of the building. To ensure the property will not become a future liability, lenders will require a professional structural review, including roof and mechanical. A lender will also want to know that it is not lending against a property that could be considered an environmental hazard. To satisfy that demand, you will be required to provide a Phase 1 Environmental Study report that says, at a minimum, "mostly clean." When a Phase 2 report is ordered, "just to be sure," the cost involved can push a real estate deal past the point of economic return. These reports must be planned for in advance as they do take some time and are an added expense.

  Some lenders will not lend in small towns without CMHC insurance.

- **Vacancy rate:** Virtually every lender will want to look at your actual vacancy rate and at the prevailing vacancy rate for the municipality where your building is located, based on CMHC data. If your numbers differ, your deal could be at risk, so make sure you can demonstrate how you got your numbers. Don't be surprised, however, if the lender uses CMHC rates regardless of what your actual vacancies are. This can have a significant impact on how the lender defines your income and, as such, your loan amount.

- **The covenant:** This is all about your pledge. Be prepared to show that your down payment is coming from your own sources. Commercial lenders may allow some flexibility compared to residential lenders when it comes to verifying self-employed income, which is great for self-employed borrowers who do not declare all of their income. But this should not be misconstrued as a way to qualify if you're unemployed and show no income. Do not think you can qualify if you're unemployed.

  Generally speaking, investors and deals that score high in the above categories have a good chance of qualifying for CHMC funding. If you are weak in one or two areas, expect higher rates or fees and a lower loan-to-value ratio.

 **Key Insight**

Everything associated with commercial lending is more expensive than a residential mortgage deal. You need to be aware of this before entering into a commercial deal so as to avoid frustration and disappointment, but you should not let the additional costs involved intimidate you. The rewards can be significant and worth the extra costs. Shifting your portfolio to multi-family commercial can be an excellent transition for the investor who has capped out or can otherwise no longer qualify for a residential mortgage.

What do you need to do?

Talk to lenders/commercial brokers

The best rates for commercial properties will come through CMHC-insured mortgage programs with conventional sources. In fact, CMHC will lend up to 85% financing, if the cash flow from the property warrants it (and their rates, at the time of writing, were less expensive than the residential rates. Pursue those first.).

 **Key Insight**

Commercial real estate investment deals are not the same as residential investment deals. The one thing both demand is a positive working relationship with a lender/broker. If you take away only one point from this chapter, make it a new understanding of the investor/lender relationship. Your investment success depends on it. Get a strong referral from a successful investor or from your local Real Estate Investment Network chapter.

NOTES:_____

_____

_____

_____

_____

_____

_____

_____

_____

TIP #27: COMPILE A SOPHISTICATED INVESTOR BINDER.

When it comes to securing a mortgage, presentation matters.

This section of the book has taken you through some key tips on mortgages and financing. You're now ready to look at the number one reason sophisticated investors get their deals done—and get their deals done faster.

Sophisticated investors know lenders need high-quality information to make decisions about mortgage financing. They know bankers and mortgage brokers must look at everything, from a potential client's credit history to the financial background of joint-venture partners.

They also know lenders/brokers are busy people who must prioritize their workloads. Therefore, anything you do to make their jobs easier will make your deal more palatable. The Sophisticated Investor Binder is the best way to make it easy for them to say yes. *That's right. Anything you can do to make their jobs easier will make your deal go faster. If you are working with a mortgage broker, help them help you.*

The Sophisticated Investment Binder will make that happen!

 **KEY INSIGHT**

The Golden Rule of Real Estate: He who has the gold makes all the rules. In this case, the banks have the gold, so learn to play within their rules!

WHAT TO YOU NEED TO DO?

Buy a one-inch binder

Get a one-inch white binder with a clear overlay that lets you slide in a title page.

Create a cover letter

This is a business letter personally addressed to your broker. That letter must include:

1. Contents of the binder: All the information the reader needs to know about you showing that you are a sophisticated investor waiting for a positive response to this particular application.

2. A reference to working with this broker in the future.
3. The date you expect to hear back from him. (And do make it reasonable. A too-short deadline is another reason to reject your request!)
4. An invitation for the reader to call you immediately regarding any questions.

Show proof of income

You need to establish that you can repay a mortgage.

If you are an employee, get a letter from your employer, on company letterhead, that states your position, salary and the number of years of service at the company. If possible, have your employer personalize it with comments about your character. Make sure the letter includes a reference who is happy to speak with the lender. A lender will accept a letter up to 90 days old, but the more recent, the better.

⊗ KEY INSIGHT

Due to an increase in fraudulent job letters, virtually every bank will call your employer directly to verify the information on the job letter, so accuracy and honesty are key. In addition to a job letter you will need to provide two of the following four items:

1. Your most recent T-4
2. Your most recent pay stub showing a year-to-date (YTD) amount
3. Your most recent Notice of Assessment (NOA) from CRA
4. Your T-1 Generals from your most recent tax return

We recommend that you include most if not all of this in your binder so that your broker can choose what to provide to the lender, depending on which lender they choose.

If you are self-employed, you must provide documentation of your income. The Canada Revenue Agency provides a Notice of Assessment after you file your taxes. Include copies for the last two or three years. You will also require two to three years of your corporate financial statements along with two to three years of your P&L statements.

In addition, ask your chartered accountant for a formal letter to your banker that clearly defines your business's actual income. This will include your salary, money received from shareholder loan repayments, expenses like rent from a home-based business, dividends, retained earnings, depreciation and other items you may find on an income tax statement. Along with this letter, provide your broker with a paper trail of documents that supports your accountant's claims. A lender for residential mortgages will not use the income from your accountant's letter to qualify you, but it will assist them in determining your true income.

 RED FLAG

Your accountant may not understand the importance of this letter. If that's an issue, draft the accountant's letter yourself, then ask him to modify it and sign it. Make sure your accountant is willing to be contacted for more information. This letter helps demonstrate your willingness to cooperate with a lender's needs.

Be thorough

Sophisticated investors speed up the mortgage application process (and build goodwill!) by giving a broker what he needs, when and where he needs it. That's why a sophisticated investor never waits for a broker to ask for information needed on the mortgage application.

Complete an application for your broker up front. The application form is likely available online and will save your broker a lot of time by not having to re-input information that you have provided on a generic form. Be prepared to provide all supporting documentation.

Do not write "see attached information" when completing the application. If it's information they need, make it handy!

 RED FLAG

In the new post-recession era of lending in Canada, banks have become extremely cautious and conservative in their lending habits. This is a perfect example of how a pendulum swings. In 2006, Canadian banks were becoming very loose with their lending habits and now have swung

Red Flag continues

in the opposite direction. But like all pendulums, they tend to swing back over time. In the meantime, your job as a sophisticated investor is to be patient with the process. Deals today will take more time than they did in 2006. They will require more scrutiny. They will require more paperwork and they may be declined more often. A sophisticated investor knows that this situation is temporary and knows how to play the game. By providing the banks what they want today, you will separate yourself from the crowd of investors who are stuck in the past and constantly complain that the banks are unreasonable. Remember, he who has the gold . . .

Include a cash-flow summary

A detailed cash-flow summary includes all sources of income and helps show the lender you can make monthly payments. Summarize income from other revenue properties as "net real estate income." Make sure these numbers support information from employers or Canada Revenue Agency. Accuracy is key!

Get a credit bureau report

Every time you sign a mortgage application, you authorize the bank to check your credit bureau report. But that report may contain inaccurate information!

By securing one for the bank, you get to check its accuracy before your banker sees it. To review the basics of a credit report, re-read Tip #14. In most cases, the bank will pull its own credit bureau record on you. By providing one in advance, you show them you are looking after the key details.

Include a net worth statement

A net worth statement takes time to compile, but it's critical. The statement must be current and list all your assets (including RRSPs) and liabilities (all loans and credit-card balances). To simplify future updates, use a basic Excel spreadsheet or a financial management program like Quicken to write the statement. You can find an example of a net worth statement in *Real Estate Investing in Canada*.

RED FLAG

Make sure the money you're using as a down payment is listed on the net worth statement and always sign and date your net worth statement. If someone is gifting you money to buy property, make sure your binder includes a letter signed and dated by the giver. It needs to state the amount, the date you received the money, and the fact the gift is completely non-repayable.

Add a real estate assessment statement

This statement shows all the details of the property you own, including mortgages held by you or others. It is especially critical when you own multiple properties and want the broker to apply an offset policy. This statement should clearly outline the equity that is in each property along with the cash flow they create. This form is often referred to as a Rental Cash Flow Analysis and is available in an Excel worksheet form. It is critical that the information you provide your broker on this form is accurate. There is nothing worse than to have a broker submit your information on your behalf only to find out later that it is inaccurate or does not match the paperwork used to verify what is on the form. This discredits both you and your broker and will hinder your ability to finance future deals. Like any relationship, make sure that it gets off on the right foot.

Make sure the totals match those in your net worth statement and that the amount of rent you claim on your cash flow analysis matches your lease agreements. Include maturity dates of each mortgage. This shows your lender you may be a source of future business.

Create a computer version of this statement for easy updates.

RED FLAG

This statement may be more difficult to explain to a lender who's not familiar with real estate investment (which is another reason to keep shopping until you find a sophisticated mortgage broker for your team!).

Make three copies

When the first Sophisticated Investment Binder is complete, make two more copies—immediately! This gives you one for your broker and two as backups. One of the backups is ready in case another deal comes along. The other is a master copy you'll update as needed.

Given today's technology, most brokers would prefer to receive your binder in electronic format. You can save all your information onto a CD or in a zip file that can be e-mailed through a secure network.

💲 SOPHISTICATED INVESTOR TIP

The Sophisticated Investment Binder takes time to put together. But all of the information it carries is relevant to *every* deal you make with a lender. In other words, you can present the information at the beginning of the mortgage application process, or scramble to find specific pieces under the tight time constraints of a pending deal. More importantly, a Sophisticated Investment Binder gives novice and experienced investors a distinct advantage. It shows a level of professionalism not always evident in the investment business. The first tip of the next part of the book puts that into sharper perspective. You can do the work in advance, or scramble later and risk looking like every other investor.

NOTES:_____

_____

_____

_____

_____

_____

_____

_____

_____

_____

_____

_____

_____

_____

_____

_____

_____

_____

_____

_____

TIP #28: GO THE EXTRA 10% AS A SOPHISTICATED INVESTOR.

Now take that binder—and make it shine!

Your Sophisticated Investor Binder will take many lenders and brokers by surprise. Even if they are used to working with knowledgeable real estate investors, they probably won't be used to working with investors who are so organized!

The lasting beauty of the Sophisticated Investment Binder, however, goes well beyond the financial data you've included so far. Successful investors are those who "put in the extra 10%." A few more additions to your binder will make sure it packs a powerful communications punch.

WHAT DO YOU NEED TO DO?

Put a face to your investment plans

The first section of your binder should include a 5 × 7-inch colour photo of your family. Make it a formal shot, or something fun. Any copy shop can produce the print you want. Just make sure it's a top-quality print. This changes the transaction from bare numbers to a more personal decision.

Add a biography

Now add a one-page bio of you (and your family). Tell your lender who you are, what you're interested in and what your background is. Make sure you include a sentence (or five!) about where you're heading with real estate. This will help your broker package your deal as well. The more they know about you, the more they can sell your deal for you.

Include your property analysis

The next two parts take you through a tip-by-tip look at what it takes to know whether a specific property is worth your time and money. These tips form the basis of your property analysis and due diligence checklist (see the appendix).

Put a copy of a completed checklist in your binder. This shows your lender you did your due diligence *before* asking to borrow money.

🔑 KEY INSIGHT

Rookie investors who compile a Sophisticated Investment Binder gain a definitive edge when meeting with lenders. Why? Because strict attention to quality due diligence shows that you understand what it really means to make the details of due diligence part of your investment system! As your investment experience grows, updated versions of the binder will demonstrate your ongoing commitment to making business decisions based on due diligence. Lenders will appreciate your commitment to clarity—and you'll appreciate how the binder keeps your business firmly focused on success. Better yet, your homework reduces your lender's risk and you may be compensated with a lower interest rate or better terms on the mortgage. Build a strong relationship by using the Sophisticated Investor Binder for *every* property, even if your broker has one from the last transaction.

NOTES:_____

_____

_____

_____

_____

_____

_____

_____

_____

_____

_____

_____

_____

_____

_____

_____

_____

_____

_____

TIP #29: LINE UP THAT MORTGAGE.

Put that binder to work.

Your Sophisticated Investment Binder is a great way to open communications about a specific property with a potential broker. But what happens if you've used the Property Goldmine Score Card to target a community worthy of more research, but you haven't yet lined up a property? Use your binder to line up a mortgage.

The Sophisticated Investment Binder carries all the information you need to get pre-positioned for your first investment mortgage.

WHAT DO YOU NEED TO DO?

Call lenders or mortgage brokers

Contact qualified mortgage brokers recommended to you by other investors. Make a list of appointments. Look for a good personality fit and learn about their experience with creative real estate investors. Your first conversation should be about getting pre-positioned. Once you have been pre-positioned through a consultation, provide the broker with the binder. Your broker will use the information provided in your binder to gather all the pertinent documents they know the lender will need. If you collect and provide this information ahead of time, you can be in a perfect position to move quickly when you do find a property to put an offer on.

Ask the tough questions regarding "grey-area transactions." Can they get quality financing without forcing you into a situation that may be considered close to fraudulent?

Tell them outright that you won't play any grey-area games.

 RED FLAG

Remember who's in charge of the interview process. They're looking for new clients. You're looking for someone you can add to your support team. This should be a win-win relationship, but you need to make sure it will work for *you*.

 **KEY INSIGHT**

Your lender and broker will always be one of the most significant members of your investment team. Cultivate that relationship. It will matter.

PART 3

How to Make Your Investment System Work

TIP #30: RELATIONSHIPS, RELATIONSHIPS, RELATIONSHIPS . . . NOT LOCATION, LOCATION, LOCATION.

Beginner or veteran, it's critical to surround yourself with a great team.

Successful real estate investment is about *what* you know (and in Part 4 we'll discuss the 12 fundamentals that drive the real estate market) and *who* you know. This may well be the most important tip of this book. If you only remember one thing, make it this tip: *For true, long-term success, surround yourself with experts and fellow investors who have the same vision. If you surround yourself with short-term, get-rich-quick thinkers, you will be so distracted by their vision you'll never achieve your own!*

For this reason, it pays to be selfish when it comes to your time and your vision. Protect them as if you were guarding your last dollar. Time is a non-renewable resource that should not be wasted.

Building the right relationships takes the extra 10% effort—a message we will constantly reinforce. It means doing the extra 10% other investors just aren't willing to do. Applied to the relationships you need for investment success, the extra 10% effort discussed in Tip #28 means acknowledging the need for a strong team—and then doing something about it!

It is, in essence, a choice. You can take the easier and more successful route to your goal, or choose the more difficult and more stressful. I highly recommend the former.

WHAT DO YOU NEED TO DO?

Build key relationships

Build solid, mutually beneficial relationships with people who can nurture your success in real estate investment. (Review Tip #3 on how to choose a real estate agent, broker, accountant and lawyer.) There are enough dream-stealers out there, so make sure you avoid them whenever possible.

Learn as much as you can about the business goals of potential team members and see if they mesh with yours. If they plan to take six months off every year, or they only want to work two days a week, their plans won't fit yours if you are in the prime acquisition period of your plan; such a relationship won't benefit either of you. At least one of you will find it frustrating and stressful.

Every one of the experts you choose should be a member of a governing body. Check with the appropriate body to ensure they have clean records and are in good standing (e.g., call the local real estate associations, CGA Canada, CAAMP, provincial law associations, etc.).

Find a group of like-minded investors. Their positive support will go a long way to keeping your vision clear and keeping you on track to achieve it. Make sure the investment group you choose is a legitimate group with views that match your own. Even here, you still need to keep your eyes open. If you are going to do a deal with a fellow investor, for instance, make sure you do your own due diligence on the deal. Don't let yourself be blinded by another investor's reputation as an investment star or award winner.

Empower your team

Once you have a strong team in place, get out of its way and let the individuals do what they do best, which is pay attention to the details. This frees you to do what you do best—find properties. Don't try to outguess your lawyers, real estate agents, property inspectors or other investors.

Practise excellence in all that you do

Do everything in real estate at a level of excellence, and demand the same of your team. If they are not willing to play at your level, you may wish to trade them for another expert and a new first-round draft choice.

Practise your due diligence system so it becomes second nature. Find out how to mesh your system with that of your team, and chaos will start to disappear from your life!

Be accountable

No matter who's on your team, you are still the CEO and president of your real estate investment business and you are accountable for all the results. You did the extra 10% when it came to choosing your team—now apply it to the details. Read every document you sign, have them explained to you if you don't understand them and never be embarrassed to ask questions.

🌀 SOPHISTICATED INVESTOR TIP

Many studies over the years have proven that your net worth and income end up being roughly the average of those you hang out with. If you want to increase your net worth and income, spend your time with people who earn more and have a higher net worth than you.

TIP #31: ADOPT A PROVEN SYSTEM: IT'S THE DIFFERENCE BETWEEN LONG-TERM WEALTH AND LONG-TERM FRUSTRATION.

A proven real estate investment system is the foundation on which you will build your wealth.

Adopting a system that has been proven over and over again will make all the difference in the world. A system is a tool or way of investing that will help you remove the emotions from the investment decisions as much as possible. It forces you to ask the key questions so you can truly analyze a property and predict how it will perform.

 SOPHISTICATED INVESTOR TIP

It is not a system if you can't easily repeat the actions and create the same or better results. Be wary of "new" systems that claim to be the latest hot thing. Approach them like you do a car in its first production year. Let someone else figure out all the bugs! Sophisticated investors adopt systems so they can quickly and easily make real estate investment decisions that fit their personal goals. A real estate system helps investors zero in on the type of property they need to buy to be successful. It helps them locate and purchase property in a particular geographic area — and it keeps them from buying property that's a bad fit with their long-term business plans.

Sophisticated investors use their systems to stay on track.

WHAT DO YOU NEED TO DO?

Find a system that works

A system that works is one that has proven successful for at least a decade. It must also be proven to work in the types of properties you want to own. If you are into buy-and-hold properties, don't waste your time with a quick-flip system.

The Authentic Canadian Real Estate (ACRE) system detailed in the book *Real Estate Investing in Canada* is a Canadian-specific system, and long-term investors have used it to purchase over $3.3 billion of Canadian investment real estate across the country. There are other systems with long track records. Just make sure they work in your area—and are truly designed to help you achieve the personal goals you have set for yourself.

If you are considering buying a system from an expert, make sure you check it out first. Never get caught up in the "there are only nine packages available tonight" hype. Make sure local investors have tested the system and proven it works.

Aim for quality

A quality investment system will include the following:

- A way to analyze the boom or bust cycle.
- A foolproof way to assess property.
- A specific plan of action regarding the kind of property you want to buy, buy and hold, or buy and sell.
- A detailed guide to financing, including strategies that help you get the financing you need to make your system work.
- Specific, proven strategies for placing offers and closing deals.

🔘 KEY INSIGHT

There's no need to reinvent the wheel. You can learn a lot from proven investment systems and experienced investors. Just remember that you need to make the system your own. That means you're in charge of the kind of properties you buy and you're in charge of how they're bought and managed.

NOTES:_____

_____

_____

_____

_____

_____

_____

_____

_____

_____

TIP #32: STICK TO THE CASH FLOW ZONE.

Rules like this will save you money—and time.

Flip open one of your local real estate newspapers or magazines and you come face to face with the number-one reason real estate investors discard the majority of properties they encounter—volume!

The simple truth about this business is that there are many products on the market. Some have great potential to generate investment revenue, a lot more do not! And that's why you need a filter.

What do you need to do?

Apply the cash flow zone filter

Our number-one filter is the Cash Flow Zone Formula. It's a simple but powerful formula that keeps you away from properties that won't deliver a positive return. Simply apply the following formula as the first step in your property analysis.

(Gross Annual Rent*/Purchase Price) × 100 = Cash Flow Zone %
* Gross Annual Rent = Monthly Rent × 12

The key number to look for is **10%**. If the calculation tallies 8% or more, there's a good chance the property will provide positive cash flow. If the number is less than 8%, review the property's fundamentals.

💲 SOPHISTICATED INVESTOR TIP

While 10% is the benchmark for positive cash flow, a sophisticated investor may be able to make a property work if it scores between 8% and 10%. Always conduct your due diligence before you buy.

❶ KEY INSIGHT

Get over the idea that any deal is the "only" deal. Time is a non-renewable resource. You may miss out on a deal if the Cash Flow Zone Formula discounts a property that might generate positive cash flow, but that's a cheap price to pay for the vast amount of time you'll save by not looking at properties that aren't worth your time.

TIP #33: USE THE PROPERTY GOLDMINE SCORE CARD. IT'S YOUR REAL ESTATE TREASURE MAP.

Believe it or not, this one piece of the system will tell you whether a city or town is poised to go up in value, or poised to drop. Use it no matter what investment system you follow.

The Property Goldmine Score Card has been developed from over 18 years of investing experience by the Real Estate Investment Network. The score card (see the appendix) will guide experienced and novice investors through a series of questions about a specific property. Even if you don't have a full grasp of the economics that drive the real estate market, this one tool will force you to see behind the curtain so you understand exactly which way the market is headed.

By the time you're finished reading this part of the book, you will see how this one tool lays the foundation for an investment system that bases business decisions on solid, market-based information, not hype or emotions.

WHAT DO YOU NEED TO DO?

Study the score card. Understand the questions

If you're intimidated by the concept of a real estate investment "system," turn to the appendix and study the Property Goldmine Score Card to see just how simple the steps can be. Next, use the score card to analyze a particular piece of property that's caught your eye. If that property earns six checkmarks or more, it may be worth a closer look. If it fails to earn at least six checkmarks, you know your system just saved you some hard-earned cash!

You may need to contact a local politician or economic development officer for the area you are investigating for information. If they can't answer your questions as per the score card, keep digging. The Internet is another great source of answers to score card questions. The score card is critical. Completing it is where you start to reap the rewards of putting in that extra 10% effort!

 **KEY INSIGHT**

Many of the questions on the Property Goldmine Score Card require you to compare a local area or neighbourhood's statistics to those of a larger municipality or province. Your goal? Find the areas that outperform the averages.

Make copies of the card

Keep copies of the Property Goldmine Score Card in the glove compartment of your vehicle and in your briefcase. Practise using the card to "test" areas. The questions will soon become second nature and you will start to see opportunities where others don't.

You will find yourself studying the media for opportunities others don't see. The announcement of a new highway or commuter train is big news. By using the Property Goldmine Score Card, you'll know these announcements signal important investment opportunities. While others yawn in indifference, you will jump all over the announcement and find the hidden real estate opportunities around it.

The great thing about a checklist is that it hones your instincts. The more you use the list, the more you understand how the various criteria can positively or negatively impact each other.

KEY INSIGHT

Sophisticated investors know their systems depend on checklists like the Property Goldmine Score Card. This tool is critical to investment success. They take time to complete. They also save you time and money—which means they make you time and money!

NOTES:_____

_____

_____

_____

_____

_____

_____

_____

Tip #34: Let Quality Research Drive the System. Never Again Get Caught by a Slick Sales Job!

Some of the best sources of information are free!

Novice investors find the questions on the Property Goldmine Score Card to be a breath of fresh air. Instead of fuelling an investment system with the excitement of nervous tension, the score card gives them a series of specific questions carefully designed to take them calmly and rationally to where they want to go. All they need now are the answers to those questions.

Veteran investors use the score card to ramp up their "buying machine" and target only areas with huge upside potential. These include towns or neighbourhoods that earn 10 or more checkmarks, meaning they have a distinct advantage in the marketplace. Quality market research is a prerequisite of quality real estate investments, so don't ever skimp on your fundamental research. If you do, you dramatically increase the risk and will likely be caught in deals based on emotions. Worst of all, you could be the last to know the property is a loser—and your own laziness will be your only excuse!

Quality answers to score card questions are not difficult to find and, better yet, are often free! There are people out there who are paid to give you this information. These include economic development officers, statisticians and politicians. All you have to do is ask!

🕐 Key Insight

Never buy a property blind! It doesn't matter who is selling you the property and what story they have told you, it is imperative that you, or a very trusted partner, go to the area you're thinking about investing in and spend time investigating the economics. If you've already got a property in mind, make sure you or that trusted partner do a detailed inspection before you buy.

What do you need to do?

Pick up a newspaper (or three)

Whether you get quality information online or delivered to your door, economic articles and announcements should be the first thing you read every morning. Is the government trumpeting huge job increases (or losses) in your target investment area? Is a new company moving in and bringing employees, or is a well-established one moving out? Have officials just confirmed a new local transit system improvement, or identified where new stations will go? How about a new overpass or a major new residential development? These are examples of the kind of announcements that sophisticated real estate investors recognize as yielding significant investment opportunities. Most people ignore these signs, then call others "lucky" because they take advantage of the investment potential others missed!

🕐 KEY INSIGHT

The information you use to assess market fundamentals can be from online or offline sources. But make sure the information is credible, supported by facts and not written with a hidden agenda.

Don't pay too much attention to the "national average" numbers that are often quoted in the media because they don't help you to see what's happening in your local area. Relying on these national averages is like saying your head is in a hot oven and your feet are in the freezer, so on average you're doing fine. Your investment system depends on quality information. Dig deep!

Continually review the display and classified advertisements published in your target area. They will tell you a story you can't find anywhere else. This includes current market data on the *true* vacancy story, which holds that a higher-than-usual number of rent ads equals a higher vacancy rate and vice versa. Current ads also give you a realistic look at rents in your target market. That information will help you make market-savvy adjustments.

Drop by the public library

Check out local directories, newspapers and community newsletters. They will tell you lots of "street" news the major media won't cover because the stories are too small. Crime rates and the location of grow-ops that were busted are front-page news. So are new schools and hospital expansions.

Pay attention to business moves

Take a look at who's moving in and out of a community. If a Walmart, Costco or Canadian Tire is moving in, someone else has done a lot of research for you.

The key is to look for employment-level trends, both good and bad. The economic development departments will have the most up-to-date stats for who's moving in and who's moving out.

Also, be aware of long-term trends. If it is a forestry town, look at demand for the products it produces. If long-term demand is good, find out if there is a large enough disease- and bug-free source of mature trees to feed the local mills. Ditto with mining towns and stable supplies of ore. This long-term approach avoids the hype and emotion of current headlines that could lead you to inaccurate conclusions.

Study housing prices

Royal LePage releases a quarterly survey of Canadian housing prices that's worth its weight in gold. It lists most major towns and cities and can be picked up at any Royal LePage office, or on the Internet. Combine these stats with stats from the local real estate boards to get a true picture of the market.

Look at vacancies

Call your local CMHC office to see if it has stats for a particular community. As these vacancy rates may be dated in smaller regions, make sure you check the date the survey was taken and *not* when it was published. The implications are enormous. For instance, if you investigate a college town and the survey shows high vacancy rates, there's a good chance the survey was done when school was out for the summer.

Use the information in local classified ads published in traditional and online sources to gauge local competition and vacancy rates for a particular municipality or community. This data will give you rental market shifts from month to month, and the data is apt to be more up-to-date than formal surveys.

Visit the local chamber of commerce

Talk to staff about what's going on in the region and tell them you have suites for rent in the area. People from out of town often call the local chamber of commerce to get some direction about where to look.

Join the chamber and network. This helps keep your finger on the pulse of the local business community. Announcements of business expansions or contractions are often shared at meetings and you can use that information to fine-tune your investment strategy.

Visit local business owners

Strike up a friendly conversation with every business owner you can. In small communities, the owner is often behind the cash register and will have an ear to the ground as to the health of the town's economy. Ask them questions such as: Are sales up or down? Are they re-developing any regions? Are the mayor and council business-friendly or not?

Collect municipal data

Visit the local municipal office and ask for a zoning map, a copy of the official community plan and a copy of the bylaws.

Speak with the local economic development departments; they are there to stimulate economic development, and that is what you are doing as a real estate investor—bringing money into their community. The savvy economic development people will welcome you with open arms. That's also a good sign they will do the same when major employers consider moving into town. The less-than-helpful ones will be difficult to deal with. They'll be "too busy" to help and act like they're doing you a favour. That same growth-impeding attitude will likely prevail when companies and employers come looking for their help. If this is what you experience, look into whether the economic development staff's lack of development acumen is sending economic opportunities off to more welcoming towns.

Meet the locals

Cab drivers, bartenders, newspaper editors and local politicians can be a very good source of information and give you a good sense of the community.

Talk to real estate agents

Talk to a number of different agents. Ask to see reports such as the Royal LePage real estate quarterly report. Interview the agents you like; then select one and bring her aboard your team. Make sure you fact-check all the information you are collecting on neighbourhoods, etc.

Pick up MLS books, hot sheets and other listings

Pick these up at the local real estate office. The back of most Multiple Listing Service (MLS) books lists prices and properties sold for the last six to 12 months.

Visit real estate boards on the Internet

They often have great stats on current and historical real estate prices. Sometimes the data is free, while other times you'll pay. A good real estate agent on your team should be able to access any of the information you require.

Talk to property managers

Talk to several property managers. They can be a good source of information on what's really going on in the rental market. Be aware that many are overworked and underpaid, factors that may cloud their comments, even in a booming market. Others may attempt to earn your business by being overly optimistic!

Sophisticated investors will tell you they won't buy until they've lined up a good manager for that property. So consider this part of your due diligence background work for the next phase: purchase and management.

Tap into provincial statistics

Provincial departments often have specific information on particular cities and towns. Staff can also direct you to other departments (economic development, agriculture, industry) that may have other useful information on what's happening in a community.

Overall provincial stats are what you'll compare your local numbers against to see if your target area performs better or worse than the provincial average.

Access information from Statistics Canada

Statistics Canada has excellent economic and population data. It's often in "raw" form and you'll need to wade in to find what you need. (Remember: you're looking for information other investors don't have!)

Stats Can fees depend on the data you want. Sign up for their free advisory service, a daily e-mail announcing their latest findings and press releases.

Look for research reports put out by the Real Estate Investment Network (REIN) and other credible research companies

The Real Estate Investment Network and other economic research firms across the country release investment information such as reports and press releases. Get on *every* credible research report e-mail list you can find and use the data to stay on top of the latest trends. Here are a few organizations to check out:

Real Estate Investment Network: www.reincanada.com
Royal LePage: www.royallepage.ca
Statistics Canada: www.statcan.ca
Cutting Edge Research Inc.: www.twitter.com/DonRCampbell
Canadian Real Estate Magazine: www.canadianrealestatemagazine.ca

Buy a street map of the area

Last, but not least, a good street map will get you where you want to go, literally! It's especially helpful if you're buying in an area you don't frequent. Look for everything a tenant will want to have access to, including parks, schools, shopping, transit and transportation. This is easy to do with a map but is far more difficult if you're just driving around aimlessly!

Always locate your target property on the map and see if there is potential in the surrounding neighbourhoods.

NOTES:_____

_____

_____

_____

_____

_____

_____

_____

_____

_____

_____

_____

_____

_____

_____

Tip #35: Control the Paper Tiger with a Proven Filing System.

Win the paper war with a filing system that buys your time back!

One of the first things you find out as a real estate investor is that you will be responsible for signing a lot of documents and that you will accumulate reports and other data from your research. You can let it overwhelm you, or opt to not tear your hair out by using a proven filing system that lets you find specific documents in seconds.

The Power Paperwork System was developed by the Real Estate Investment Network (REIN). It is easy to use, compatible with Canada Revenue Agency rules regarding paper trails, provides the best results over time—and can be used when buying single or multi-family properties. *Put this in place now—or set it up before you buy your first property!*

What do you need to do?

Buy a filing cabinet that will house legal-size documents

This is essential. The legal documents and paperwork you need to file your taxes must be kept in an accessible place. This is the absolute best way to do that.

Buy good-quality file folders and hangers

You need four different colours of folders and hangers. Every time you buy a piece of real estate, add four new file folders to your cabinet.

Red: for all tenant information. This includes all rental information, move-in and move-out inspection reports, the completed tenant questionnaire, lease or rental agreements, a CD of property pictures and all correspondence with the tenant.

Yellow: for property miscellaneous. This is where you put general property information, warranties, your master key and all maintenance and inspection information.

Blue: for all legal documents. Because this file won't be accessed very much after closing, blue files go into the bottom drawer of the cabinet. Documents will include a copy of the offer to purchase, all due diligence documents, the survey (or title insurance certificate), the appraisal and all closing documents.

Green: ongoing monthly receipts. This is the file you will open most often. It holds all of the receipts for any expenses related to that property. At the end of each month, gather all of the receipts from a file and put them in a #10 envelope marked with the month and year. On the outside of the envelope, list the company name, the amount paid for each receipt and the classification (office expenses, marketing, maintenance). This greatly speeds up your computer accounting records and provides a replicable record if your computer crashes or you are audited.

Keep your accounting records up to date

All of the receipts in your green files must be entered into a QuickBooks-style accounting program at least once a month. Always write all of the key details of the receipt on the actual paper. Your accountant will love it—and it's a wonderful way to answer an auditor's questions!

 RED FLAG

Legitimate expenses will be denied if you don't keep receipts and make sure you know what they're for! Handwrite notes on every receipt!

Establish a classification coding system

Keep track of individual expenses with a proven classification system. According to information from the Canada Revenue Agency, a statement of expenses related to real estate rental investments can be classified according to the following:

- Advertising
- Caretaking
- Financing and borrowing costs
- First-mortgage interest
- Second-mortgage interest
- Condo fees
- General repairs and maintenance
- Insurance
- Legal and accounting
- Property management

- Property taxes
- Utilities
- Auto expenses

Use your system to save money!

Get into the habit of tracking expenses as you go. By using the file folder and monthly envelope suggestions outlined above, you will make it very easy for your bookkeeper and accountant to advise you about how your portfolio is performing. These systems also save you accounting fees and allow you to make decisions based on facts, not emotions.

🕐 KEY INSIGHT

Set up a simple spreadsheet program so you won't miss out on all the deductions for simple things like a $5 box of Tim Hortons doughnuts. With a program like QuickBooks, you can set it up so that you press Control D to enter a doughnut receipt.

NOTES:_____

_____

_____

_____

_____

_____

_____

_____

_____

_____

_____

_____

_____

_____

_____

_____

_____

_____

TIP #36: CELEBRATE YOUR SUCCESSES.

Make investing fun . . . and enjoy the journey, not just the destination.

Real estate investment demands hard work and patience. Sophisticated investors use a system they can depend on and sometimes the system makes real estate so simple it is boring. Don't go looking for excitement in your investments. However, that is not to say that real estate investing should not be fun and enjoyable.

The key is to not wait until you've "made it" to celebrate. Celebrate each step along the way. When an offer is accepted, take your favourite person out to dinner. When you close on a property, go do something you love. When you have all your suites rented, find a way to celebrate your success. Make it fun—and make it something you wouldn't normally do.

What you are doing is rewarding action, and the more you reward action, the more action you'll take toward achieving your goal.

Of course, when you sell a property for a good profit, treat yourself to something big—you earned it!

WHAT DO YOU NEED TO DO?

Stay focused, yet have fun

Take real estate investing seriously—it is a long-term commitment to wealth creation. But don't get so caught up in the business end of your investment life that you forget about life and loved ones.

Continue to follow your system and build in celebration points along the way. Small rewards remind us that success is a cumulative process.

Three small rewards I will use to celebrate:_____

_____

_____

_____

_____

_____

_____

_____

PART 4

FOCUS ON THE TWO TYPES OF ECONOMIC FUNDAMENTALS AND DRAMATICALLY INCREASE YOUR BOTTOM-LINE RESULTS

Part 3 walked you through the importance of following a proven real estate investment system and identified specific people to speak with to access critical market information on the road to becoming a successful real estate investor.

Now that you know where to look, this part of the book will walk you through a list of what sophisticated investors call the "market fundamentals" that will help you find towns and neighbourhoods that have the best opportunity to outperform the general real estate market. Once you understand how the fundamentals impact property value, you will be able to look at the nitty-gritty of optimizing actual investments, which is the topic of Part 5.

TIP #37: DIG FOR SPECIFIC INFORMATION AND IGNORE GENERALITIES.

Knowledge = Advantage = Long-Term Results. Never buy into hype or emotion.

Sure you can get lucky in the real estate market—many people have. But a lot more have been unlucky. The last thing you want to do as a real estate investor is rely on luck and chance. That's not investment. It's called "speculation"—and you might as well buy a lottery ticket for your retirement plan!

Successful wealth creation through real estate investment is all about uncovering the market fundamentals that can tell you whether a property is poised to increase, or decrease, in value. And the good news is that the numbers are easy to get, but most investors don't know the right questions to ask.

We're looking for markets with a future, not a past. A town or neighbourhood may show rising values today, but sophisticated investors look at how it will perform in the future. Please note that we are talking about specific town or neighbourhood research, not market generalities. General provincial or national real estate stats mean nothing to a sophisticated investor. Sure, they're interesting to read, but they are really useless to an investor because they don't drill down into a specific target area.

For example, you may hear a media report that the average national or provincial real estate values increased by 5% year over year. That number is generally useless. It could mean that some markets are up 10%, while others are down 5%, thus averaging 5%. If you based your investment decisions on such a general number, you might say, "Great, real estate prices are up again, so let's buy some more." However, if you're not paying attention to local numbers, you could be the one buying in a region where prices are dropping.

WHAT DO YOU NEED TO DO?

Understand the two types of fundamentals

Some market fundamentals are passive, meaning they're outside the investor's control. Although passive, they often have the largest impact on the long-term value of your properties.

Other fundamentals are within the control of the investor, such as "sweat equity." The key is to find properties where you have a combination of both. You need to understand how both kinds of factors impact the investment environment.

Review the Property Goldmine Score Card

As you read this tip, refer to the Property Goldmine Score Card in the Appendix. You should develop a strong appreciation for how this checklist can support your investment system and power your decisions with real-world information.

 RED FLAG

The Property Goldmine Score Card will help you pinpoint the market fundamentals of a particular community, thus narrowing your search for a property to buy. You can also use it to "test" a particular property in a specific community. Either way, the power of the market fundamentals holds true: Find a town or neighbourhood that, according to the checklist, delivers the most potential.

WARNING! Don't just buy *any* property in a region that offers great fundamentals. The property must also fit detailed investment criteria. Not all properties will work, even if the fundamentals are there!

> **Market fundamentals: The foundation upon which your real estate portfolio is built**
> Build your portfolio on a strong foundation of fundamentals and it will create long-term wealth. Build it on hype and poor fundamentals and it becomes higher risk and could invite financial disaster.

Here's a quick overview of the real estate investor's fundamentals discussed in detail in *Real Estate Investing in Canada*. The fundamentals discussed here will play a major role in your long-term success as an investor. Fundamental market research is provided to investors from groups as diverse as the economics departments of RBC (Wealth Effect & Affordability Index) and TD (Increased Job Growth & Gentrification), to regional bureaucracies (infrastructure expansion, zoning and renewal), real estate sales firms

(Royal LePage) and specific research firms such as the Real Estate Investment Network. Make sure that you tap into as many unbiased resources as you can, study their reports and become a knowledgeable investor.

1. Passive factors: Use them as indicators of future strength
These factors wield a direct influence on market strength, but are outside an investor's control.

- Mortgage-interest rates
- Wealth effect
- Affordability index
- Increased job growth
- The boom effect
- The economic development office's attitude
- Infrastructure expansion
- Gentrification and renewal

2. Active factors: Where you can have a direct impact
Market-savvy investors know these factors help them boost investment value.

- Maximizing zoning and value
- Direct renovations
- Stand out from the crowd
- Divide and profit
- Speculating on tips

NOTES:_____
_____
_____
_____
_____
_____
_____
_____
_____
_____

TIP #38: LOW MORTGAGE RATES ARE A NEUTRAL FACTOR FOR INVESTORS.

Sophisticated investors know interest rate hype when they see it. Learn why low interest rates are a neutral factor for investors and often an increasing interest rate is a good thing!

Mortgage rates, hockey and the weather are national obsessions. Most Canadians assume low mortgage rates drive values upward and high interest rates keep values down. If that's true, then a low-interest-rate environment should benefit real estate investors.

Sophisticated investors take a general statement like this and dig a little deeper. Interest rates play only one role with respect to value increases in real estate. They are talked about so much because the relationship between interest rates and value sounds logical. But to get the truth you must dig a little deeper.

WHAT DO YOU NEED TO DO?

Ask the obvious: What does a low mortgage rate really mean?

The answer depends on your investment system and your portfolio plan!

A low interest rate for a mortgage keeps an investor's expenses down by allowing access to investment funds more cheaply, which is great in the short term. However, low mortgage-interest rates also allow more renters to become homeowners. While this increase in demand for real estate will drive the values upward, it will also expose the investor to higher vacancy rates. Investors will be competing for a shrinking cohort of renters. So, where an investor wins on the interest rate side, they lose on the vacancy side; that is, if they only use obtaining a low interest rate as the reason to invest.

Since values increase lock-step with vacancies, low interest rates are a neutral issue for investors.

Don't generalize about interest rates and investment

If you're buying and flipping properties, low interest rates are good for business, providing you with a larger market of buyers.

If you're buying and renting to generate a long-term source of passive income and long-term wealth, slight increases in interest rates can be a good thing over the term of your investment. If interest rates are in the historical low zone (but not at historic lows), then the investor has a much more balanced market.

Remember that long-term mortgage rates and the Bank of Canada's prime interest rates are not always heading in the same direction. Always access information relevant to the current market.

- Which way are interest rates going today? Up? Down? Flat?
- How does that compare to historical numbers? Low? Average? High?

 **KEY INSIGHT**

Keep your perspective when interest rates shift. If, for example, the interest rate on a $100,000 mortgage increases to 5.25% from 5.0%, it really is only a $20-per-month difference. If this $20 a month turns your investment deal into a money-losing deal, it was a bad deal to begin with!

NOTES:_____

_____

_____

_____

_____

_____

_____

_____

_____

_____

_____

_____

_____

_____

_____

_____

_____

_____

TIP #39: STUDY THE NET WEALTH EFFECT.

There is a direct correlation between property values and how people feel about their wealth and disposable income. Use this data to predict future value.

The key number here is *not* average income, but average "disposable" income. Disposable income as defined by sophisticated investors is *available income after taxes and regular household expenses* are deducted. In other words, money that is left over at the end of the month. The factor that has the most impact is, of course, the tax component (both on property and income). This number can differ dramatically from region to region.

Of course, if incomes are increasing quickly in a given area where taxes are increasing as well, real estate values will not be positively affected. On the flip side, you may find a region where incomes aren't skyrocketing, but taxes and living expenses are decreasing, even dramatically, as we witnessed in Alberta between 2000 and 2004. This combination led to a spike in real estate values.

In real estate markets, perception is reality. If people can, or think they can, afford higher real estate prices because they feel wealthier, then prices move up. If they feel constrained by high expenses, high real estate values or high taxes, values will flatten. This ties directly into the Housing Affordability Index in the following tip: *As a region's populace feels increasingly "wealthy," real estate values will move upward because of the perceived rise in affordability.*

WHAT DO YOU NEED TO DO?

Identify where affluence lives

Identify a town or community where people tend to spend more money on retail items than is the average. This is a sure sign that the wealth effect is in place and you will see real estate values increasing more quickly than the average. Focus your investment strategy on towns where income and retail sales are increasing at a higher rate than the provincial and national averages.

Track media stories

Follow Statistics Canada's income numbers, then drill down to the provincial and local numbers. Save articles from print and electronic media discussing increases in retail sales or disposable income measurements. Remember to compare the numbers to the provincial and national averages.

Watch for anomalies!

Beware—there are communities that break the rules.

In communities with a lot of retirees, for example, demand for quality housing may drive market values upwards. However, net disposable incomes will decline and the perceived Wealth Effect will be negative for long-term values in the region. These communities may offer some good opportunities for short-term or specialized housing investments, but without an increase in the Wealth Effect, real estate value growth will not be sustainable over the long term.

 **KEY INSIGHT**

Sophisticated investors look for information others miss. You are looking for a community that outperforms the rest of the marketplace, in regions where the overall tax burden is decreasing. Even when the values across a whole province are on the rise, a community with a higher-than-average gross wealth effect will often outperform its peers. Just look at what has occurred in Fort McMurray, Alberta, in the last decade.

NOTES:_____

_____

_____

_____

_____

_____

_____

_____

_____

_____

_____

_____

_____

_____

_____

_____

TIP #40: APPLY "AFFORDABILITY" DATA.

Use the Housing Affordability Index to test a community's investment potential.

Economists at the Royal Bank of Canada produce a quarterly report that analyzes the affordability of housing in specific markets across the country. Get the latest Housing Affordability Index report by visiting www.rbc.com/economics . This tool has proven to be a very accurate source of real estate market health across Canada.

In these reports, you will find the percentage of median income that is required to purchase a median home in each province, as well as in select major cities; in a recent improvement, the report breaks out different housing types. This helps investors determine whether a market is overpriced or undervalued compared to the rest of the country.

As a rule of thumb, a well-balanced market for investors is a market that has a Housing Affordability Index of about 33%. That means that it takes 33% of pre-tax income to make the monthly payments for a median piece of property.

 RED FLAG

Cities and towns that are above this rate are often overpriced for investors. Even though prices may be skyrocketing, if the city's index is 5% or more above this mark, it indicates the market is turning speculative and the fundamentals are getting out of balance.

WHAT DO YOU NEED TO DO?
Look for 33%

Read the RBC's latest Housing Affordability Index Report and focus your extended research on areas where the index shows 33% or less. If a community meets that test and the rest of your indicators are strong, you may have zeroed in on an area that will outperform the rest of the market—but only if other fundamentals are in place. A low affordability index doesn't necessarily mean it's destined to go up. Some regions just happen to always outperform in this fundamental.

Be wary of regions where the Housing Affordability Index is too low, as this is a sign that renters are able to become homeowners quite easily.

Do your own calculations

For most towns and cities, you will have to do your own math to determine where the town sits on the scale. Yes, it is worth the effort as the majority of investors isn't willing to do that extra step to uncover the real investment gems. This is one of the most important indicators of a community's investment potential.

NOTES:_____

_____

_____

_____

_____

_____

_____

_____

_____

_____

_____

_____

_____

_____

_____

_____

_____

_____

_____

_____

_____

_____

_____

Tip #41: Identify Where Increased Job Growth Is Occurring.

Look for an area where people are moving to fill tremendous job opportunities.

Savvy real estate investors know it pays to read the newspaper and Internet news sites, and watch the media. Always be on the lookout for major announcements of new jobs, major expansions or new employers moving into an area. This is a good sign of a future increase in residential housing demand. It's also a signal of an increasing Wealth Effect.

Here's how it works. When companies or governments make a major announcement of new jobs or new business relocations, the announcement will trigger a significant increase in housing demand. Naturally, the housing supply takes time to catch up to this demand, but often never does. From this increased demand and fixed supply, real estate prices are driven upwards in a given area more quickly than the regional average. You can see this occurring today in regions as diverse as Maple Ridge, B.C.; Calgary, Alberta; and Waterloo, Ontario.

What do you need to do?

Look for jobs, jobs, jobs

When analyzing a region, look for cities, towns and neighbourhoods in high demand because of what's happening in the local labour market in terms of an increase in jobs or easier access to jobs.

Your goal is to find areas where the population is growing faster than the provincial average due to an influx of jobs. In some towns, the population will be growing because the town has become a retirement haven or is a cheap place to live, but this does not always lead to increased real estate values. You want to find cities, towns and neighbourhoods that are gaining a reputation as great places to live and have a growing economy.

Visit the Economic Development Office of towns you have picked for potential investment. (You'll discover more about the importance of this office in Tip #42.)

Study both components of new residents

People moving into a town to fill new jobs come from two main sources. *Immigration* occurs when people move from other countries into a new country; *intra-migration* occurs when people move from one part of the country to another. People, generally speaking, look for rental properties until they are settled (usually for two years). After two years, those with savings look to buy a home, so investors win in both cases. They have a market for their rentals and a stable market for the properties they wish to sell in the future.

These sources of in-migration can exist independently of each other, or combine to provide a very strong market. What you'll generally find is that if a region is creating a lot more jobs than the average, the immigration and intra-migration numbers will be very strong. As people migrate to your target region, you will need to make adjustments to your marketing plan. Make sure you know which type of in-migration your plan will focus on.

 **KEY INSIGHT**

Work with the human resources departments of the employers who are hiring. Become a solution to their new employees' housing concerns. Make it easy for them and they'll make it easy for you.

RED FLAG

If you discover you have targeted a region where there is a net loss of migration and immigration, seriously reconsider any long-term real estate investments in this region as your market will continue to shrink while available housing units will increase. Less demand + fixed supply = decreasing prices.

NOTES:_____

_____

_____

_____

_____

_____

_____

_____

Tip #42: Surround the Boom for Best Results.

It's not always a great idea to invest right in the boom, as the best deals may have disappeared. However, the Boom Effect will have a major impact on the surrounding area's real estate.

When a specific area experiences a boom in residential real estate prices, it impacts real estate markets in the surrounding areas in a delayed fashion. There are two reasons why this occurs: first, demand for the less expensive real estate surrounding a boom area increases rapidly, because those who can't afford the higher prices in the boom area move out into the surrounding regions.

Second, perception becomes reality. That's right, human nature once again kicks in, and those who live in the boom's surrounding areas begin to believe that their area is also going to boom and therefore drive prices up. People will begin to ask more for their properties, right when the demand is increasing. A perfect economic storm occurs.

For a sophisticated investor, it is often easier to invest in areas that surround the initial boom, because the prices will be lower there and the rents will be very similar to the initial boom region. This lag can be from anywhere from six months to six years, depending on how far out from the initial boom the property is located and how many other of the Key Factors are in place driving the region's market.

On a macro scale, for example, Calgary had a late-1990s boom and property values in areas surrounding the city were pushed up quickly along with it. The value of real estate in towns closest to the city increased first, and then in areas farther out. You can witness this effect in every area across the country where there has been a marked increase in value. In Toronto, in 2003, when prices began to outstrip what the average income earner could afford, property values in the surrounding cities and towns really started to take off as people chose to move farther out so they could still live the dream of home ownership.

The same effect occurs on a micro scale. When a neighbourhood is redeveloped or goes through a gentrification, the older, untouched neighbourhoods near it also increase in value.

Some investors develop their investment strategies around the Boom Effect. They identify the boom, then analyze areas outside the boom and use that information to buy properties at great prices before the positive boom affects the area.

WHAT DO YOU NEED TO DO?

Focus on facts, not speculation

Never be the first into an area you "think" will benefit from a close-by boom. Instead, make sure the value increases have already kicked in, thus reducing the risk of buying in a region the boom may silently pass by.

Since blind speculation is risky, always review the facts of the region and property. Zoning changes, for example, do not mean a development will proceed. Announcements of new condo developments don't mean that they will always be built. Let the speculators take the first dollars off the table as they are the riskiest profits. After the boom has truly taken a grip, that's when the risk is diminished and sophisticated long-term investors move in.

🎯 KEY INSIGHT

Look for new neighbourhoods being built in or near older neighbourhoods. The micro-ripple effect will dramatically increase the values of the neighbouring older homes. Another reason to buy resale instead of new as an investment is that over a five-year-plus timeline, resale property values increase more quickly than do new-home property values.

NOTES:_____

_____

_____

_____

_____

_____

_____

_____

_____

_____

_____

_____

_____

TIP #43: BUSINESS FRIENDLY EQUALS REAL ESTATE FRIENDLY

Jobs and taxation directly affect real estate values. Look for regions where development is wanted, not shunned.

Real estate investment is a complicated business impacted by the local economic development office. In a perfect investment world, you want to invest in an area with the potential to attract and sustain a good supply of quality renters and eventual buyers. That means an area with strong economic growth potential in terms of new industries and new jobs. *It also means finding a business-friendly environment with minimal taxation (personal and property) and with a fair landlord-and-tenant-law structure!*

If you find a region with dynamic and forward-looking economic development officers, you have just identified an area that has a great potential for attracting employers. Their job is to "sell" the region to major employers, and if they understand this role, you will know by your first conversation with them. Discuss potential deals they're working on, look at their overall plans, and make sure the region still has land to be developed to attract major employers.

If, on the other hand, while doing your due diligence and asking the key questions on your Property Goldmine Score Card you feel you are constantly being blocked or even directly put off by the local office, be wary. This attitude will be a deterrent to investment by potential employers. You'd be surprised at the number of economic *development* offices that act like economic *deterrent* offices.

ⓢ SOPHISTICATED INVESTOR TIP

The authors acknowledge that economic development offices across the country differ significantly. Some of the best to work with are located in Maple Ridge and Vernon, B.C.; Edmonton and St. Albert, Alberta; and Hamilton, Orillia, Barrie and Kitchener/Waterloo/Cambridge, Ontario. Visit or Google these offices to learn more about what a quality economic development office can offer a real estate investor looking for information.

Remember, no matter what your political leaning, if you wish to be successful in the business of real estate investing, you want to have a business-friendly atmosphere that is designed to attract people. You want a town or city that promotes itself and actively attracts investment, as this will help your business succeed. Real estate investing is a business, so you want to look for business-friendly atmospheres.

A macro-level analysis of a province's tax and tenant laws is just the beginning. You will find provinces and municipalities that offer a distinct advantage in both of these areas. You also must look at municipal tax structures for both business and property.

WHAT DO YOU NEED TO DO?

Learn who's who

You do not need to contact local or provincial politicians on a regular basis, but it is a good idea to know who's who, and it makes sense to call or e-mail local and provincial politicians with your reaction when you hear about plans that positively or negatively impact your business.

Be politically active on subjects that will help your business succeed. It is easy to sit back and complain like the masses do, but as a real estate investor, you can make a real difference by making your voice heard on key subjects like income, business and property taxes, and zoning bylaws.

Look for regions where the government and bureaucracy support what you want to do—avoid regions where the support doesn't exist. There are enough areas of opportunity available to you, so why add the risk of a poor political climate into your portfolio?

Get involved

Join the local landlord association and/or a local real estate investment network. Through the association you will have access to the decision makers and be able to keep your finger on the pulse of your target investment region.

Do your homework

Find out why nearly identical properties in different communities are priced differently. Get your information from people who live and work in the community, including real estate agents.

Take a look at how local tenancy laws impact the region's real estate investment opportunities and learn how actual or proposed zoning bylaws can nourish or strangle local property values.

See the Appendix for a list of support tools and key contacts that can help you find out about landlord and tenant laws across Canada.

TIP #44: TRAINS, PLANES, AUTOMOBILES (AND SEWERS): PAY ATTENTION TO REGIONAL INFRASTRUCTURE GROWTH.

Access, access, access—that's all that matters.

Paying attention will pay you dividends. When you read an announcement of a major infrastructure improvement in the works, get off your couch and check it out, using the "what's behind the curtain?" approach to analyze the potential benefits. These announcements could be the annexation of new land by a city, a new transportation development, or a new sewer or water plant—all of which show signs of a region looking forward to growth potential.

There are many towns in the country that have the potential to grow, and have a number of economic fundamentals going for them, but they lack the capacity to add to the sewer system, are running out of industrial land that could bring in more jobs, or are very difficult to get to. All of these factors will negatively affect long-term values in the region.

 **KEY INSIGHT**

Transportation infrastructure: Picture in your mind an area near your region that currently has a highway servicing it. Now take away that highway and picture how that would affect access to the region—and its desirability. In most if not all cases, you will see that the region could never have grown to its current status without transportation infrastructure.

Now, the reverse is also true. Once the transportation improvement is completed, the serviced region will grow at a much faster rate. Demand for real estate will increase, more jobs will move to the region and, best of all, people will follow. This is just one of many infrastructure improvements you can take advantage of.

When Calgary, Alberta, started building its CTrain several decades ago, some local real estate investors thought CTrain proximity would hurt long-term property values. Sophisticated investors, backed by the experience of investing in major metropolitan markets like Toronto and Montreal, saw what others missed: Proximity to light-rail transportation commuting routes pushes property values up by giving commuters better access to the downtown core.

It is not just new transportation that drives these values. Watch for widening of highways and the construction of highway extensions and overpasses. Such infrastructure changes will reduce commuting times and push up property values and rents.

WHAT DO YOU NEED TO DO?

Keep informed

Read the major media; watch for any announcement of major infrastructure improvements being announced in your target investment region. These will identify a region that is set to grow when other regions are in stasis or decline.

Read the local press of the region you are targeting for investment, as this is where the real gems will be found. Befriend the local economic development department, as the staff will be able to keep you informed of major infrastructure proposals and projects being built.

Always analyze a neighbourhood as if it were a town on its own

Ask yourself:

"Where do the people who live here work?"

"Is the investment value of residential property recognized and respected by municipal leaders when they make decisions about area roads and land-use changes?"

"What will the demand be like when the infrastructure improvement is completed?"

RED FLAG

Governments like to announce, then re-announce and re-announce again, infrastructure improvement projects, a great vote-buying scheme. Never invest based solely on announcements—many projects never come to fruition. Sophisticated investors wait until they "see the smoke"; in other words, they wait to see the project actually being worked on, making it less likely to be stopped.

TIP #45: LOOK FOR GENTRIFICATION AND RENEWAL. RENEWAL WILL RENEW YOUR BANK ACCOUNT.

Is it shabby or chic? Watch for clues that show a neighbourhood is moving from one economic class to the next.

Often described as tough but funky, older neighbourhoods that turn into good investment opportunities typically got their start as working-class communities on the "outskirts" of a more centralized hub. Many feature once well-kept homes that slid into disrepair—and out of residential real estate favour—as suburban neighbourhoods sprouted in the 1970s and 1980s.

These days, these regions are easy to recognize. They tend to have a few houses that show signs of recent renovation, located alongside a mix of older, unrenovated character homes. These regions often turn into great family neighbourhoods, as they have larger lots or older landscaping, and are close to transit or job locations.

Before you invest in these renewal areas, you *must* drive through them to look for signs of increasing pride of ownership. These include tended gardens, new paint or siding being added to properties, and newer cars in the driveways. These properties will be surrounded by others that have not yet begun this transition; these are your target properties. Look at what has occurred in the Junction area of Toronto, Inner City of Calgary and the Yaletown neighbourhood in Vancouver; then you'll see the real impact.

🚩 RED FLAG

Never buy the best property in the neighbourhood. Buy the worst and bring it up to the neighbourhood benchmark and you will get the biggest bang for your investment dollar. And never be the first to invest in a renewal area, as sometimes the gentrification doesn't fully take hold and neglect still characterizes the neighbourhood. To reduce the risk, wait for the renewal to really take hold.

These transitional neighbourhoods aren't all located in neighbourhoods just outside of a community's "inner core." Some of these neighbourhoods are right downtown, where old, run-down warehouses are being refurbished as apartments or upscale luxury condominium lofts.

In other regions, look for dilapidated industrial buildings that are being torn down or renovated. These include in-fill developments, where developers knock down old buildings and construct narrow, zero-lot-line houses or townhouses.

 **KEY INSIGHT**

You can use these redevelopments as part of your Boom Effect fundamental strategy. As the region's older industrial buildings are redeveloped, the areas surrounding them will dramatically increase in demand.

WHAT DO YOU NEED TO DO?

Look for clues

How do you know if you've caught the neighbourhood in the right time? Look for telltale signs of continued improvement. These include a mixture of older-model cars and new vehicles. The gentrification is more advanced if the number of new cars has outstripped older models.

Look for media stories about neighbourhoods whose long-time and new property owners talk about "taking back" their neighbourhood from prostitutes and drug dealers. Meet with the local Neighbourhood Watch or neighbourhood community group to see what's going on and where they want to take the community. Like people in the economic development departments, you will find groups that have a forward-looking vision and others that don't have this quality. Invest in regions where the leadership is strong and they want to renew their neighbourhood.

Exercise prudent patience

Renewal areas have long-term profit potential. But you do *not* want to be the first investor into an area you believe is going to be in transition.

 RED FLAG

When you invest in a neighbourhood where renewal has begun, it often means you are buying into a neighbourhood with a more transient tenant profile and lower-than-average rents. The tenant situation will improve and the values increase as the renewal progresses, but it will take time. You will need patience to buy in transition areas.

🔑 KEY INSIGHT

Local investors are often the last to discover neighbourhoods going through the process of renewal. That's because they let their personal beliefs about where they would live obscure the fundamentals of their investment system. They let their emotions and past history affect their investments. This is an example of what goes wrong when you make decisions based on emotions instead of facts—you miss the biggest opportunities.

NOTES:_____

TIP #46: MAXIMIZE VALUE AND ZONING OPPORTUNITIES.

Always look for ways to make a good deal better.

The types of property available for investment are as varied as people's investment needs. Sophisticated investors learn to look at a property's physical attributes, where the property is located and what it's currently used for. Then they examine how they may be able to change that property's use—called Divide and Profit—to optimize return, an investment strategy that goes way beyond renovating an existing property to add resale value.

For example, you could purchase a rundown hotel and convert it to condominiums or rental units. This takes the property from a below-average performer to its highest and best use, with positive cash flow. The same can be true if you are buying raw land and selling it off by the building lot, thus increasing the overall value of the property.

Another example—and a much simpler one—involves buying a property that is currently a single-family dwelling and converting it to a multi-family or student-housing property. This is done by investors across the country, every day. You will need to know your local zoning and tenant regulations to make this transition successful; however, these changes will dramatically affect not only the value of the property but the income you generate from it.

Zoning will always be the key determinant; it is not just the simple act of making changes to the property. You have to do it so that it fits all of the local rules and regulations—and there are many.

WHAT DO YOU NEED TO DO?

Explore the zone

When you're looking at an area, always check into the zoning and what it allows. Examine the city's redevelopment or long-term plans for the region. Do you have the opportunity to change the zoning to fit their plans? That strategy is easily applied to a plot of raw land on the edge of a growing city or a small town, or to an area where the city would like to see an increased housing density.

Ask yourself key questions like: Can warehouses or old office buildings be transformed into trendy loft-style apartments or condominiums? Can a single-family home near a university or college be turned into a home that's rented out by the room (in other words, be "suited")?

Simple math shows how a four-bedroom home that typically rents for $1,000 a month could generate $1,600 if each renter paid $400. You would need separate lease agreements with each tenant. Rooms left vacant over the four-month summer break could be rented to summer students via short-term agreements.

Be certain you understand exactly what needs to be done to ensure changes meet local zoning requirements and safety codes.

 **KEY INSIGHT**

It costs money to change the way a property is used, and profitability may depend on getting those changes in place. If you don't have the knowledge or funds to make the changes happen, partner with someone who does.

 RED FLAG

Learn to think outside the box, but never "assume" a property-use change will be a) easy or b) possible! Avoid costly mistakes by getting the facts before you buy or make it a condition of the purchase contract. Look for opportunities that others can't readily see and you will have no lack of properties to invest in.

Take another look at that garage or storage shed

If the property has an unattached garage, think about renting it out separately if bylaws allow. Sophisticated investors rent unattached garages for anywhere from $50 to $300 per month. They rent the garages to the tenants renting the house, or to someone else who wants the space for storage or parking. The additional income vastly increases monthly positive cash flow.

This is also true of extra parking you may have on the property, especially if it is near a major employment region with limited parking. The same thing goes for property with separate storage areas. Look at the local economy to determine possible renters. Would the site be attractive to people with large recreational vehicles?

⑤ SOPHISTICATED INVESTOR TIP

If you do rent out that garage, you need to know that, in most provinces, garage rental is not covered by the landlord and tenant laws. In all cases, use a separate and non-residential lease for the garage. This improves your ability to set garage rents. Market-savvy investors also arrange for their garage leases to end during the wintertime. They know it's much easier to renew the lease when the weather is colder!

NOTES:_____

_____
_____
_____
_____
_____
_____
_____
_____
_____
_____
_____
_____
_____
_____
_____
_____
_____
_____
_____
_____
_____
_____
_____
_____
_____
_____

Tip #47: Buy Below True Market Value.

There is a huge difference between current market value and true market value. Discover the difference and see profits where others can't.

There's an old stock market joke that says everyone can make money from stocks as long as they follow the cardinal rule: Buy low and sell high. Real estate investment has a similar axiom. Fortunately, at least for real estate investors, the buy-low/sell-high supposition actually works for those who understand hidden values in properties—and how to buy substantially below true market value.

True market value is defined as the final retail value that an investor can garner for a property after he has fixed a problem and maximized its use. Sometimes this entails a massive restructuring, as in turning raw land into a subdivision. At other times it is a much simpler process, such as buying an apartment building and selling the individual units as condominiums.

Buying below market value is one of the real estate investment industry's least understood aspects, but there are a number of investors who focus their efforts on this smaller yet very profitable investment strategy. It is something that all investors should keep their eyes open for. This happens in several ways.

Foreclosures and Pre-Foreclosures: Not as Simple as They Seem

In this instance, you buy properties from lenders who have foreclosed on unpaid debt, or from homeowners trying to avoid bankruptcy or increase their cash flow—fast. In Canada, unlike many other countries in the world, accessing these properties is not as simple as it may sound. Our privacy laws are very strict, making it much more difficult for investors to identify potential foreclosure properties and obtain owner contact information. In the U.S., the process is much easier.

The best market is the pre-foreclosure market, where proactive advertising can help an investor attract property owners who have too much property and too little income. This strategy helps you solve their problem by paying them a fair value for the property, which helps them to save their credit rating. It's a true win-win. *Never ever* be a vulture and try to steal their property from them for next to nothing just because they are desperate.

CONDOMINIUM CONVERSION

Investors may purchase a larger, multi-family property, such as an entire apartment building, then convert the property so each suite has an individual title. As individual units, the units are worth far more than they were valued as a single multi-family unit. The process is known as *condominiumization* or *stratification*.

In some regions, these individual units can be sold immediately. In other areas, you have to hold them in your portfolio for years before you can sell them at a worthwhile profit. During this holding period you can rent them out to create income until it becomes time to sell.

The development of raw land is also covered under this scenario. Here, you buy the land and convert it to individual lots to be sold at retail. Although not a strict condominiumization, you are still buying a large block and selling it in smaller pieces.

 RED FLAG

Condominiumization tends to increase demand and property values in neighbouring areas. Remember this fact when you are assessing a property's long-term prospects. Will your investment benefit your own long-term wealth creation? Will it improve other local property values faster?

WHAT DO YOU NEED TO DO?

Build a network of motivated vendor contacts

Find out "who knows what" on the pre-foreclosure front in your target area. Foreclosure lawyers and trustees, for example, do look for buyers they can count on to make a deal go through. Their job is to get a fair market value for the property.

Advertise for motivated vendors who need your help with getting out of the property. Be creative!

At the same time, you need to build your list of buyers who want to buy the properties from you now or in the future. Most investors forget about building their buyer's list when, in fact, this is the most important and often most difficult list to build. Once you build a portfolio of prospective buyers for the properties you buy and convert, you will be able to confidently purchase an ever-increasing number of under-true-value properties.

Learn the art of the "simultaneous close." Here, you use your contacts to buy an under-true-value property. You then assist a new buyer in purchasing the property from you for a slight profit on the same day you take possession. Make sure that full disclosure is used to all parties and that you are only selling the property at true market value or below. The person buying from you often pays less than the appraised value (remember, always leave some profit on the table for the next owner), but probably has to do a certain amount of work to get the property ready for the traditional market. The initial vendor will be happy because you solved their financial situation, your new buyer will be happy because you were able to offer them a property below market value, and you will be happy because you will have made a small profit on the deal.

Scout condominiumization prospects

Identify multi-family properties where condominiumization is possible. Speak to a local expert who has worked on conversions and be aware that the local government will have a big say in whether they will allow it and what steps you must do to get it condominiumized. Issues will include fire-code standards all the way to more political concerns that conversions will deplete the rental market stock. In all cases, the local politicians and bureaucrats will have a lot to say about your conversion. Follow The Condominium Secrets at www.reincanada.com .

 RED FLAG

Condominium-conversion investments take deep pockets and expertise to get started. You must realize that all of your costs are up front and your return is derived only from the sale of the property. Your business plan must take this into consideration. If you need to hold individual units in your portfolio for several years, make sure your business plan reflects that reality!

NOTES:_____
_____
_____
_____
_____
_____
_____

TIP #48: ADD VALUE WITH A MARKET NICHE.

The more focused your real estate business, the more profitable it will be.

Newcomers to the real estate investment market often follow a pretty linear train of thought. They see real estate investments as generating long-term wealth in one of two main ways: You buy and hold quality rental properties that appreciate over time, or you adopt a quicker-cash strategy via the reno-and-flip deal.

Reality paints a different picture and savvy investors will explore niche-market opportunities like those outlined below.

RENT-TO-OWN

With this strategy, you will find quality tenants for quality properties and set up a formal agreement whereby they can graduate from renters to owners. The renter gets a limited down-payment rate in return for owner financing and proving they are a good credit risk. (This subject is covered extensively at Real Estate Investment Network workshops and has proven to create tremendous relationships between landlords and tenants.) Tenant hassles disappear as tenants begin to treat the property as if it was their long-term home, and tenants save money every single month towards their purchase. This is a great way to give back to society, as it shows people who thought they would never be able to own a property how they can become homeowners.

FURNISHED SUITES FOR RENT

A highly mobile workforce means large urban centres have a growing number of employees who only live in their cities on a part-time basis. When major construction or engineering projects are announced in a region, an instant opportunity arises. These large projects attract experts from across the country for short stays, often in hotels. However, many would prefer to stay in a rental property, as it is not only cheaper but much more comfortable (especially in smaller centres). You furnish your rental property with comfortable yet simple furnishings and then get creative with your marketing to attract these professionals. The rent is often

50% to 100% above market rents for an empty suite, and is still cheaper than a hotel.

There are literally dozens of these unique niche strategies you can use to increase your investment returns. Make sure that you are following one that has been proven to work in Canada over a long term.

WHAT DO YOU NEED TO DO?

Educate yourself

Identify your target demographic and figure out who needs your "product." Learn what's important to them in terms of amenities (schools, work, recreational areas) and investigate market prices for a similar product.

If small families are your target for a building, look for unique ways in which to attract them. (Use your advertising to alert people to local schools and daycare facilities, extra-large washers and dryers, etc.) Identify a niche and then put yourself in the tenant's shoes. Advertise where they read, talk directly to them in your ads. (Do not write generic ads—be creative. See Tip #51.)

Develop a quality marketing program that zeroes in on your target market.

Be service-oriented

Tenants most interested in the rent-to-own category may have encountered bankruptcy, or be close to that position. They may not know they could qualify for a new mortgage a year after declaring bankruptcy. To improve the deal's rent-to-own success, include financial counselling in their rent-to-own agreement.

Find out what amenities (Internet, cable TV, on-site parking) your furnished-suite clients need most and then supply it. Also make sure your kitchens and bathrooms are well equipped. Do your suites offer a toaster, blender, microwave, good set of knives and a hair dryer?

 RED FLAG

Make sure your niche actually exists and is reachable. For instance, don't try to force furnished suites in an area that already has too many hotel rooms. Check the student-housing situation before considering them as a target. If the local schools are growing, then you have lots of potential; if the student population is declining, then the demand will already have been filled, so look for another niche.

TIP #49: STAND OUT FROM THE CROWD: THE DIFFERENCE BETWEEN PROFIT AND LOSS.

No matter what real estate strategy you are following, you will have competition. Learn how to get your message out so it's heard!

Everything you do in your business must have a consistent and clear theme. From the first contact with a vendor, to attracting new renters and working with your bankers, consistency in message is critical. As U.S. business guru Dan S. Kennedy states, "No matter what business you're in, you're always in the business of marketing." And that is especially true in real estate.

The important point to note here is that we're not talking about marketing or selling a property—we're talking about your whole message.

Small, focused marketing steps can make all of the difference in the world. Once again, it is all about knowledge and learning what your target is looking to hear. From classified ads to billboards and flyer drops, marketing is the engine that drives your real estate. Marketing includes everything from how you answer the phone, to getting your prospect to the door, to curb appeal and inside-suite condition. How the prospect is treated while viewing the suite is also part of the marketing strategy. Indeed, every step of the process must be thought of as a marketing opportunity.

⑤ SOPHISTICATED INVESTOR TIP

Matching your message to your prospective target is critical. If you are trying to get a mortgage, target your message and presentation to a banker's point of view. If you are trying to attract motivated sellers for your property, make sure you are speaking their language. In other words, put yourself in their shoes, think about what they will be looking for—then give it to them wherever possible.

WHAT DO YOU NEED TO DO?

Get educated

Read all you can about marketing in the real estate industry. Then put the best nuggets into action.

Define your market

Clearly define whom it is you are targeting and what you want your ads to achieve once people read them. Define your niche, get into prospective tenants' heads, and figure out exactly what they are looking for from you. Then make your message match their needs. This may sound obvious, but if you look at most ads today you will see that they target a general public—and ads like this will not produce results. The more you speak directly to your prospect, the better results you will have. (See Tip #51 on classified ad writing.)

Turn every conversation into a real estate discussion. Be proud of what you do and tell everyone. You never know where your next renter, property or investor may come from, and everyone you know is a potential dealmaker for you.

NOTES:_____

_____

_____

_____

_____

_____

_____

_____

_____

_____

_____

_____

_____

_____

_____

_____

_____

_____

_____

_____

Tip #50: Never Advertise—Always Market!

Hone your ad-writing skills and generate the data you need for other marketing materials.

The great thing about a great classified advertisement is that the process you use to write that ad will help you develop other marketing materials, including reports you plan to give to prospective investors.

The most important thing you need to remember about a quality marketing program is that it is designed to deliver business, pure and simple. *Research shows that a quality marketing program yields higher-than-market rents and premium property values.*

What do you need to do?

Become a student of marketing (not advertising)
Read all that you can about street-smart direct-response marketing. Direct-response marketing means the ad is designed to have the reader take immediate action. It has nothing to do with creating a brand!

Identify who needs your business
Design your marketing program to promote your business to renters and sellers.

Target media and on-line spots where your prospects will be reading or gathering. For instance, if you need renters and you are near a local hospital or school, why not use their bulletin boards for marketing?

🌑 KEY INSIGHT
Use lead-generating ads: Are you building your list of prospective buyers for your properties? Do you want to line up future renters, rent-to-own clients or joint venture partners? Most of these are part of an ongoing business plan that requires constant new leads.

Create your data sheet
List everything you can think of about your product and service. Include facts (spacious kitchen, new siding, rent price) and benefits (client can make

money by buying and renovating your property, immediate access for a family looking to rent, etc.).

Be creative. Identify the details that caught your eye and made you think about the property as if you planned to rent or buy it. ("Recent renovations mean your work is done." "Basement games room ready for action." "Private deck ideal for entertaining.")

Use the data sheet as part of the "Free Report" you give to prospective clients and investors.

Work with the powerful words list

Review Tip #51's list of powerful words. Where appropriate, work them into your other marketing materials, including the data sheet.

NOTES:_____

_____

_____

_____

_____

_____

_____

_____

_____

_____

_____

_____

_____

_____

_____

_____

_____

_____

_____

_____

_____

_____

_____

TIP #51: LEARN AND USE CLASSIFIED AD-WRITING SECRETS.

Never follow the crowd if you want real results!

Classified ads, both on-line and off-line, are a crucial part of any real estate investor's plan, providing you with renters, buyers, sellers—and much more. Because of this, it is important to learn the secrets to writing classified ads that work. The good news is that since so many people do such a poor job of writing their classified ads, it is quite simple to write ads that stand out from the competition.

Newspapers and on-line rental sites provide you with targeted prospects. Since their readers are actively looking for what you have to offer, your job is to make them choose your product over the hundreds of other advertisers.

Most sites and newspapers filter your prospects for you by geographic region, so you are truly only talking to a very select group. For example, the *Ottawa Citizen* or the *Saskatoon Star Phoenix* services a particular geographic area. Because advertisements are grouped by product (for example, "Suites for Rent" or "Single Family Homes for Sale"), motivated readers save search time.

WHAT DO YOU NEED TO DO?

Think about your client

Review your amenity list and rate each item on a scale of 1 to 5 in importance to the individual who will buy or rent your property. Put yourself in the shoes of your prospects: What are they *really* looking for in a property to buy or rent? How do you convey this to them in your ad?

Write a catchy headline

Choose the top two items you rated as being the most important features your client wants or needs. Now choose two items that make the home unique. Take one or two of these top four items and use them to write a creative classified ad headline that attracts immediate attention.

Examples:

"Get Naked with a Good Friend" (features a two-person tub)
"Free Utilities—Free View" (free utilities and a great view of the city)
"Warmth in the Winter" (fireplace on main floor and in lower-level recreation area)

Go bold with the headline, but don't use only capital letters (they make a headline hard to read!). Avoid abbreviations and do be creative! Use eye-catching phrases ("Must Rent—Off to Cuba") or name the benefit the buyer or renter will receive from your property ("Finally—A Place To Call Home. Be Proud Every Time Your Friends Visit!").

Address the potential renter's needs and wants

Think like one of your prospects and make your classified ad stand out by using catchy sentences and adjectives to paint a "word picture" of what the owners/renters can expect. "Bright Kitchen" and "Private Deck" have lots of appeal. "Instant Access" and "5-Minute Walk to Two Elementary Schools" offer peace of mind.

Write as if you're talking to one person, not a group. The words "you" and "yours" are very powerful—use them often. ("Come home to your 3-bedroom bungalow located on a quiet cul-de-sac just minutes from schools and shopping.")

Make the ad only as long as it needs to be

Keep your sentences "tight," but don't sell a property short by leaving important details out. You want to attract a long-term tenant who will pay you thousands and thousands of dollars over the time of their tenancy. Don't cut down on words to save a few dollars, thus missing out on attracting the right tenant. The people reading your ad are already looking for a specific product. Tell them what they need to know so they can make an informed decision!

Pique the prospect's interest with talk of benefits and when they call, make sure you (or your voice-mail) give them an even more visual picture of the property and the area. No more, "You've reached Bob, leave a message after the beep." Be eloquent; spend a minute describing benefits that you couldn't fit in the ad.

Leave readers with a feeling or emotion

Use emotive words such as *home, comfort, enjoy, private, bright, relax, easy* and *instant*, and back them up with pertinent details about the area ("Walk to school parks and the river valley"). Tell readers about the lifestyle your property offers ("Enjoy the sunset in your fully fenced backyard" or "Warm days on your private deck—warm nights by your fireplace").

Once you create desire for your property, add a call to action and ask for the sale or tenancy, such as: "This home can't last. Don't wimp out! Call today."

RED FLAG

Writing a classified ad takes time and effort, but it is well worth it to learn what works and what doesn't. Watch for ads that you yourself respond to. Assess what elements really stood out. Keep ads you like and look for ways to use their ideas in your own.

Use advertising's most powerful words

Re-edit that classified ad. Where possible, use real estate advertising's most powerful words. They are:

Free (utilities)
Discover (quiet lifestyle)
Proven (safe)
You, your
Save (on heating)
New (renovated)
Easy (access to transit)
Announcing (rental rebates)
Home
Warmth
Bright
Clean

Free report for readers

Register your book and get the latest version of the Classified Ad Secrets report. By visiting www.realestateinvestingincanada.com and registering your book, you will receive an e-mail outlining exactly how to receive your free copy. Written by Don R. Campbell, it will clearly give you all the tips you need to write classified ads that jump off the page and have readers grabbing their telephones to call you.

TIP #52: RENOVATE SMARTLY: IT'S A DUSTY AND DIRTY WAY TO WEALTH.

Renovation shows proliferate on TV today (and it's not as easy as they make it seem). Don't buy into the dream without having very specific knowledge. See the direct warning in Tip #64!

Renovating properties has been and always will be one of the most popular real estate subjects. There are dozens of books and at least that many TV shows, all devoted to the massive results you can create with a little paint and floor coverings. Sadly, this has really muddied the waters for real estate investors.

Let us be clear—the renovations you complete on your own home differ dramatically from the renovations you should be doing on your rental or re-sale suites if you are interested in making a profit.

All warnings about the downside of do-it-yourself (DIY) projects aside, many investors get into real estate to renovate and resell properties as a way to build their own pool of working capital. That approach can work, but only if you know what to renovate and what to leave alone. Not every fixer-upper is worth your personal sweat equity. Make sure you value your time and you learn the secrets to properly estimating and renovating a property.

Canadian renovation secrets

You can get a Canadian-specific renovations system titled "Renovation Secrets: Renovating & Flipping Houses for Quick Cash." Written by two experts who have transacted over 788 properties, it has been tested and proven for over a decade. The results that Canadians are achieving with it are quite amazing. It is available to readers of this book at a special discount by visiting www.realestateinvestingincanada.com and clicking on the Renovations Secrets menu item. This program will literally save you thousands on your renovation projects.

WHAT DO YOU NEED TO DO?

Identify the right property

Be picky. Increase the odds of success by adopting proven strategies for the renovate-and-resell market. Look for quality-built properties in areas that show an increase in pride of ownership and always use a qualified house inspector to make sure the property is structurally sound. Never compromise on this step. Major structural repairs are seldom worth the dollars you might save on the purchase price.

Properties that are slightly neglected can be a goldmine, because repair and clean-up costs may be less than a major renovation. Similarly, "cosmetic" changes are the simplest and least costly but these can include new flooring, drywall, paint and cabinets.

Assess those changes or upgrades that could prove expensive. Be honest with yourself. Your focus should always start and end with curb appeal; those upgrades that will make the property attractive to the renter or buyer.

 RED FLAG

Skip the property inspection at your own peril. Use an expert inspector to avoid major post-deal issues related to problems the untrained eye might not see, including mould due to water damage, roof repair problems or hazards linked to electrical wiring. A comprehensive inspection report also gives you a kind of quick list for repairs.

KEY INSIGHT

Many investors take a DIY approach to renovations on the first one or two properties they buy to renovate and resell. Then they start to use trusted contractors to do the improvements. You will start to really make money when you focus on buying properties with potential and then let others do the physical work.

NOTES:_____

_____

_____

_____

_____

_____

_____

_____

TIP #53: JUMPING THE GUN: INVESTING ON A WISH AND A PRAYER.

Speculation is not investment—it is fraught with risk. Know the difference between investing and speculation.

Speculation in the real estate market can lead to significant financial gains. Speculators who jumped into the Sea-to-Sky Corridor between Whistler Mountain and Vancouver, B.C., soon after Vancouver's Olympic bid was accepted, rapidly drove up property values. There, speculators made money because values rose and stayed high, giving initial speculators a chance to bail out, cash in hand. The fundamentals showed that prices were not sustainable and there wasn't much supporting them; however, values continued to skyrocket. Why? All because of speculation.

As a speculator, you can make massive amounts of profit in a fairly short time; however, this is not the same as investing. Investing is based on long-term fundamentals, whereas speculation is based on taking advantage of a unique and often short-term increase in demand. As an analogy, investors are to value-stock investors as speculators are to day traders. Money can be made in each, but the risk levels are very different.

We don't discuss speculation in *Real Estate Investing in Canada* or any of our other books because it doesn't fit the ACRE system of investing, and speculation is not a "system" per se that you can duplicate. You can't consistently read the markets when speculating; you're reacting to quick market shifts and acting on gut response. For a system to prove itself, there must be results that can be duplicated. With speculating there are too many variables that are out of your control and the risks are high—too high for investors who keep their eye on their own Personal Belize.

🚩 RED FLAG

Get the facts. Speculation on a single deal can put your whole portfolio at risk. Sure, it's tempting to get rich quick; that's why you see so many late-night advertisements, but sophisticated investors are long-term value investors.

WHAT DO YOU NEED TO DO?

Recognize the danger signs

When the excitement of the deal detracts from the fundamentals and emotions become more important than market facts, it's easy to be drawn into the hype. Remember, it is your job to ask the tough questions so you cut through the hype and get to the facts. To get your plan back on track, pull out that Property Goldmine Score Card.

Refuse to play the game

Speculative investments throw market fundamentals to the wind. When you run across a speculative deal, recognize the hype for what it is. If your goal is long-term wealth, then keep asking the questions until you get the answers you need. Speculation, and those who engage in it, operates on the premise—and promise—of quick cash to distract you from your fundamentals. Watch out for the "Gotta Act Now or You'll Miss Out!" sales pitch. It's a good sign the deal is speculative (and someone else is out to get rich quick).

NOTES:_____

_____

_____

_____

_____

_____

_____

_____

_____

_____

_____

_____

_____

_____

_____

_____

_____

Tip #54: Analyze a Property Right Down to the Last Nickel.

It's time to crunch numbers—even "future" numbers.

Many beginning investors only analyze the absolute basic expenses when deciding whether a property's income will cover the operating expenses. The most common cry of the soon-to-be-broke investor is, "I found a property and the rent will cover both my mortgage and my taxes!" Sadly, this uninformed view of investing has led these neophytes into some very bad deals.

Once again the critical key is to be brutally honest about a property's potential. Assess the "true" income that it can deliver (rather than what you hope it will) along with all of the ongoing expenses you'll need to cover with this revenue (much more than just the mortgage and taxes).

This is also true of the costs of closing on a property. Many beginning investors fail to assess the true cost of buying a property, which adds up to much more than just the down payment and legal costs. Sophisticated investors know that there are many additional costs that need to be budgeted for well in advance.

What do you need to do?

Crunch the numbers

Take a harsh look at all properties you will be investing in. Don't ever get caught wearing rose-coloured glasses when doing your analysis. Sophisticated real estate investment comes down to bare-bones number analysis. (At the end of this tip, we'll give you a checklist you can use to ensure you are analyzing a property in detail.)

Be thorough

Remember all the talk about how successful investors go the extra 10%? This is another place where that 10% saves and makes you money. Leave no details out. Sure it takes an extra few minutes, but this analysis will tell you the truth about the property and save you from getting caught in a bad deal.

Cash-Flow Analysis Numbers: Make sure you get accurate numbers for all of these and any others that are specific to your property:

Income:
Rent
Laundry
Parking
Other

Expenses:
Heat
Electricity
Water/Sewer
Property Taxes
Condo Fees
Insurance
Property Management
Vacancy Allowance
Repairs & Maintenance
Snow Clearing/Landscaping
Mortgage Payments

Closing Costs:
Legal Costs
Legal Disbursements
Professional Inspection
Appraisal
Title Insurance
Property Survey
Mortgage Fees
CMHC Fees
Land Transfer Tax
Property Insurance
Renovations
Reserve Fund

NOTES:_____

_____

_____

_____

_____

_____

_____

_____

_____

_____

_____

_____

_____

_____

_____

_____

Tip #55: Perform Special Due Diligence on Vacation Property.

The fundamentals for vacation property are a little different.

There are two kinds of recreational property: personal use and pure investment. Make sure you are honest with yourself as to what is driving your recreational property investment. If it has a personal-use component to it, feel free to let emotions come into the equation; however, if it is truly an investment piece, then emotions *must* be taken out of the equation.

The wonderful thing about owning recreational property is that you may be able to use it for revenue and your own R&R. The drawback about buying recreational property as revenue property is that it could compromise your whole system, leading to less R&R—and way more stress.

The most important thing to understand here is that due diligence regarding vacation property involves more than the basic market fundamentals.

🚩 RED FLAG

It may not be a real estate investment, even if it looks like one!

This is true in all types of real estate investment, but is most common in recreational or tropical property. It is only a real estate investment if you have full, 100% control over the title of the property. You will get a full certificate that outlines your exact suite or property, and you have the regular real estate market to sell it into if you ever wish to.

Unfortunately, many people believe that buying a time-share or a percentage interest in a property is a real estate investment when it is really a security like a stock.

The key is full control of a specific property. If you don't have control so you can solve problems, increase value, increase rents, do renovations and all the things that sophisticated investors do to increase value—you aren't investing in real estate.

Another test as to whether it is a true real estate investment is available exit options. A true real estate investment will provide you many and varied exit options that are in your control. An investment that limits your market (i.e., there turns out to be no market for your time-share or your percentage

Red Flag continues

interest in a property), or puts limits on who you can sell to, is *not* a real estate investment.

Make sure you are taking the emotions out of these decisions. Base decisions on fact. If you are buying a security supported by a property, it is still a security. And *always* review your exit strategies; if they are limited, the value will be greatly diminished in your portfolio. If you can't cash in your profits, the profits are no good to you!

WHAT DO YOU NEED TO DO?

Check emotions at the investment door

The recreational market is not like a traditional market for revenue property. For one thing, demand for recreational real estate usually spikes during its peak-use season, putting upward pressure on prices, too. If you are going to buy in the recreational market, buy in the off-season when there is less competition.

Let your strategy lead. If it's a summer property, return to the area in the winter when purchasers are few and far between and vendors are much more motivated. Also, it will help you identify the underlying strength of the region's economy. If the economy and therefore the strength of your investment is based on a short three-month season, you may wish to consider whether your investment money will perform better in a 12-month, fundamentally strong region, and use a portion of those profits to rent the best place on the best beach for the whole high season in the recreational property area.

Never ever be influenced by a smooth sales pitch. Never be embarrassed to ask the tough questions! It's your hard-earned money. Don't throw it away.

Exercise a higher level of due diligence

The amount of due diligence you need to apply increases along with the distance you have to travel to see the property.

If it is being rented out on your behalf, make sure you are digging deeply into the management company and its track record. Sadly, you will find inexperienced managers running the show because they don't cost as much, but this will cost you more in the problems and vacancies that will arise.

Establish ownership

Sounds too easy? This can be a bigger problem in some foreign countries. You need to know who owns the title to the property and precisely where the property's lot lines are. (Can renters using your oceanfront cabana actually access that ocean?)

It may sound exciting to own property in a tropical paradise. Just remember, though, "You're not in Canada anymore," so you can forget the rules and regulations we have all become used to.

In some regions, squatters can move onto your property and in just 30 days become the rightful dwellers on your property. You can't kick them off, no matter what your ownership papers say.

Visit the property

Get past the marketing messages. You've got to see it to believe it. Also be wary of promises like "a new development" or "future airport." You want to be sure everything's in place before you buy. You *must* differentiate what is real from what is marketing hype.

If you are going to buy in a foreign locale, especially in tropical countries, visit it in the high season as well as the low season. Try to live in similar conditions as the property you are buying. We've seen many people visit a region, stay in a five-star hotel and love the experience. Then, when they return at another time to try out their "investment property," real life hits home and paradise is not all that it seems.

Learn the language, speak with the locals, and ask about the property. The locals will know the current owners, how they treat people, what problems they have and much more. (This holds true for any locale you are investigating.)

Beware the mark-up

When you visit the property, find out how much similar properties cost on the local market. You may find comparable properties at dramatically lower prices.

You will find that many properties that are being sold at a distance are overpriced compared to the reality of the local market. This is because our *perception* of property value inflates prices.

If you seriously want to buy in a region (especially recreational or tropical), visit the place and start looking for yourself. Never use the excuse that it is too much time or hassle. While there you will discover just how much these distant marketed properties have been marked up. Not doing this type of homework is like buying in a small town in northern Canada because the prices are cheaper than where you live. That kind of unsophisticated investing leads to trouble.

Use your own lawyer

Vet the deal through your own lawyer/solicitor, not one used by the seller. You need solid details on everything from your property lines (how close to the shoreline do you own?) to restricted uses, dispute procedures and how money will be transferred to you.

A different legal system and culture also puts different legal issues into play. What are the squatters' rights for the area, for example? What about the responsibilities and liabilities of the owners? Each country has different rules and, sadly, even the sales team or developers don't know all the rules.

Be accountable

Ask yourself, "Who will be 100% responsible for your investment?" It won't be the "local representative" noted in the contract—so invest accordingly!

🕐 KEY INSIGHT

The property can be down the street, around the corner, or across the world. But if you're buying it as an investment, the fundamentals of your investment risk strategy always stay the same. Look at every property for what it is: an investment in your future. Don't get caught with the lure of "tropical or lake-side paradise." Make sure you have done all of your homework well in advance. Remove the emotion!

NOTES:_____
_____
_____
_____
_____
_____
_____
_____

PART 5

DATA, BRICKS AND MORTAR:
THE PRACTICAL SIDE
OF WEALTH CREATION
THROUGH REAL
ESTATE INVESTMENT

TIP #56: ASK THESE CRITICAL QUESTIONS BEFORE BUYING *ANY* PROPERTY.

Uncover the hidden problems and opportunities. Never skip a question.

Pilots never skip their pre-fight checklist—and neither do sophisticated real estate investors. No matter how thorough a sophisticated investor becomes in completing his or her due diligence, he or she knows that a checklist of questions will help avoid potential pitfalls. And when it comes to real estate investing, avoiding problem properties is just as important as finding solid investment properties!

Here are the questions you must have answered before you even consider buying a property.

WHAT DO YOU NEED TO DO?

Ask: Is this the right area?

Step one is to determine that you are looking in the right area. You answer this question by working through the macro questions outlined on the Property Goldmine Score Card (located in the Appendix).

Ask: What does your due diligence tell you?

Here, you dig into the micro questions of a particular property by getting answers to the questions in the Every Property Due Diligence Checklist (see the Appendix). These questions help you determine the facts on the specific property. They cut through any of the hype or emotion that surrounds purchasing the property.

The more often you ask these questions, the faster you'll get to the answers. To speed up the process, many sophisticated investors have their real estate agents get answers to these questions *before* they even present the property to the investor. This saves the agent and investor real time, since they both get to focus on properties that fit the investor's system. When you focus on the facts, you fine-tune your system and improve your portfolio!

KEY INSIGHT

If you have trouble getting answers to your questions from a vendor, that's a sign there could be some hidden problems they would rather not discuss with you. This is great news, as you now know you either need more clarity, or you need to walk away from a potential problem property.

SOPHISTICATED INVESTOR ACTION STEP

Due diligence accomplishes more than you might think! Once you are happy with the answers to the questions on your checklist, you can present your findings to your lender when applying for a mortgage. This extra due diligence gives your banker more good reasons to say yes to your loan. For a refresher on the value of quality information delivered in a quality presentation, review Tip #27.

NOTES:_____
_____
_____
_____
_____
_____
_____
_____
_____
_____
_____
_____
_____
_____
_____
_____
_____
_____
_____
_____

TIP #57: COVER YOUR ASSETS WELL.

You've worked hard to build your portfolio. Make sure you spend time to ensure you're insured properly.

Not all insurers are created equal, and not all properties can be insured equally. Insuring rental properties is much more difficult than insuring your home. There is a lot more to consider, especially since many insurance companies have dramatically reduced their coverage of rental or investment properties, further complicating the whole issue of asset insurance. The crux of the matter is that every insurance company has its own rules and guidelines, some good and some bad. That's why it is critical to have a veteran investment real estate insurance broker on your team.

The different insurance regulations on rental properties take beginner investors by surprise. You need to understand that insurance policies have *exclusion clauses*. In other words, insurance covers some things—and not others!

Insurers may, for example, require an upgrade of electrical service before the company will insure a residential property, while others will accept it as is. You will want to have this discussion with your insurance agent *long* before you remove conditions on the property.

 **KEY INSIGHT**

Insurance companies are revising their policies all the time. As a purchaser, then, ensure that your purchase offer includes a clause that gives you time to have a property analyzed for insurability. Many unsophisticated investors don't consider the insurance needs of a property until after they have removed conditions. They then run into difficulty when they find out that they can't get insurance on the property without investing in extensive renovations. A finance company will not provide funds on an uninsured property. *Never* remove conditions of a purchase without first confirming insurability.

 RED FLAG

Many insurance companies won't insure a residential property with 60-amp service. They will stick to this guideline even if it costs them the rest of your business. Others might not insure a home with suites that share 100-amp service. They require a 100-amp panel per suite. Be clear with your insurance broker as to what is required, well in advance!

What do you need to do?

Put an insurance agent on your team

Find an insurance agent who has worked with owners of rental properties. Make sure he or she knows what you're doing and understands your real estate investment portfolio. There is a vast difference between an insurance broker with rental property experience and one who has only dabbled in it. Find a veteran and tap into their expertise. If your broker often turns down your insurance requests, you are probably working with the wrong broker.

Discuss discount opportunities for bulk purchases. Ask about their discount levels and how you can achieve them. Discounts are often based on the number of properties or the value of your complete portfolio.

Make appropriate insurance a condition of closing

To avoid closing a deal on property that's difficult to insure, add the following to your offer: *"Subject to Vendor arranging appropriate insurance on property within 10 days of acceptance."*

Talk to your insurer before you remove the final conditions on the property and you won't get caught in a bind at the last minute.

Talk insurance specifics

Ask your broker about policy exclusions. Determine whether you need a basic policy, a mid-level policy or a premium policy. Learn about the differences in costs and coverage.

Be aware of hidden rules. Find out, for instance, what your liabilities are if the property becomes vacant. You may have to pay an increased premium. Be specific and ask whether the coverage is still in effect, since some policies become void if the property is vacant.

 RED FLAG

Your insurance will not cover tenants' personal property. Make sure they know that and encourage them to insure their belongings. Insurance companies offer tenant insurance. As many tenants aren't aware they're not covered, you can pass this information on to the tenant as a service.

Find out about replacement-cost and rental-loss insurance

Make sure your property is covered with replacement-cost insurance. This applies to condos, too. When buying a condominium, have your professional review the insurance policy the condominium corporation has on the building. Look for specific provisions such as the replacement cost if the property should happen to burn down.

Do your best to arrange rental-loss insurance. This will cover you in case your property becomes uninhabitable due to an insurable event. It will pay you what your monthly rent would have been until the property is in condition to rent out again. This simple clause has saved investors hundreds of thousands of dollars over the years.

🕐 KEY INSIGHT

The banks will want their mortgage payments even if a property has been burned and is uninhabitable. Rental loss insurance will provide you this critical source of revenue. Discuss this with your insurance agent up front.

NOTES:_____
_____
_____
_____
_____
_____
_____
_____
_____
_____
_____
_____
_____
_____
_____
_____
_____
_____

TIP #58: A MULTI-FAMILY PURCHASE GETS COMPLICATED—FAST. BE PREPARED.

These deals promise easier management. But they're definitely more complicated.

Multi-family purchases (MFPs) are a great way to optimize your time and cash flow. Instead of six tenants living in six separate properties scattered across the region, you can have all six living in a six-unit dwelling at one address. This can result in far fewer hassles and often yields substantial monthly savings on your operating expenses.

Imagine only one roof, one heating system, one yard to maintain. That is a positive aspect of multi-family unit ownership. But the good news comes with a buyer-beware codicil. If single-family homes are at the first level of real estate investment complexity, then multi-family properties are a definite step up—way up. With multi-family purchases, the purchase and due diligence are more complex and you have additional issues with choosing tenants who will get along (or at least not bother each other).

WHAT DO YOU NEED TO DO?

Apply the MFP rules of due diligence

As discussed in Tip #26, the due diligence required of an MFP is more complex and more expensive because it takes you into the world of the "large commercial lender." With an MFP, you often deal with what the industry calls a commercial mortgage lender. And these lenders have a completely different set of rules.

In addition to all the regular analysis and due diligence, you will often be required to undertake an environmental study of the land and an engineering report on the infrastructure of the building. This will cost you substantially more than single-family-home due diligence.

Understand the environmental study

Almost all commercial lenders require a Phase 1 environmental study to help them determine if there are any current or future environmental issues that will devalue this property. If the Phase 1 study uncovers potential issues, you may be required to go to Phase 2, and that is where costs start to skyrocket, potentially into the tens of thousands of dollars.

Know the fire code

Your due diligence should also include reports from the local fire department to make sure the property meets the required fire code. Many jurisdictions now require multi-family owners to bring their properties up to current fire codes, even if the property was built decades ago, under a different code. These repairs easily run into the tens of thousands of dollars, and if you are not aware of them, they can make a good deal go sour very quickly.

Get the building inspected

Most lenders will be very specific on the building infrastructure inspection. They will require an engineering firm to sign off on the complete inspection. Obviously, this makes it much more expensive than a regular house inspector's report.

 **KEY INSIGHT**

A detailed inspection gives you the approximate costs of any required repairs. This information gives you an opportunity to negotiate purchase conditions with the vendor. You can present the "third party" report from the engineer and require that the repairs be done before the purchase is finalized (closes), or negotiate a discount off your purchase price. The inspection will also help you decide whether to purchase or not; if the building requires substantial repairs and you are not getting it at a substantial discount, it may be better to walk away.

Examine the MFP record

Many municipal jurisdictions keep records of complaints against residential properties. The emergency response department (ERD) may not go out and search properties for violations, but it may keep records of properties against which complaints have been filed. If those complaints led to a work order and that work order was not completed, you may be responsible. (Example: Basement windows that are smaller than current requirements for that property type. If you don't complete your due diligence by checking with the city bylaw enforcement team, you could be stuck with an order to immediately replace each and every basement window at your cost.) If, on the other hand, you find this out in advance of removing your conditions, you can go to the vendor and negotiate compensation.

RED FLAG

The MFP record and ERD file are especially important if the seller doesn't have, won't provide, or insists on an "as is" condition regarding a property you haven't been able to inspect. Any time your questions go unanswered, you need to see it as a sign of hidden trouble. Dig deeper!

Get the tenant files

We will discuss the basics of tenancy. Here we will just say that regardless of whether you have one tenant, or many, the rules are the same: You need to confirm tenant information *before* you remove conditions or take possession of the property. Too many investors are left with a very bad deal simply because they did not confirm the tenant information in advance. For example, a vendor may embellish the rent rolls or promise certain rental incentives. If you don't get confirmation from the tenants in advance, you will be stuck fulfilling these promises even though you did not budget for it.

Ideally, you need to obtain tenant files to ensure there are written leases signed by both parties. Then review each tenant file with the lease, the move-in report and the tenant application. Record this information on a spreadsheet if you can't take copies with you.

Know your lender's requirements

Most MFP vendors provide buyers with an opportunity to review the rent roll and ascertain the vacancy levels. If you're getting new financing, the new lender will likely demand a certified rent roll where the seller warrants that the vacancies are at a certain level. Your lender then approves the mortgage based on a certain vacancy level.

If at closing (perhaps two or three months later), the vacancy level is higher than the level at which your mortgage was approved, most lenders will hold back some of the funding until the approved vacancy level is achieved.

In extreme cases, the lender can refuse funding and reverse their mortgage approval if the vacancies (and, therefore, the income) are not at the level agreed to in the mortgage-confirmation letter.

Get a post-closing adjustment agreement

With your offer, include a post-closing adjustment agreement. Add this as a schedule to your contract and ask that it be signed and returned with the contract. A post-closing agreement allows your lawyer to hold back some funds to take care of anything the vendor promised to do but didn't complete. In most cases, these funds aren't required because the vendor fulfils his or her obligations. The funds are then immediately transferred to the vendor. The agreement protects you from cases where the required work is not complete. This holdback for post-closing adjustments is there for you to complete the work without the money coming out of your pocket.

You'll also want to have the tenants sign rental confirmation forms to confirm the amount of rent they are paying, when it's due, the amount of their security deposit and any side deals they may have with the vendor. Once you receive these forms, make sure you compare them to the information you have from their tenant files and the certified rent roll that was provided you. This is another use for the post-closing holdback of funds.

Spend some time on that vacancy issue

While the deal is conditional, get your lender to state clearly in writing what vacancy level he or she will accept. Compare the lender's vacancy requirement against the current building situation.

Make sure your seller knows what your lender wants and negotiate further how the lender's requirements will be achieved. After you have removed conditions, even though you haven't yet taken possession, you may wish to assume responsibility for choosing tenants. As the current owner will no longer be responsible for long-term tenant choices, this ensures you won't get stuck with less-than-desirable tenants.

Factor in "normalization"

No matter how thick the contract and how diligent the research, you can expect some unforeseen time and expense associated with assuming an MFP.

There will always be a normalization period after you take over the property. During this period (often three to six months, depending on the quality of the building), don't expect to be taking out much in the way of positive cash flow. There will always be surprises and these surprises inevitably cost you money. Make sure you are prepared for this and budget accordingly.

TIP #59: PROPERTY TAXES ARE INEVITABLE—SPREAD THE PAIN!

Make property taxes part of your monthly cash-flow calculation.

Real estate investment is all about managing cash flow. Sophisticated investors know the mental pain involved with writing a large cheque for property taxes every year. They also know monthly tax payments will ease that pain—and help them stay on top of important information about how their property is performing every month. *This tip is especially critical if you have a number of properties with taxes that fall due on the same date!*

WHAT DO YOU NEED TO DO?

Work with the local tax authority

Call the local tax authority and find out what you need to do to make regular monthly payments instead of a large lump-sum payment. Set it up so these payments come directly from your bank account. This makes them part of your monthly cash-flow calculation.

☯ SOPHISTICATED INVESTOR TIP

If this monthly approach is one you would like to adopt, implement it in January. All of your quarterly, semi-annual and annual cash flow assessments will now include a critical piece of information.

NOTES:_____

_____

_____

_____

_____

_____

_____

_____

_____

Tip #60: Be Realistic About Subdivisions.

These developments look like a great way to "get rich quick." In reality, they are much more complicated and expensive than most think.

We've all seen the advertisements for future subdivisions. There may be ten acres of pristine land overlooking a beautiful pond with geese tranquilly swimming around, plus good access to a commuting highway and utilities that run right up to the property line. The land's currently zoned as agricultural. But hey! It's obvious the parcel is destined for residential subdivision success and all you need is the cash to start making it happen.

The dreamiest part? You'll recoup that initial cash payout and use the money to build your own dream home in a neighbourhood you put together. Pull in a few other investors and you even cut the cost of the initial risk. Sad to say but this is often a pipe dream. If you don't have the experience and contacts to put together a subdivision deal, you will often bump up against some solid brick walls.

What do you need to do?

Find out what's really involved in such a development

Sophisticated real estate investors know there's money to be made in land development. They also know these deals are much more complex than buying and owning residential rental properties. Before you ever try to bring a subdivision to birth on your own, consider the following facts:

- Development agreements require a good working relationship with the local municipality. If it's the business you want to be in, make sure you know whom you'll need onside. With these deals, politics can be as important as subdivision experience.
- Never assume a zoning change will happen, or will happen in a particular time frame. Take the timeline you have planned and double it. Remember to factor these extra costs into your model.
- If the land includes lakefront property, expect other levels of government to be involved with issues concerning land use that impacts the shoreline and water quality.

- Utility providers: Get as many details as you can regarding their expected timelines for delivering their services into your potential subdivision—then double these timelines.
- Utility provision costs money. Find out exactly how much it will cost to service the lots you plan to sell.
- Hire a team of experts in the subdivision-development business. If you jump in yourself, hoping that it will work, you will invariably be shocked at hidden costs you never even considered. These experts are worth their weight in gold.

 RED FLAG

Lenders will not advance millions of dollars on a good idea, and sophisticated investors wouldn't dream of asking for it! With this kind of deep-pocket project, your due-diligence package must be extremely detailed and include a full business plan, market research on target buyers and a backup plan if the deal doesn't come to fruition. The lender will be looking at the property and at the experience of the people involved. And don't expect full 75%-plus financing—or to get all the money at once.

Beware the debenture

A debenture is an unsecured bond that is backed by the credit of the issuer but not by any specific collateral. There are two things you need to know about debentures:

1. They can be an efficient way to share the financial risk of an expensive project.
2. They can be an efficient way for many people to lose money on a single project.

Before you buy into a debentured real estate investment, do your own research. Run the project/site plan through the Property Goldmine Score Card. If you are thinking of being a financial partner in a subdivision, you are still obliged to do your own full due diligence. Consider the Property Goldmine Score Card as a bare minimum. If you blindly go in without doing your own homework, you compromise your portfolio with unnecessary risk.

Demand details from the developer

Look at the developer's background and subdivision experience. Find out if the company has enough staff to complete the project and whether it has access to the cash the project needs for completion. Check to see what safeguards are in place to make sure money raised to support this project won't be used on another. Find out what the reporting structure will be like. When will you receive reports? When will you get paid out—with the first dollars or the last? All of these are key considerations.

Also, remember that this is not a true real estate investment. Here, you are a financial partner. You are buying a type of security, not a piece of property. This greatly limits your exit strategies.

NOTES:_____

_____

_____

_____

_____

_____

_____

_____

_____

_____

_____

_____

_____

_____

_____

_____

_____

_____

_____

_____

_____

_____

_____

TIP #61: GET UP CLOSE AND PERSONAL WITH THE RESIDENTIAL ZONING CODE.

Is that suite legal, illegal, conforming, non-conforming or something else altogether?

Sophisticated real estate investors learn to survey a property for innovative ways to optimize their cash flow. They see a detached garage and think, "I can rent that out." They see a separate entrance to the basement and think, "This single-family home can accommodate two renters."

So far, so good.

The problem with some of the "obvious" revenue-generators is they may not fall within a particular municipality's regulations regarding residential zoning laws. Many jurisdictions across the country do not license additional suites in property they designate as single-family homes. This means the city or municipality may knock on your door (at any time!) and shut down your secondary suite, turning your great investment into a poor one in a single day.

Of course there are thousands of secondary suites across the country. Some areas have very clear guidelines that, if met, will allow you to license your basement suite and rent it out. Other municipalities appear to turn a blind eye, knowing that if they shut down all "non-conforming" suites there would be a housing crisis in the town.

If you are considering secondary suites in your property, make sure you know the regulations and the level of enforcement.

 RED FLAG

> Most regions will ignore your secondary suites until there is a complaint. This complaint can come from anyone: tenants, neighbours, friends or jealous family members. Make sure you do not rely on this added income to make your deal work.

WHAT DO YOU NEED TO DO?

Get the facts

Call the municipal government's development office to ascertain the latest rules and regulations. Find out how a particular municipality defines "self-contained dwellings located in a larger detached dwelling." If one is allowed, do you need to have separate cooking, sleeping and bathing facilities? Are legal parking spaces (usually, these are narrowly defined) required for each unit within a home?

Ask how you can determine if a particular suite (sometimes called a "secondary suite") is a "listed" use or a "discretionary" use. Speak with fellow investors in the region to discover what their experiences have been with the local authorities as they pertain to secondary suites.

Now dig deeper

Vendors who advertise a house with a "basement suite," "in-law suite" or "non-conforming suite" may know their suite doesn't meet the code, or meets only certain aspects of it. A non-conforming suite may be one grandfathered into that particular dwelling. It may also be "vendor-speak" for illegal! The vendor might know that, in some municipalities, development officers don't have time to investigate claims made in real estate advertisements. If the suite is non-conforming, then the value of the property is less to you as an investor. Factor that in when negotiations begin.

Be sure—before you buy!

Make sure your investment is based on fact, not conjecture. Secondary suites are not allowed in some zoning classifications. Some suites may have been "grandfathered" into new zoning regulations, while others may never have been legal. There is a definite risk in buying an investment property that does not meet local zoning requirements!

Take the address to the local planning department to see if the suite is actually conforming—*before* you remove your conditions.

🅚 KEY INSIGHT

Real estate investment has developed a certain amount of its own "lingo." Make sure you base business decisions on what that lingo really means. A "suite-able" dwelling isn't so sweet if the building and zoning codes don't actually allow another tenant. Sure, you may be able to run the nonconforming suite for a while, but you will not be able to plan on that income over the long term, since there is always the threat of this second income being taken away.

TIP #62: OBTAIN A FULL SURVEY OF THE PROPERTY—OR USE TITLE INSURANCE TO COVER YOUR FUTURE.

The survey will immediately advise you of noncompliance issues. These issues can become very costly if you haven't done your homework. Base your purchase decisions on the hard facts of a real property report.

The survey certificate is called many different things across the country (including a real property report and a surveyor's real property report). Drawn up by surveyors, it is a two-dimensional picture of your property and locates the buildings, including garages, tool sheds and decks, on the land. It also outlines how far each building is from the property lines as well as any easements or rights-of-way on the property.

Compliance is the term that describes what happens when a municipality looks at that property report and decides it meets its bylaws. Compliance issues include the physical location of all buildings, which must be a certain distance from property lines. Compliance occurs when permits for these buildings are properly issued.

Compliance also covers land- and property-use issues. You can't generally keep farm animals within an urban municipality. Without the right permissions, you also can't turn a single-family home into a rental property with self-contained living quarters on the upper and lower levels.

The reason you need a real property report and compliance is that the real property report tells the lender (and you) there are no compliance issues on the property. This means you won't have to take the garage down because it is too close to the property line, or change an overhang that passes over the property boundaries. Your lender uses the information to protect its investment and make sure you will not have to decrease the value of the property to make it comply.

 RED FLAG

Noncompliance issues cost real estate investors cold, hard cash. You may have to remove an illegal basement suite. A nonconforming deck that encroaches on a municipal right-of-way may have to be torn down at your expense. Be aware.

WHAT DO YOU NEED TO DO?

Perform your due diligence

Never, ever, take a vendor at his or her word. Real property reports and compliance are not hassles—they're documents that support your due diligence.

Write contracts that stipulate the seller will provide the real property report and evidence of compliance 10 days before closing the deal. Make it the seller's responsibility. Once you get the report, keep it in your files so you can provide it to the person who purchases the property from you in the future.

Be forewarned that decks, especially covered decks, often are noncompliant. The encroachment of decks on the utility right-of-way is a major (not a minor!) encroachment. In a worst-case scenario, the municipality can order noncompliance issues rectified immediately—even *before* it will allow the property to be transferred at the land titles office. The municipality can refuse the permits and order that the deck be torn down and removed. If a deck encroaches on the municipal right-of-way and it interferes with any work the municipality has to do in the future, you could be responsible for the cost of removing that deck.

A vendor's lawyer could claim you are being unreasonable in not wanting to close a deal despite issues related to permits and encroachments. This could lead to a demand that you pay late-closing interest costs. It can be a significant amount of money—and such an aggravation is avoidable if you've stipulated that being provided with real property reports and compliance are part of your closing terms.

If encroachment is the issue, have the vendor's lawyer obtain an encroachment agreement from the municipality. A standard agreement will state that:

- If the decks are ever removed they cannot be built in the same place; and
- If the municipality ever has to work in the right-of-way, the property owner assumes the risk if anything happens to the deck, as well as the responsibility to repair it.

🔑 KEY INSIGHT

A real estate-savvy law firm may not start a title-registration process unless it has seen a real property report or that title insurance is in place. Its goal is to make sure you understand the legal implications of a purchase and the risk of buying property that doesn't match a real property report or meet municipal compliance.

ⓢ SOPHISTICATED INVESTOR TIP

Title insurance has become increasingly popular in Canada. It is used extensively in the east and is slowly being adopted out west. Title insurance is used in place of, or in addition to, a formal survey certificate/real property report. It provides you with select coverage in case the property is found not to conform in the future. In addition to many other benefits, some title insurance policies will even pay for the renovations required to make it conform—so make sure you shop around! Title insurance also helps you close on a property more quickly than if you were to arrange a new survey certificate.

NOTES:

TIP #63: KNOW THE BASICS OF CONDO-PROPERTY MANAGEMENT.

Multi-unit rental projects owned by individual investors require three levels of management.

The legal and practical aspects of property management are quite different when a strata-titled multi-unit rental property is owned by numerous individual investors. Investors should understand the basics of the three management levels, and know how one builds on the other.

Each province has its own set of rules that control the operations of a condominiumized property. Make sure you become well versed in your obligations as a condo owner and learn what the regulations state for rentals, reserve funds and special assessments.

WHAT DO YOU NEED TO DO?

Understand the three levels

Owner/occupiers and the occasional investors who do their own management would be at Level 1 strata or condo management. Investors who do not want to be part of a management pool would be at Level 2 (tenant acquisition and administration), and most other investors would be at Level 3 (rental-pool management). In projects owned by one investor, the distinction between the three levels is much less important.

🚩 RED FLAG

Property management is not cheap and, as with most purchases, you get what you pay for. Find a property-management company with extensive condominium experience. Its personnel will be much more aware of key and hidden regulations and, more importantly, know how to deal with issues that arise. These condo experts are often *not* the same management companies that will be managing your single-family or smaller multi-family properties. Go with the experts; the extra costs will be well worth the hassle-free management they'll provide. That said, don't assume a company offers better management just because it charges more than the market average. Get *lots* of references.

🔑 KEY INSIGHT

Get into the habit of reviewing all property-management costs on a project before you invest, then review the costs again after you've owned it for a while. Watch for "fee creep." This occurs when small, incremental fees are added by management over time. You'll find that most management companies are 100% above board. But it's your business and you want to ensure the people you have put in charge of your business are doing their job for a fair "wage."

NOTES:_____

_____

_____

_____

_____

_____

_____

_____

_____

_____

_____

_____

_____

_____

_____

_____

_____

_____

_____

_____

_____

_____

_____

_____

TIP #64: PUT YOUR RENOVATIONS TO WORK. (IT'S NOT AS EASY AS MOST THINK!)

Factor renovations into your investment plan, and make sure you finance the work with profit in mind.

We all know renovations can make you money. However, it can be fiscally dangerous to jump into a renovation project without following a system, especially since the rules about renovating a rental suite are substantially different from those involved with renovating your home. When it comes to your home, emotions are allowed to run wild. Unless you are thinking specifically of resale, you can choose colours, textures, fixtures and appliances based on your personal taste. In a rental property, that same approach drives the budget up beyond economic hope. It can also make your property difficult to rent.

Treat a rental suite reno like it's part of your business. You need to remove your personal preferences, replace them with information about what your target renter wants—and still be cost effective. A whole book could be written on this subject! A proven Canadian-specific system is available for investors looking to know exactly what renovations to do and which ones to avoid at all costs. It is titled "Renovation Secrets" and is available at www.realestateinvestingincanada.com .

You need to make sure the renovation *financing* won't eat away the profit from that new kitchen—or flush the cost of a new bathroom down the drain! When estimating the cost of the renovations, make sure you add a 50% buffer to cover the issues that will inevitably arise. Remember to be honest with your banker. Presenting an honest reno budget is further evidence of your willingness to do the extra 10%!

THE LOC OPTION

A line of credit (LOC) may be the best way to finance a home renovation that costs less than 75% of the home's value. A LOC can be registered as a second mortgage, leaving the first mortgage in place.

Canada's chartered banks can't lend a homeowner more than 75% of the value of a home without having the loan insured. Those premiums can add a significant cost to a renovation project and must be factored into your business plan. (A 2% insurance premium on a loan of $90,000 would cost a borrower $1,800.)

THE PPIL OPTION

A purchase plus improvements loan (PPIL) is used when buying a home where improvements are necessary to add value to the house. PPILs are also good for renovations. The key? They must add value to the house. PPILs can save you money because lenders will let you borrow based on the post-renovated value. That negates the 75% rule—and saves the insurance premium.

WHAT DO YOU NEED TO DO?

Calculate the real costs

Determine the pre-renovation value of your house and the cost of the renovations.

Get an appraisal

Have the property appraised as-is and request the appraisal include an "after-renovated value." Take both of these to your banker or mortgage broker. The bank will give you the mortgage based on the post-renovated value. The catch? The renovating cash (a cash holdback) will be held in trust or by the bank until the renovations are done. Once that happens, the holdback is released.

🅞 KEY INSIGHT

A failure to calculate accurate renovation costs is one of the main reasons greenhorn investors don't turn a profit when re-selling renovated properties. Fixing up a basement in a single-family home is a bad investment for most investment properties. You won't recoup this $25,000 in the increased value of the home. However, the money spent on the above-ground floors (especially on the kitchen, bathroom and light fixtures) will give you an immediate return on your investment. Remember to always follow a proven system, like the "Renovation Secrets" program mentioned previously. The small subtleties make all the difference. Never guess what the renter or next purchaser wants—go with the facts. You can and should learn from the mistakes of others. Make sure your plan for the property covers the added costs of the borrowed funds used to complete the renovations.

TIP #65: DON'T CRY THOSE CONTRACTOR BLUES: PROTECT YOURSELF WITH CONTRACTS IN WRITING.

Quality contractors can be tough to find. Use written contracts to protect both parties–and to build solid business relationships with contractors you can trust.

You can build a home, renovate a personal residence or make over an investment property, but the cardinal rules of contractor negotiations remain the same:

1. Get quotes and contracts in writing.
2. Decisions regarding quality and cost are not interchangeable.

WHAT DO YOU NEED TO DO?

Meet the contractor

This is an obvious requirement for most projects you are about to begin. But many forget to do this when buying a property where a renovation has already begun and the contractor is already on-site. Here, your relationship with and trust of the contractor's ability to get the job done on time and on budget is very important. A dependable and knowledgeable renovator is your best friend when working on fixer-upper properties. Treat him like gold.

Put the deal in writing

Even though you have developed a relationship based on trust and professionalism, make sure you have a clearly written contract in place (hence the name *contractor*). The contract should outline all aspects of the renovations, including plans, price and timing. It should also cover payment schedules—what needs to be completed and at what stages of completion you will make payments. It must have a clear definition of what occurs if the work is not up to your stated standard, or your timeline. Penalties and holdbacks are very commonly used to keep the project on time and on budget.

Any changes to the timeline, plan or pricing *must* be given in writing and be agreed to by all involved so there are no disputes at the end.

Contractor checklist: what your written deal should cover

The job

What's to be done? Make sure the contract describes the job completely and correctly. Go for detail.

The material

What materials and products will be used and who will make those decisions?

The permits

Who will obtain the appropriate zoning approval and building permits?

The business

How will you handle deficiencies and mistakes? How will payment be determined? (Pay-as-you-go? Instalments? Upon completion?) Who provides workers with the space, access and utilities they need to do their jobs?

Insurance requirements

Define what insurance the contractor must have in order to work on the property and to fulfil the requirements from your insurance company.

Make quality a business priority

A quality renovation project needs to suit the requirements of your business plan. At the most basic level, contracted improvements need to:

- be good
- last a long time, and
- have a positive impact on your business plan's financial bottom line.

In other words, the work has to make your property more valuable for the resale or tenant market.

That might not mean granite countertops and hardwood floors, even if that is your taste. What you're looking for is a solid return on your renovation dollar with quality products and quality craftsmanship.

To protect your investment, expect the following:

Your contractor must:

1. Be licensed.
2. Perform the work as contracted and then take responsibility for making sure changes are authorized in writing.
3. Hire skilled trades to your level of expectation.
4. Oversee the work.
5. Maintain liability and property damage insurance.
6. Maintain workers' compensation insurance.
7. Have extensive experience in your type of renovations. Don't hire a high-end craftsman to do a quick reno on your rental suite; you will be wasting his time and your money.

SOPHISTICATED INVESTOR ACTION STEP

Aim to build relationships you can count on with quality contractors and tradespeople. If the relationship is not working, do your best to fix it or move on. Learn to recognize the contractors who understand what you need and are capable of doing the work to your satisfaction. They become a "partner" in your business. Treat these relationships with the respect they deserve. Many novice investors launch their portfolios buying under-valued property they renovate with the help of family and friends. That can work, and it can also prove disastrous. To avoid costly errors, including cost over-runs related to time, make sure your "partners" share your commitment to the business plan.

NOTES:_____

_____

_____

_____

_____

_____

_____

_____

TIP #66: D.I.Y.? IN MOST CASES THAT WASTES A VALUABLE COMMODITY.

Time is a non-renewable resource that you should not waste. Make sure you spend your time where it matters most.

Many people have difficulty understanding the concept of valuing their time. In fact, we as a society are so focused on price we often forget about the time it takes us to make savings.

For real estate investors this is particularly true. Investors create wealth when they identify and buy properties that are undervalued and have positive cash-flow potential. Sadly, so many investors get caught up in the "I can do it myself and save myself some money" syndrome, they miss the point of real estate investing.

It is true that many of us could paint the property, or fix the drywall. But while we are busy doing that, a good investment deal will pass us by. In fact, we'll be so busy we won't even know it passed us by. Investors make the most money when they buy properties and rely on other trusted team members to do the other work, like management or renovations.

If you ever think that all the good deals are going to other people and there are none left for you, recognize that thought as a real indication that you are not spending your time on the things you need to focus on. Protect your time even more closely than you do your money. Money can be regained—time cannot.

🕛 KEY INSIGHT

Every job you do could probably be done by someone else for much less than your time is worth. Even if you were ridiculous and started to pay a painter $50 an hour to paint your suite, it would still be cheap in the long run. Why? Because during the time that you are *not* painting, you could uncover a deal that nets you $15,000 or more. So even though you dramatically overpaid your painter, you still came out substantially ahead of where you would have been if you'd painted it yourself and "saved yourself some money."

Arlen Dahlin, a good friend of the authors and a very successful investor, says, "Most people are programmed to step over dollars to pick up dimes." Don't let yourself be one of those types of investors! Stay focused on the most profitable use of your time in the business.

RED FLAG

D.I.Y. is also a life killer. Think: No time, no fun, and no family or friends left to enjoy your long-term investment dream!

You are obliged to bring your talents to your business and to help it to become its most profitable at the net bottom line. If you still choose to go the do-it-yourself route, that's perfectly okay. Just know that as you are scraping off the old wallpaper, other investors are out there grabbing up the great deals.

WHAT DO YOU NEED TO DO?

Pay yourself

Factor in a management fee even if you plan to manage the property yourself. This upholds the most basic of investment advice: Make sure you get paid first.

Apply a clear and accurate cost to your time. Ask the question, "What am I worth to my investment business on an hourly basis?" Once you have this number, try to only do tasks that meet or surpass this number. Will you be perfect at this task? Probably not. However, the more time you focus on these higher-paying tasks, the more profitable your investment business will be.

Be real

Property management is a 24-hour-a-day, 7-day-a-week job. If you have the time and the inclination to add an additional full-time job to your life, feel free to do so. Just know that the time spent managing investment properties limits the time you can spend finding and buying good properties. Keep a perspective on real costs. You can expect to pay 4% to 10% of your monthly rent to a management company. At $850 per month, an 8% fee only adds up to $68. That's an amazingly cheap way to buy back your time and still get 24-hour coverage, seven days a week.

 **KEY INSIGHT**

Savvy real estate investors do two things right:

1. They guard their time like it's a product of the Royal Canadian Mint.
2. They know investors make most of their money buying properties, not managing them.

Tip #67: Calculate the "Sweat Equity" Equation.

Your sweat equity has a price tag. Learn it.

Still not convinced you should put an actual price tag on your own sweat equity? Consider this: The renovation-and-resell market is one component of the real estate investment market where you can always find people making money. But take a closer look. *It's also the one area where you're going to find more than a few people losing their financial shirts!*

That's what makes this tip so sweet. Believe it or not, you can put a price tag on your sweat equity. And you can use that price tag to determine whether a particular reno-and-flip project is worth your time.

What do you need to do?

Practise the Sweat Equity Equation

The Sweat Equity Equation says the first 100 hours you put into a moderately neglected property will increase its value by 10%, as long as you follow a proven system for renovations and you know what you are doing. Just putting in time will not increase the value, but putting in time in the right areas can make a *huge* difference.

Example:

You buy a house for $100,000.
100 hours of "sweat" will typically increase its value by $10,000, perhaps more.
That equals $100 per hour.

You can make this $10,000 in two hours by finding a property that is below market value and buying it. Which would you prefer to do? Two hours for $10,000 or 100 hours for $10,000? Keep this in mind when you put pencil to paper to figure out the investment value of the specific reno-upgrades outlined in the next tip!

 RED FLAG

We have all met investors who like to "hide" in their renovation projects so they don't have to face other things that are occurring in their lives or their investments. If this is true for you, just acknowledge it for what it is. And be honest with yourself: Is this the best use of your time?

Tip #68: Figure Out the Best Bang for Your Reno Buck.

Learn to identify what needs doing—and what makes you money.

There are a lot of fixer-uppers on the real estate market and investors with a good eye for the renovate-and-resell market are always looking for ways to increase property values without compromising their investment system's cash flow.

Wise investors typically follow a quick checklist. It helps them zero in on the specific upgrades that need to be done, after which they can assess costs and calculate returns. Make sure you check out the complete "Renovation Secrets" program at www.realestateinvestingincanada.com .

If you are considering renovations, learn from others' mistakes. Spend the dollars where they will have the biggest impact on either rental or resale and always put yourself in the shoes of the prospective buyer or renter. Try to think like they do and walk into your property with a fresh pair of eyes, looking for things that would turn you off the property.

What do you need to do?

Consider a facelift

Some of the least expensive upgrades include cosmetic features like paint and carpet and floor cleaning. These simple upgrades are not structural and usually require more time than money, but they dramatically increase the perceived value of the property, thus allowing you to charge higher rent or a higher selling price.

Specific additions include new lighting, which has an immediate impact on perceived value and is very cheap to upgrade. If you paint, go with warm, neutral colours—not typical "renter beige." You want shades that are likely to match almost any furniture the new buyer owns, yet not be boring.

Fix anything that is obviously broken. Windows, doors, locks, countertops and chipped bathtubs and sinks headline the list. If not fixed, these become instant turnoffs and show the prospect that you just don't care.

Boost curb appeal

Mow the lawns, weed the gardens, trim the shrubs and repair and paint the fence. Replace the house numbers with large numbers (*not* the stick-on kind!). Install a new mailbox or slot.

Take another look at that front door: It is the first item that most prospects touch on the property. Make sure it feels "safe and secure" and is in good shape. You may want to replace it with a new bevelled metal door with a small decorative window. New doors provide tremendous return on investment.

Check all the locks and door handles both in and outside the property. This is how your prospect interfaces with the property and if these are cracked, broken or loose, the prospect gets a poor perception of your property no matter what else you've done to increase its curb appeal.

Upgrade the appliances

This is where an investment in renovation starts to get costly. Upgrading the appliances, however, is often worth the money because it boosts your monthly rental charge, can attract a better class of tenant (which is "investor code" for tenants with fewer property-management issues!) and can dramatically reduce the chance of appliance-repair bills.

There is no need to go to the top of the line. But do make sure that they match (white or black preferred) and that they are in great working order.

Ⓢ SOPHISTICATED INVESTOR ACTION STEP

If you own a property with three or more suites, find out how much it will cost you to install a coin-operated washer and dryer. If you share the revenue with the coin-op company, you remove the hassle of broken-down washers and dryers from your life, since the laundry company is responsible for maintaining and cleaning the machines.

Add a suite

This is one of the best ways to increase cash flow on a rental property. A suite in the basement of a single-family home can increase your monthly cash flow by 30% to 60%.

Suites can also add significant value to the property. When you're looking at a single-family home, look at the basement. A partially finished basement could significantly drop your reno costs, especially if you plan to develop lower-level space for an additional tenant.

Make sure that the space you're considering fits the local zoning laws and that you provide the tenant with easy, private access and egress to their suite. Review Tip #61.

Go for the major overhaul

This category is for the handyman's special and fixer-upper. Like development, this arena is fraught with traps for the rookie investor. It sounds very alluring to buy a junker and turn it into a quality rental or resale property. But knowledge is critical. If you plan to use the major overhaul strategy, make sure you have a talented team around you. This is not recommended for the faint of heart.

 RED FLAG

This is a good place to lose a small fortune! The biggest mistakes beginners make when analyzing a junker deal is to overestimate what the property will be worth after a major renovation is done and to drastically underestimate what it will cost to renovate the property. They may also forget to value their own time into the deal.

Change the property's use

Change of use is a wonderful way to add value to a property. There are many strategies that you can follow. For example:

- Change the property's zoning to allow subdivision of a larger piece of land.
- Buy an apartment building and convert it to individual condominiums for sale on the open market.
- Convert old derelict warehouses into funky lofts.
- Add a suite or two to a property that is under-utilized within the current zoning.

The strategies are truly endless. Complications aside, this kind of deal could push up your property value by 100%, 200% or even more.

 RED FLAG

These investments carry significant risks. Deep pockets are often required for a change-of-use strategy. Are you prepared to hold the property for 10 or more years if the zoning application is turned down?

Increase the income

Increase the Net Operating Income (NOI: gross income less expenses) of a revenue property, and you increase the property's value. Here, the investor identifies multi-family properties with below-average rents, then undertakes a cosmetic-level facelift and raises the rents.

Calculate your Net Operating Income (NOI) as follows:

Gross Rental Revenue + Laundry Income − Vacancy Allowance − Operating Expenses = Net Operating Income.

Revenue Increase Example: You buy a 10-unit apartment building where units rent for $400 a month, but market rent for those units is $450. Increase that rent by the $50, producing an extra $500 a month or $6,000 a year.

To estimate how this affects value, multiply the NOI by 10.

NOI = $6,000/year × 10 = $60,000.

Each region will have its own prevailing rate of return on a rental income increase. Speak with a quality investment real estate appraiser to discover your local multiplier. However, for rough estimates, 10 is an easy number to use.

🅘 KEY INSIGHT

There are other key formulas you can use to quickly get value estimates. They are:

Approximate Market Value. This calculation will give you an approximate price for the property based on prevailing market conditions and the Net Operating Income. Although this value is not the "true and final" market value, it does provide you with a number from which to work.
Approximate Market Value = Net Operating Income ÷ Prevailing Capitalization Rate.
Capitalization Rate. This calculation tells you if the vendor is in line with the prevailing marketplace. You will need to know the asking price and the Net Operating Income.
Cap Rate = (Net Operating Income ÷ Asking Price) × 100

Decrease expenses

Most investors are focused on driving income upwards and pay only a small portion of their effort toward reducing expenses. That's short-sighted, since cutting monthly expenses by \$1,000 achieves the same NOI as increasing rents by \$50.

Remember, it is what comes out at the bottom line that counts, so make sure you are continually looking at ways to reduce your expenses without being detrimental to the property.

 RED FLAG

Don't fall into the trap of deferring needed repairs and maintenance. This will (absolutely) cost you money in the long run. A smart investor can, however, often find simple and easy ways to decrease the property's operating expenses. These include installing low-flow taps and toilets, increasing the efficiency of the furnace, adding insulation, re-caulking windows and installing long-lasting light bulbs.

Identify other income sources

Garages and storage buildings can be mini-goldmines when rented separately from residential buildings. You can also buy land with harvestable timber. If you recoup your investment by selling off a portion of the timber, it's like getting the land free!

NOTES:_____

_____

_____

_____

_____

_____

_____

_____

_____

_____

_____

_____

_____

_____

_____

_____

PART 6

NEGOTIATE THE DEAL YOU WANT (PRACTICE MAKES PERFECT)

TIP #69: IDENTIFY MOTIVATED VENDORS. AVOID BEING BAITED.

Your investment success depends on closing real estate deals. Save yourself a ton of time by learning to avoid unmotivated vendors.

Regardless of how you meet a potential vendor—through a realtor, a friend or an ad in the newspaper—it is critical that you quickly discern two things. First, you have to find out if the property has a remote chance of working as a real estate investment. Second, you have to assess how motivated the seller is.

The higher the vendor's level of motivation and desire to close a deal, the better a chance exists to strike a deal that is fair for all parties. No matter what you are purchasing in your life, be it a new car, refrigerator or an investment property, the quality of the deal is determined by one thing: the vendor's willingness and eagerness to sell.

You always need to take a step back from the emotion of a possible deal and remember that an unmotivated vendor can waste a lot of your very valuable time and leave you with nothing in the end. We call these vendors "fishers." They are the people who drop their bait into the water just to see who bites. They have zero attachment to whether they sell and they're often just looking to see what their property is worth. In other words, they are not going anywhere and have all the time in the world to hold out for their price and their terms—no compromise.

All markets, hot and cold, also have vendors who want (or even need!) to sell their properties. As an investor, it's your job to help them do that. Motivated vendors will be much more flexible on price, closing dates and other terms. Remember, you are not taking advantage of their situation. You are helping them move on to the next stage of their lives, whatever that may be. A motivated vendor will be predisposed to making a deal—and you can help them do that.

But how do you know one from the other? Sophisticated investors will tell you time is money—and they don't like to waste it. They'll ask a potential vendor a few simple (and very direct!) questions, and then use his answers to guide their next steps.

SOPHISTICATED INVESTOR ACTION STEP

Never give up outright on a property you would like to add to your portfolio. Time and circumstances change a vendor's motivation level. If a vendor is currently unwilling to work with you on a deal, send him a short note that states that you would like to discuss purchasing his property when the time and circumstances are right. Provide your contact information and then just forget about it. I have heard of deals coming back to investors up to six months later. When that kind of call comes out of the blue, it signals that the vendor is now motivated and much more open to making a deal.

RED FLAG

Never second-guess whether a vendor will eventually become motivated. There is an old theory that says vendors become motivated after their property has been on the market for a "long period of time." This is utterly false. Even if a great deal of time has passed, a vendor may not be in a rush to sell. Unless his circumstances change, you'll find the same old unmotivated vendor no matter how many times you go back! The willingness to make a fair deal arises only when there is a corresponding willingness to sell.

WHAT DO YOU NEED TO DO?

Assess the vendor's motivations

You need to determine the seller's underlying motive—why is the property on the market? Is it because the vendor has elected to move as a lifestyle decision (downsizing to a condo, for example), or is the sale necessitated by a divorce proceeding? The degree of motivation is very different in each case.

Be serious about getting answers to your questions. If you can't talk to the vendor personally, write your questions down and ask your real estate agent to get you the answers. Also, look at the property records to find out how long the vendor has lived in the property. If it has been many years, your plans to ensure the property is well maintained may help negotiations.

Study the motive and figure out how you can help

Once you understand the vendor's motivation, start thinking about that motivation as a problem you can help solve. Does the vendor need money fast? Have they already bought another home? Do they want to stay in the home until their kids have finished the school year?

Learn how motivated vendors help your business

Motivated vendors have a problem to solve and they will welcome virtually any opportunity to help them sell their property. Remember not to take advantage of a desperate seller. By helping them solve their problem, you will be rewarded with some or all of the following:

- A below-market price. This is not your biggest concern but it's a definite bonus if the deal works out this way.
- Terms and conditions that suit you. You may get a closing date that is months into the future, but includes a locked-in price that protects you from market increases. You may also get a lot more fixtures or chattels than you would with an unmotivated vendor.
- Access to the property before closing so you can do minor renovations and conduct showings to potential renters/buyers. This condition gives you a wonderful opportunity to get the property ready for your renter. As long as you are not doing major renovations, you will find that most vendors will allow this. Even if you don't plan to fix up the property, the ability to show it to potential renters is a great advantage.

🔑 KEY INSIGHT

Sophisticated investors know that purchase price is one of their least concerns. While the masses may zero in on price, investors choose to focus on terms. That's why most high-quality investors advise others to "buy at market value today and sell at market value in the future." They know you will lose many great deals if you argue over the last one or two thousand dollars, since that kind of cash means very little in the end. A more successful strategy demands you keep moving forward. If you lose a property with a $50,000 profit potential because you argued over the last $1,500, you prove you are a master at "stepping over dollars to get to dimes!"

Always ask the following critical question of *every* vendor you speak with, whether you are buying from him or not: "Do you or anyone you know have any other properties you are thinking of selling?" You will be surprised at how many people say yes to this question. It's a low-effort way to learn about more properties you might want in your portfolio.

Tip #70: Negotiations Make The World go 'Round: Learn The Secrets.

Negotiation does not mean you argue over a price. Negotiation means coming to terms. Follow these rules for best results.

Many people are intimidated by the word "negotiation." That's because their only experience with what they think of as "negotiation" occurred when they bought a car. Let us be brutally honest. That is not a negotiation. That is a discussion about price between two people with opposing agendas.

Negotiations in the purest sense have something to do with price, but that's only a small part of the equation. Even if the other party believes that price is your primary motivation, you can use your knowledge about the real purpose of the negotiation process to get to a deal that works best for you. To see this in action, learn as much as you can about negotiation, then put that information to work. And don't wait until you are a master before you buy your next piece of property. Since the vast majority of vendors lacks negotiation skills, investors who apply the following rules will be far and away ahead of the game!

There are many wonderful books on negotiation strategies. For real estate investors, we have boiled it down to very clear and concise strategies (all of which are described in detail in Chapter 15 of *Real Estate Investing in Canada*).

 **KEY INSIGHT**

Use these negotiation strategies in all aspects of your life, not just real estate.

What do you need to do?

Study the rules of negotiation (all 15 of them!)

There are 15 rules of negotiation you can master. The first three are about preparation and they lay the foundation for negotiation confidence. Never skip these first three!

Practise the rules of negotiation

The Rules of Negotiation

1. **Set goals and write them down—every time.** Know your limits, including the most you can pay for the property and the earliest you can take possession. These are your outer limits: Stick with them and you will never get stuck with a bad deal.

2. **Have an agenda and a plan.** Negotiating by the seat of your pants is the biggest—and most common—mistake people make. (Re-read Rule 1!) With a clear agenda and an action plan firmly in your hands, you will know exactly where you are going and the path to get there. This prevents distractions and lets you keep emotions completely out of the equation.

3. **Create a relationship, not an armed camp.** Pay attention to the person on the other side of the table. Find out their likes and dislikes and if you have anything in common. Use this information to create a relationship rather than a confrontation. This will help both of you negotiate terms with a clearer head.

 RED FLAG

Adversarial or confrontational negotiations get you a quick, stress-ridden trip to nowhere. This approach also wastes time, because people dig their heels in—for no real reason. Always try to get to the point of the discussion. If negotiations become unmanageable or overly confrontational, walk away. There are many more great deals out there, and, since your time is money, you'll want to spend it wisely.

4. **Seek the win-win deal.** Of course you want to get the best deal for yourself, but don't try to take the last dollar off the table in every situation. Veteran real estate investor Tim Johnson taught many investors to "always leave something on the table for someone else." It's a credo the authors of this book live by.

5. **Separate the people from the problem.** Unsophisticated investors make negotiations personal. Your key is to completely separate the personalities from any real problem that arises. If the discussion gets personal, bring it back to the facts.

6. **Focus on motivations, not positions.** As we discussed in the previous tip, you need to learn the vendor's real motivation and work with that information. You accomplish this by being a good listener. It is a powerful negotiation strategy to find out where the vendor's motivations lie and help fulfil them, without jeopardizing your own. You'll find this to be much easier than you think.

7. **Search for agreement.** Throughout the negotiation, use the magic words, "Do you agree?" This strategy helps set the stage for a positive final agreement. The more small items you agree to, the easier it is to remove emotion and personality from the process.

8. **Listen only to reason, not pressure.** If someone gives you a deadline or tries to pressure you to make a decision, avoid getting pulled into their trap. The seller's agent may tell you, "Another offer is just about to come in, so you better deal now so you don't miss out." This may be the case, but we stress "may." Explain that you can only deal with your own offer and you can't control whether another offer comes in. That approach turns the tables.

9. **Be willing to walk away.** This is the most powerful tool sophisticated investors use. The masses believe they'll miss out if they let a single deal go. Sophisticated investors know another deal will come along— and may even be more profitable. Say, "It looks like we can't come to a fair agreement for both of us. Call me if things change in the future as I would like to buy this property." Those words work like magic and flush out any bluffs they may have been playing on you.

10. **Remember: Silence is golden.** When in doubt, keep your mouth shut and let the other party do the talking. The other party will invariably want to fill the silence, and often will fill it with a concession to you.

11. **He who mentions a number first, loses.** Let the other party state the price they want. Ask them to state their bottom line and work the price down.

12. **Negotiate only with the decision-maker.** Never get caught negotiating with someone who doesn't have the authority to make the agreement. If a property is jointly owned, both partners must be in attendance to approve the deal. Some nefarious vendors will negotiate a deal with you, then come back two days later saying their "partner" doesn't agree to the terms and the discussions have to start all over again. This is the real estate version of the old "good cop/bad cop" routine we've seen in movies for years.

13. **Be patient.** Allow the deal to take what time it needs—but don't get caught up if it becomes an obvious waste of time.

14. **Be confident.** You may need to fake this rule until you can make it ring true. But be honest with yourself: If you have followed the first three negotiation strategies, you already have a huge advantage over the other party and you deserve to go in with confidence. If you can't muster the conviction, be clear and calm in all your discussions, as this will give you the air of confidence.

15. **Follow through.** Once the deal is done, fulfil the terms you agreed to.

 **KEY INSIGHT**

This list reiterates some points covered in other tips! But that's the wisdom of system duplication. When rules are proven, practise them to build success.

NOTES:_____

_____

_____

_____

_____

_____

_____

_____

_____

_____

_____

_____

_____

_____

_____

_____

_____

_____

TIP #71: THE PROBLEM WITH PHONES.

Cell phones and telephones are great for setting up meetings; they're not so great for negotiation.

Every real estate investor will eventually find herself having to handle some negotiations over the phone. *Rookie investors should avoid this like the proverbial plague!*

When you can't avoid the situation, be aware of the potential for problems. Veteran negotiation trainer Randy Shuttleworth of The Training Company put together a tremendous supplement for real estate investors who are forced to negotiate by telephone. Follow these guidelines for the best results.

SOPHISTICATED INVESTOR STRATEGIES

Extra tips for negotiating on the phone

Because of the busy schedules we all have, there comes a time when negotiating over the phone is unavoidable. Here are some common pitfalls that you must keep in mind:

- The caller always has the advantage of surprise and is the best prepared.
- Important points are easily omitted or assumed.
- It is impossible to read the other person's body language.
- It is much easier for the other party to say *no* when they don't have to look you in the eye.

Avoid negotiating over the phone whenever possible. But when using the phone is unavoidable, take it seriously! Here are some quick do's and don'ts:

Do's

1. Talk less! The less you talk, the more your opponent will feel the need to fill the space.
2. If your opponent calls you, just listen and take notes. Then call him or her back with your side of the story. This will allow you time to prepare a proper response.

Sophisticated Investor Strategies continues

3. If you have to initiate the call, develop a checklist to avoid omissions and assumptions.
4. Re-state agreements in your own words and confirm the terms upon which you both have agreed.
5. Have an excuse ready to break off the discussion. This will allow you to bow out gracefully if needed.
6. *Be prepared!* Don't ignore rules just because this is a phone call instead of an eye-to-eye meeting. Telephone negotiating can work, but only if you are prepared!

Don'ts

1. Don't push yourself into a quick decision. Telephone negotiating can create a false sense of urgency where parties feel pressured to close the deal.
2. Don't negotiate an issue to conclusion until both parties understand the process for solidifying the deal. For example, how will things be put into writing? By a lawyer, a letter of confirmation, notations on a faxed order form, etc.?
3. Don't negotiate when you are involved in another activity (e.g., during a meeting or staff review, as you will not be completely focused on the negotiating process).

(Source: The Training Company, www.training-company.com)

NOTES:_____

_____

_____

_____

_____

_____

_____

_____

_____

_____

_____

PART 7

PURCHASING AND CLOSING:
THE ART OF THE DEAL

TIP #72: FOLLOW THIS DUE DILIGENCE PRIMER ON PURCHASING AND CLOSING.

Your investment system's success depends on closing deals. Do it often. But do it right.

Closing on properties that fit your system is something you really can't do often enough. Once you complete your due diligence to the point of purchasing a property that fits your system and remove emotions from the decision-making process, it is time to get that deal done and add that property to your portfolio. The next step is to carry out due diligence on the closing. We will offer specific advice on what you can do to make sure you get the deal you *think* you've agreed to. Sometimes, it differs from what all the other parties believe.

To ensure you are fully informed, we'll look at closing from the buying and selling sides.

🄐 KEY INSIGHT

A lawyer who specializes in real estate from an investment perspective is a critical person to have on your team. Make sure these types of transactions are the lawyer's number-one focus; that way you won't end up paying for their mistakes or oversights long into the future. Never hire one lawyer over another based solely on price—go discount shopping somewhere else, but do not do so with your legal or accounting advice. Make sure the decision you make is based on the lawyer's amount of experience. Once the lawyer is a member of your team, make sure he or she reviews all documents and agreements.

Our goal is not to produce fear, but to get you to acknowledge facts. *Due diligence is the foundation of a successful real estate investment system. When you follow it, you plan for success. When you ignore it, you invite trouble.*

Even if you're working with trusted business partners, or face a great deal that demands a quick decision, never skip a step. Here are five tips in one, each of which could save you literally thousands of dollars and hours of wasted time in your upcoming transactions.

WHAT DO YOU NEED TO DO?

Read your mortgage approvals from start to finish

Your lending institution will send you a written mortgage-approval document, whether you are buying a small property or a multi-unit building. No matter what the lender tells you verbally, this document specifies exactly how the mortgage is going to be structured. It will include details such as the amount, the interest rate, the payment schedule and the list of fees.

To this point you have relied on certain unwritten statements to bring the deal close to completion. These may or may not be reflected in the mortgage-approval document you have in your hand. So, check for specific conditions that you believe were agreed upon. Match up the numbers, interest rates and other figures and dates with your notes. If you find something in the document you do not understand, ask to have it clearly defined.

If all the terms fit, and your lawyer concurs, sign it. If there are changes to be made, no matter what your timeline looks like, never agree to the terms just to get the deal done.

 **KEY INSIGHT**

Never ever remove the financing conditions on your offer to purchase based solely on a verbal agreement. More often than not a verbal approval can turn into an outright rejection or saddle you with mortgage terms and conditions that are not what you required. Wait until you see it in writing before you call the vendor to remove your conditions.

RED FLAG

Mortgage and legal documents bind you to action. Never sign anything you are not in full agreement with or don't understand completely! There are no stupid questions—ask until everything is clear.

When selling, keep the keys

Simply put, never give the keys to a buyer until the deal is done. Once a buyer, even a trusted friend, has the keys, he or she may lack motivation to finish the deal. Getting the purchaser to the table with his or her money, lawyer and motivation is much easier when you still hold the ultimate prize—the keys to the property.

Once everything is in place for a timely closing, you can work with the purchaser on providing early access to show the property to prospective tenants.

Let your lawyer be your lawyer

Never let the vendor's lawyer become *your* lawyer at closing. Although this sounds like a way to save a few dollars, it can be a recipe for disaster. In these transactions, you need a lawyer who represents your interests and requirements alone. With one clear focus, he or she can protect you where needed and point out opportunities or problems. Expecting a lawyer to act for both sides of a deal puts her in the position of advising one party who might not realize he's not getting the best deal possible.

Get the facts on arrears

Assumable mortgages can make a sweet real estate investment deal. The buyer gets a good price on the property. The seller gets to move on.

When you get a number from the lender, have it broken down into:

- The principal being assumed
- The arrears total
- Legal fees.

Without this information, you could find yourself planning for an assumed mortgage based on the principal, then find out you're responsible for the other costs as well.

Stick by your own rules

Every investor develops his or her own approach to due diligence. The rules are based on what works, or what hasn't worked in the past. Every time you break a rule, you compromise your system.

Never let anyone force you to deviate from your proven system. Often these deviations have an underlying reason that is not explained to you. It may be to make someone else's life easier, or so they can get their commissions faster, or to save the lawyer time in his busy schedule. The bottom line? They work for you, not the other way around. Take control of your system, run it the way you need it to go and stick with it.

Never, ever skip a step in your due diligence just to make it easier on someone else. That skipped step will eventually come back and bite you financially, be it tomorrow or five years from now.

Tip #73: Fix Your Closing Cash Payment.

Make sure your cash payments stay fixed.

In some cases, a vendor's current mortgages can be assumed at the time of purchase. Almost everywhere in the country you will still have to qualify with the bank to take over the mortgage. The exception is Alberta, where you can still find mortgages that are fully assumable with no qualifications. These are becoming increasingly rare, but they still exist.

When assuming a mortgage, with or without qualifications, you will come to an agreement with the vendor on the specific amount of cash you will be putting into the deal. If you are not careful, this number can fluctuate at closing due to mortgage and tax adjustments, etc.

As a sophisticated investor, it's your job to ensure the cash amount stays fixed. You can do this by attaching a Fixed Cash Schedule. (See the sample form below.) On an assumable mortgage, if the mortgage goes down, the cash goes up, so make sure you have the right figures when you first negotiate the deal.

WHAT DO YOU NEED TO DO?

Get the right numbers
When it comes to having the "right figures," don't take someone's word for it; get it in writing from the lender.

Know your options
If the figures change and you don't want to put in more cash, add something like a second mortgage. It can fix the total purchase price and cash at the rate to which you and your partner first agreed.

 **KEY INSIGHT**

Use a formal written document, like the one printed on the next page, to fix your cash amount.

The following form was developed and implemented by veteran real estate investors Arlen Dahlin and Valden Palm. Use it to fix your cash amount!

Fixed Cash Schedule Form

Addendum to Agreement of Purchase and Sale

RE: PROPERTY: _____

SELLER: _____

BUYER: _____

1.1 If, on the date of closing, the actual, verified balance of the existing mortgage is less than the figure stated on the "Assumption of Mortgage" line, the difference shall not be added to the total of all deposits, but shall instead be deducted from the Total Purchase Price, and the Total Purchase Price shall be amended accordingly and so indicated on the Statement of Adjustments.

1.2 If, on the date of closing, the actual, verified balance of the existing mortgage is more than the figure stated on the "Assumption of Mortgage" line, the difference shall be deducted from the total of all deposits, and shall not be added to the Total Purchase Price, it being understood and agreed that the total of all monies paid to the seller, either by deposit or balance payable at closing, shall reduce by the amount of the said difference, with the Purchase Price remaining the same.

1.3 If the seller places a new mortgage and the buyer will assume, the Statement of Adjustments will be prepared crediting the buyer for the original principal balance of the new mortgage. The mortgage will be assumed without adjustment credit to the seller for any pay down of mortgage principal.

The purpose of the above clauses is to confirm that the total buyer's cash, as stated in the "Initial Deposit," "Additional Deposit" lines and "Balance Payable at Closing" are indeed maximums, and shall not be adjusted upwards for any reason. The minimum total buyer's cash shall always be at least $1.00 so that there is never a negative cash to close for the seller to pay. In addition, the following clauses also apply.

2.1 The buyer shall get the benefit of any property taxes already paid or to be paid by the seller to the tax collection authority or to a mortgage tax account with a lender and shall not be reimbursed or adjusted for by the buyer.

2.2 The seller is responsible for the current year's taxes, without adjustment, as well as any property taxes in arrears by the seller at the closing date or adjustment date shall remain the responsibility of the seller to pay.

_____	_____
Witness	Seller
Witness	Seller
Witness	Seller
Witness	Seller
Witness	Seller

TIP #74: CALCULATE THE *TOTAL CASH* REQUIRED TO CLOSE.

Savvy investors base their bottom-line calculations on solid data and informed estimates.

Ask a group of real estate-wise investors about the "hidden costs" of a real estate deal and you'll see knowing smiles cross their faces. That's because, at one time or another, they have been caught with a "hidden cost" at closing. They forgot to factor something in, or some cost came as a total surprise. Sophisticated investors only get caught once! Then they take that experience and add the item to their due diligence checklists.

The reality is that it takes money to close a real estate deal—much more money than you need to cover the down payment and legal costs. Novice investors may try to tell you that the up-front costs of a real estate purchase are pretty easy to calculate. If you buy a $100,000 property, a conventional first mortgage would be about $75,000. That means you need $25,000 for a down payment and $1,200 for legal costs and you're in. Right? Wrong!

Sophisticated real estate investors use the Property Analyzer Form developed by the Real Estate Investment Network (REIN) (see the Appendix) to walk them through the total costs associated with buying a particular property. This form covers the obvious and not-so-obvious costs and it ensures you do not get caught short of cash on the day of closing. To help you prepare for the real costs, here is a list and brief description of the closing cost items most commonly forgotten.

TAXES

- GST/HST: This applies to new housing—and to some homes with substantial renovations. There may be a rebate available to investors (see GST/HST tips, Part 9).
- Property taxes: It's surprising how often these are forgotten at closing. The cost depends on how much of the tax has been prepaid by the vendor and how many months are left in the local tax year. Your lawyer and the lawyer for the vendor should make an accurate adjustment for this, but in some cases the information you get may not be 100% accurate. Do a little homework yourself.

- Land transfer tax: In some provinces the provincial government demands a "piece of the pie" every time a property passes from one party to another. Each of these provinces has its own guidelines and formulas for calculating this tax. Make sure you are prepared for this cost by knowing in advance your local land transfer tax formula.

KEY INSIGHT

> In some provinces there are situations that do not warrant the land transfer tax, such as when one family member sells to another, or when the family farm is sold or transferred to a child. Have your lawyer look to see if your situation fits any of the exemptions.

INSURANCE

- Mortgage insurance premium and application fee: Mortgage insurance is one of the most expensive life insurance options out there. It is designed to ensure that if the party responsible for the mortgage dies, the mortgage gets paid off. It's a good idea, especially for a homeowner, but most sophisticated investors and homeowners decline the bank's expensive coverage and arrange for a third-party life insurance with the beneficiary. It's set up to pay off the mortgage, with any remainder going to pay a relative or charity of their choice.
- Property insurance: It has become increasingly difficult to get comprehensive insurance coverage for rental properties, but this coverage is absolutely essential to have in place before you take possession. It will be one of the conditions of a mortgage and, from a business perspective, is a critical piece of your asset-protection plan, providing protection from loss and litigation. Because there are a limited number of quality insurance companies willing to work with the average investor, you will find the costs quite high. Check with an investment real estate insurance broker well in advance of closing on a property.

KEY INSIGHT

> Because it is getting more difficult to insure certain rental properties, it is highly recommended that you include a clause in your purchase offer that allows you to check if the property is insurable or not. Include this statement: "Subject to property being insurable satisfactorily to the buyer."

OTHER FEES/EXPENSES

- Lawyer (notary) fee: Find out in advance what your closing lawyer will charge. The lawyer will take these funds out of the monies you provide for closing.
- Disbursements: These are unavoidable government and registration fees for the transfer of the property and are often worked into the bill from your lawyer for legal fees.
- Appraisal fee: In most cases, a bank will require an independent valuation or appraisal of the property. Appraisal costs vary wildly, depending on the region and size of property. If you have a good, long-standing working relationship with your banker or mortgage broker, you can often work with them to pay some or all of the appraisal fee.
- Survey and compliance fee (real property report): This is the cost of having a survey done on the property and having the local government stamp that it still fits the guidelines.
- Title insurance: This has become increasingly popular over the last few years as a replacement for the above-mentioned survey. Although the costs are very similar to a formal survey, the added benefits are well worth pursuing. Do note that different title insurance companies offer different types of coverage. You need to research the options and make sure you get the coverage you need to fulfil your requirements at the bank.
- Prepaid utility bills: In rare cases, a vendor may have prepaid his or her utilities in order to get a discount. If this has occurred, the vendor will want compensation for any remaining credit.
- Service charges for utility hookups: There is a fee to transfer utilities from the vendor's account to yours. New investors are sometimes caught off-guard by recent utility company demands for a large deposit prior to opening up an account. We've heard of demands as high as $2,000 plus deposit for small, multi-family properties.
- Moving costs: If you are moving to the property, make sure your contingency plan includes the money to cover the move and the cost of cleaning the new property.
- Condominium fees: If your vendor is not current with his or her condo fees, you could be responsible for these missed payments, depending on the jurisdiction. This can quickly add up to thousands of dollars. Have your lawyer check on this figure early in the process.

- Home-inspection fees: For each property a sophisticated investor purchases, a detailed inspection should be carried out. Make sure it is completed by a licensed expert with liability insurance. There are many people out there who call themselves home inspectors. Make sure you're dealing with a legitimate one.
- Renovation and repairs: In about 75% of the properties you buy, some renovations or fix-ups will be required to make the property liveable or to bring it up to your rental standards. Factor these in from the beginning of your analysis. This figure can be as low as $1,000, or cost tens of thousands of dollars.
- Water quantity and quality certificate (for homes with well service): If the property is on a well and septic system, you will want an expert to test the quality of both.
- Staying Power Fund: Every rental property you have should have its own reserve fund to cover at least one month of mortgage and taxes. (More is better!) Do not think of this as money you might not need. Think of it as money you will need to cover a vacancy or repair.

What do you need to do?

Complete the property analyzer form

Review the form (located in the Appendix) and commit to making *real* costs part of your business plan. Understand that this form is a critical part of a non-emotional investment system.

 Red Flag

Never ever skip the property analyzer step. It is specifically designed to make sure you remember *all* the costs of operating and purchasing a property. It eliminates surprises.

NOTES:_____

_____

_____

_____

_____

_____

TIP #75: INCLUDE A COVER LETTER WITH THE OFFER TO PURCHASE.

Cover letters boost the chance of offer acceptance.

Do you want to give your offer a significantly greater chance of acceptance? Then add a cover letter to every offer to purchase you submit. This letter will clearly define what you are offering the vendor and why. It clarifies communications and allows the vendor to make a better-informed decision on your offer.

WHAT DO YOU NEED TO DO?

Make it deal-specific

Write a letter addressed specifically to the vendor that clearly communicates why she should accept your offer. Highlight any aspects of the offer she will find most attractive based on your assessment of her motivation for selling.

If the closing date helps the vendor's need to vacate one home for another, draw attention to that point. If the purchase price is only slightly lower than the asking price, explain why it's fair given the current market or the results of your home inspection. If you are asking for any special compensation based on obviously required renovations, clearly state to the vendor why this work must be done.

Add a line or two about your experience and perhaps a couple of testimonials from previous vendors from whom you've bought property.

Treat the vendor with respect. If the vendor is a homeowner who has taken obvious pride in the property, comment on the property's condition. If the vendor is an investor, focus on the deal's numbers.

Always sign and date this letter and include your contact information as well as that of your real estate agent.

Write one letter for every offer

Sophisticated investors may make more than one offer on a property. This allows the vendor to choose whichever offer best suits his needs. Use separate cover letters to draw attention to the details of each offer.

Avoid misrepresentation or miscommunication

A formal offer to purchase (using a form you developed for your system) helps you make exactly the offer you want to make. A cover letter helps you convey your message to the vendor. It ensures a vendor gets the message you want, versus someone else's biased interpretation of what you want from the deal. Your letter may, for example, draw attention to how your offer facilitates the resolution of a specific vendor motivation, be it a price or possession date.

 **KEY INSIGHT**

> Make sure this cover letter forms a part of the offer to purchase and is delivered directly with and attached to the formal offer.

Optimize your letter's impact

The letter should be brief and to the point. Always sign in blue ink, so the vendor knows it's not a photocopy. Staple the letter to the offer so they can be presented together.

If it is addressed to a homeowner, and you have very clear handwriting, feel free to hand-write the letter. Sometimes this can be less intimidating.

KEY INSIGHT

> Not everyone uses cover letters, or is familiar with the strategy. Ignore those who tell you "we don't do that here," or "it's not necessary." This is your strategy. Successful investors know it works and that's why you've adopted it.

NOTES:_____

_____

_____

_____

_____

_____

_____

_____

_____

TIP #76: THE LAWYER ALWAYS GETS THE CHEQUE.

This is not a tip. **It's a rule**.

You've done your due diligence, the deal still looks good and you're ready to write a deposit cheque to hold the property while the last of your conditions are being met. This is often called the initial deposit and it is sent along to the vendor with the initial offer.

A lot of trouble can arise from these deposits and there are a lot of misconceptions about their purpose. With more than 20 years of real estate investment experience behind each of this book's authors, we are confident in telling you your offer will be taken seriously as long as the deposit cheque is at least $1,000. *There is no reason to attach an initial deposit cheque for more than this amount as that will have little or no effect on the vendor's acceptance.*

What you can do is provide the vendor with an initial deposit of $1,000, then increase that to a higher amount upon removal of all your conditions. Write this into the offer to purchase and explain it in your cover letter.

After you've decided how to structure your deposit, the question always arises: To whom should the deposit cheque be made out?

The answer is very, very simple. It is *never, ever* given directly to the vendor. The legal recourse to get it back if the deal doesn't go through is long and painful and puts you in a vulnerable position. The initial deposit *must* go into a trust account that is held on your behalf. In most cases, this will be your lawyer's trust account. It is increasingly rare for this cheque to go to *your* real estate agent's trust account (not the vendor's agent).

WHAT DO YOU NEED TO DO?

- Write the cheque to your lawyer, in trust (e.g., Ritchie Mill Law Office in Trust).
- Never write the cheque to the vendor, no matter how tempting it is.
- Don't write the cheque to the vendor's lawyer in trust.
- Always keep the cheque in your control. You don't have a relationship with the vendor's lawyer or his real estate agent. This fact never changes—even if the deal is with your own mother. Your lawyer is the only human being on earth who should get that cheque.

🔘 KEY INSIGHT

In most cases, the deposit will not be a problem. It becomes a part of the monies used to close on the property and the vendor gets it at closing. However, the one time you break this "lawyer's trust" rule will be the time the deposit goes into dispute. You do not want that to happen because it will take months before you get even a whiff of your money again.

NOTES:_____

_____

_____

_____

_____

_____

_____

_____

_____

_____

_____

_____

_____

_____

_____

_____

_____

_____

_____

_____

_____

_____

_____

_____

_____

_____

_____

_____

TIP #77: AVOID THE HASSLE OF "HURRY UP AND WAIT."

"The cheque is in the mail" just doesn't cut it!

When dealing with funds for closing, you should always deal strictly in funds that are immediately cashable. This goes from the money you provide your lawyer for closing, to the funds your lawyer uses to buy the property, to the funds sent to you by the lenders as proceeds of a mortgage.

Most law firms that focus on investment real estate know that only certified or electronically transferred funds should be used. However, there are still horror stories out there from rookie investors using unsophisticated lawyers or notaries who don't understand that it takes about 10 days for an uncertified cheque to clear and another couple of days to process. If the bank or lender is not given clear instructions about how to handle this, they will post the required funds, using regular mail. This holds up closing by weeks and will cost the investor countless dollars in additional interest and possible penalties.

Make sure your lawyer has a system that eliminates the old "hurry up and wait" routine.

 RED FLAG

Veteran and rookie investors play the waiting game far too often. It is even more disconcerting when the funds don't show up on time and no one in the loop (the banks or lawyers) can advise where they may be. The whole process adds up to a financial headache for investors. In addition, if the funds are coming to you because you sold or refinanced a property, it's *your* money—but it's not in your account.

WHAT DO YOU NEED TO DO?

Use a bank draft or certified funds

Avoid the "hurry up and wait" hassle completely by asking your lawyer to use a bank draft or a certified cheque to send funds to the lender.

SOPHISTICATED INVESTOR TIP

Some experienced real estate investors take the whole issue of fund transfers to another level and refuse to use even a certified cheque. As far as the bank is concerned, the money leaves your account as soon as a cheque is certified. If that cheque goes missing, you lose that money and it's very, very hard to get it back. With a bank draft, however, you keep one copy of the draft and, if the other goes missing, you get a form from the bank, fill it out with a lawyer, then get another bank draft. Too many investors also don't realize that certified cheques can actually have stop payments placed on them with many financial institutions. Don't always count on a certified cheque being as good as cash!

Use a professional courier service

Many lenders have a policy of mailing cheques to personal addresses, but courier them to businesses. Make sure you request that any substantial funds being sent to you be couriered, not mailed. This gives you the opportunity to trace the process and avoid the "cheque's in the mail" syndrome.

Remember, no matter how large the cheque the lender is sending to you, it is small potatoes to the bank and it won't be as important to them as it is to you. Avoid problems by being clear in your instructions.

Draw attention to the right address

A surprising number of cheques go astray because they are sent to the wrong address! In real estate transactions, there is a tendency to send the cheque to the mortgage address, which in the investor's case is often an investment property with a tenant in it. Prevent that from happening by emphasizing the correct address in your letter.

When you or your lawyer advises the banker as to the address, shine a big spotlight on the address you wish the cheque to go to. If it is different from the property you are purchasing, make that abundantly clear! Make the correct address physically noticeable with capital letters in bold print, for example:

John Q. Investor
123 INVESTMENT STREET
Any Town, Any Province
Postal Code

As with anything involved with investment real estate, the small details are often the most critical. Make sure you design a checklist that reminds you of all the little details along the way. In addition, ask to see your lawyers' closing checklist to see if there is anything you wish to add to it. If they don't have a checklist, be concerned, as checklists are really the only way to ensure that nothing is missed along the way.

NOTES:_____
_____
_____
_____
_____
_____
_____
_____
_____
_____
_____
_____
_____
_____
_____
_____
_____
_____
_____
_____
_____
_____
_____
_____
_____
_____
_____
_____

TIP #78: KNOW THE ASSETS YOU'RE BUYING.

Clear communications will help you get the assets you expect—the good, the bad and the ugly.

Surprises are the investor's worst nightmare. Pressure and excitement to close a deal often lead to major mistakes because of a perceived lack of time for proper due diligence. These mistakes or surprises will cost you money, either immediately or very soon in the future.

The bottom line? When it comes to knowing what you're about to buy, you need to follow your due diligence system to the letter, including visiting every single unit you're about to buy and uncovering the real facts about the tenants.

Make sure that you never, ever get pressured into skipping any of your vital due diligence steps. Whether buying a large multi-family property or a single-family condo, the rules are always the same and they are designed to eliminate costly surprises.

WHAT DO YOU NEED TO DO?

Inspect every unit, no excuses!

There is no compromise on this point. You either know *exactly* what you are buying, or admit you're jumping in blindly. Imagine your shock when you take possession and the photos don't really match the condition of the property on possession day! It wouldn't be the first time that happened with real estate.

For instance, at the early stage of a purchase of a large multi-family property, you may be able to inspect a few sample units before you submit your offer to purchase. You should ask to see a unit that's in top condition, in inferior condition, and in average condition. This gives you a quick overview and lets you get a feel for the property and how it's being managed. Since many vendors don't want you disturbing their tenants unless you have a serious offer on the table, be prepared to get access to only a minimal number of suites before you give them an offer.

However, do *not* remove your final offer conditions until you have seen each and every room in each and every suite. This can take a lot of time, but it is critical that you know the full condition of what you are buying. Even a detailed engineering report won't cover the condition of all the suites. It is up to you to physically walk through every one. Take your prospective property manager along with you for insights into the property's potential, both good and bad.

Many sophisticated investors bring along their building inspector or handyman as a second pair of eyes on these inspection tours. Having a professional at your side is way better than trusting your instincts.

SOPHISTICATED INVESTOR ACTION STEP

Take photos of every room in every suite and keep track of which photos go with which suite. To make this easier, take a photo of the door number before entering the suite. You'll know that all the photos after it, up to the next door photo, are of that suite. Make sure you take additional photos of damage or any other condition of interest for future negotiations. These photos serve two purposes: 1) They are a visual record of the condition and the assets that form a part of your offer to purchase, and 2) you can use them to schedule and plan future renovations.

RED FLAG

Haste makes waste. If you rush through the inspection or due diligence process, surprises you would have caught if you had been more careful will raise their ugly heads only *after* you own the property. A thorough inspection saves you money.

Get the leases and rent rolls

Look at the leases and rent rolls from the month previous to your purchase. Look for anomalies (lots of move-outs, lots of unpaid rent, etc.). These may be a sign the vendor is moving the tenants to their other buildings, or that they weren't great tenants to start with. Never rely on an old rent roll and leases list.

Examine every lease and compare it to the formal rent roll. Make sure the rent amounts noted in the leases are the same as those listed on the rent roll. If you can't get a copy of the written lease agreement, use a rental-confirmation form, sometimes called a tenant estoppel certificate. It's a form an existing tenant signs stating his rent, security deposit, expected discounts and move-in date.

For more on how to avoid problems with existing tenants, see Part 8 on tenancy issues.

TIP #79: *CAVEAT EMPTOR*: NEVER REMOVE CONDITIONS UNTIL THE REPORT IS READ!

If the property is worth buying, it's worth getting the full report!

Most vendors are honest citizens, with no malicious intent. Now that we have that out of the way, you need to know you should never trust a vendor.

It is your job as a sophisticated investor to ensure you live by the *caveat emptor* credo. Loosely translated, it means "let the buyer beware" and, since you are the buyer, you must be aware.

Investing in real estate is a serious business and must be treated as such. That means every time there is to be an agreement between the vendor and purchaser, it must be detailed in writing and be signed by both parties. Verbal agreements may well be comfortable for everyone, but they are very difficult to uphold when "selective" memory kicks in down the road.

The second part of the *caveat emptor* warning involves the condition of the property and disclosure by the vendor of any "issues of concern." One legal view holds that if a seller knows something that would affect any reasonable purchaser's buying decision, then the seller has to disclose that information. This would be wonderful if it worked in the real world, but sadly it doesn't.

In real life, it is *caveat emptor*, or buyer beware. Investors should understand that *caveat emptor* is a large part of real estate law. Proof of a seller's misrepresentation is difficult to establish and there is absolutely no guarantee of what will happen if you go to court. That's why it's best to make purchasing decisions using *caveat emptor* as your guide.

For new homes, old homes and in-between homes, the sophisticated real estate investor's rule of thumb is always the same: Hire a professional home inspector and make sure his inspection report is acceptable before final conditions are removed from the deal.

WHAT DO YOU NEED TO DO?

Make inspections a priority

Every purchase should be contingent on the results of an independent, licensed, professional home inspection. Think of a professional home inspection as inexpensive insurance on your investment. If the report indicates the property has problems that will be expensive to fix, then the cost of the report is a cheap way to insure you aren't stuck with a money pit. If the report comes back relatively clean, then the money was well spent for peace of mind. A home inspection includes:

- A room-by-room walk-through of the home
- A detailed report with items ranging from a broken cabinet door to a leaking roof
- A detailed review of all the infrastructure of the property—mechanical, structural and aesthetic.

Include the following sentence in your offer: "Subject to the buyer obtaining a building inspection satisfactory to the buyer within 14 days of acceptance."

RED FLAG

Your inspector may have a software package that prints out a good-looking report, but that doesn't mean he's done a detailed inspection. A sophisticated investor doesn't care about the look of the report; we care about the quality of the building. Don't get fooled by flashy graphics and colour photos.

KEY INSIGHT

The details of a professional home inspection will help you calculate additional expenses that might be incurred with a property purchase. Some reports may lead you to walk away from a deal. Others may lead to more extensive negotiations where you ask the seller to do the necessary repairs, or to compensate you for them. Either way, a quality inspection means you're the big winner.

Get the details in writing—part 1

With *caveat emptor* as your guiding principle, get everything in the deal in writing and have it signed by the vendor. This is the rule of thumb for changes, too. If the vendor agrees to leave the lawnmower and it was not a part of the original offer, then simply write that up and have it signed and dated by both parties. Similarly, if the vendor agrees to clean up the property be very clear, in writing, what that means to you and what it will cost him if it isn't done. The written agreement for that condition could say, "Vendor agrees to remove derelict car from backyard on or before closing or will pay the purchaser $1,000 toward removal."

Get the details in writing—part 2

In some cases, a real estate agent will agree to take care of an issue as a way to get the deal done. This could take the form of monetary compensation, or stipulate specific work to be done. If this occurs, make sure you have the agreement in writing. Selective memory will cost you money!

 **KEY INSIGHT**

This tip makes it sound like you shouldn't trust anyone when buying real estate—and that is not true. In almost all cases, the deal flows perfectly well and all agreements are fulfilled. Due diligence is about the exceptions to the rule. By making sure you do your own research and require all agreements to be signed and dated, you have a strong argument toward a settlement that works in your favour. *An additional note:* If someone agrees to something but is unwilling to put it in writing, take it as a signal that you've called their bluff and now know they probably weren't sincere about meeting that promise in the first place. That's good information to have up-front. Remember, great investments mean there are no surprises!

NOTES:_____

_____

_____

_____

_____

_____

_____

_____

_____

_____

_____

_____

_____

TIP #80: AVOID PLACING FIXED DATES IN ANY PURCHASE CONTRACT.

All parties to a real estate deal should be looking for a deal they can successfully close. Learn to focus on that successful close, but avoid setting dates that box you in.

After you have been investing in real estate for a while, you come to know how long it takes to get things done. For instance, in some jurisdictions it takes at least 14 days to get a land transfer registered, while in others it takes substantially less time. In busy areas, getting a lender's approved appraiser out to the property can take weeks, while in other areas they can come the next day.

It is your job, as an investor, to know how long each step of the purchase takes and to use that information to be realistic in the condition dates you put into your offer to purchase. Conditions are clauses within an offer that stipulate items of business that must be met before a contract is unconditionally valid. The majority of conditions are set by the purchaser, but both parties can set conditions.

For example, these can include a condition for the vendor to arrange appropriate financing or a professional inspection by a certain date.

Another key date to be realistic on is the date of closing (or when you take possession of the property). If you know that it usually takes 21 days for the banks, lawyers and land titles office to complete a transfer, don't set unrealistic expectations with the vendor by telling them you'll close in 14 days.

🏳 RED FLAG

If you put an unrealistic closing date in your offer—just to get the deal done—you will box yourself in. That leaves you with only two options as the deadline approaches. 1) You will have to pay a large premium to all of the parties involved (banks, lawyers, inspectors, appraisers, etc.) to get them to move you up to the front of the line. This will cost you both money and reputation. 2) You will have to go back to the expectant vendor and ask for an extension on the closing date, thus opening you up for paying additional compensation or being in a situation where the vendor refuses, leaving you with a completely unrealistic deadline. In the worst-case scenario, you don't close on time and have to forfeit your full deposit to the vendor.

WHAT DO YOU NEED TO DO?

Always include your lawyer in the deal

Every offer should include the subject line: "Subject to the buyer's lawyer's approval within 14 days of acceptance." This clause gives you a chance to have your lawyer review the purchase contract to ensure that everything is clear and acceptable and the timelines are realistic.

If you're working with a real estate lawyer, he will want to check out your offers to ensure there are no landmines hidden in the contract. If they do find any issues, this clause allows you to address them before the contract becomes unconditional.

Be prepared for some vendors to request less than 14 days. This can work—as long as your lawyer is available in that shorter period. Check your lawyer's availability in advance.

Avoid specific dates

Sophisticated investors avoid specific dates on their contract conditions. Instead, use a specific number of days *after acceptance*. For example, rather than a statement that says, "Subject to buyer's lawyer's approval by May 11, 2006," use a statement such as the following: "Subject to buyer's lawyer's approval within 14 days of acceptance."

This protects you from being under any additional time constraints if negotiations go back and forth before the vendor agrees to the contract a couple of weeks after you start the process. Make sure you have designed the deal so the clock starts ticking after all the parties agree to the terms of the offer.

Make the possession date/closing date conditional

In most jurisdictions, the possession date and closing date are the same thing: the date the property becomes yours. Choose a realistic date that gives you time to get your financing in place and time for your lawyer to complete the transaction. This should be no fewer than 30 days from the date the vendor accepts your offer, and preferably longer. You will only know what is realistic in your jurisdiction by asking a veteran real estate investor or real estate lawyer.

Give yourself time to arrange financing

If you need to arrange financing to buy a property, include a conditional clause such as: "Subject to buyer obtaining financing satisfactory to the buyer within (insert number) days from acceptance of offer."

Always be realistic. You need to give your banker (with whom you are trying to build a long-term and mutually beneficial relationship!) time to arrange the financing deal you want. Sophisticated investors don't rush!

Speak with your banker or mortgage broker in advance to understand what timelines they see for mortgage approvals. Keep up to date on this timeline. It is a constantly shifting number based on how busy the bank's underwriters are and the region in which you are buying.

KEY INSIGHT

Note that the above clause clearly states the financing must be acceptable to you, the buyer. This clause helps you maintain the option of not accepting "any financing" you can get.

Factor in property-inspection time

We've said it before and we'll say it again. A professional and well-respected home inspector should go through each and every property you buy. Make this a routine cost of doing business by including a condition such as the following in every offer you make: "Subject to the buyer obtaining a building inspection satisfactory to the buyer within 14 days of acceptance."

A quality home inspector should provide you with a complete report on everything, good and bad, around the property. Your goal is to gain useable information to guide the purchase offer. This condition lets you walk away from a deal and get your deposit back if your inspector finds a major problem.

As noted in Tip #79, a property inspection report may lead you to reopen negotiations with the vendor. You may ask him to do the necessary repairs, or request compensation for having to do them after the deal closes.

NOTES:_____

_____

_____

_____

_____

_____

_____

_____

TIP #81: YOUR OFFER MUST *NOT* BE AN OPEN OFFER!

Every deal should include one irrevocable date. That's the date a deal works, or both parties move on.

The previous tip shows how conditional dates give you time to complete your due diligence and arrange appropriate financing. Conditional dates also make sure your lawyer has time to review a deal and enable you to make your deal contingent on the results of a quality property inspection.

The one key date that many rookie purchasers ignore is the "irrevocable date." This is the length of time your offer is valid for acceptance by the vendor—and it should never be open-ended. Your offer is a legal document that binds you to fulfil many different agreements. It is a huge mistake to allow this to be floating around in perpetuity!

 RED FLAG

> If you set a date that's too far in the future, you give your vendor or your vendor's real estate agent time to "shop your deal." This means he or she can talk to other purchasers and use your deal as a negotiating tool. You might not end up with the property. Worse yet, your hard work will be used as a catalyst to get the price higher! This is not a fair business practice. But it happens—and you can keep it from happening to you.

WHAT DO YOU NEED TO DO?

Light a short fuse

Set a date that tells the vendor how long you will keep your offer open for consideration. You want this date to be not very far in the future, but still give the vendor enough time to consider the offer. Many sophisticated investors use a time frame of "no longer than three days."

Stick with your plan

Be clear in the cover letter about how long the offer is open for acceptance. Tell them you are currently looking at a number of properties and have chosen theirs as the one you want. Let them know you can't wait forever for their decision as you will buy a property very soon and need to know whether theirs is it. The authors like to use the sentence, "Our lives are both busy, so there is no need to waste any of your or my valuable time . . . "

Tip #82: Make Possession Dates Part of the Negotiation.

Know the implications of a changed possession date.

Changing the possession date of an original deal can be a way to help out a buyer or seller. It may improve the buyer's ability to have repairs or renovations done before the property is placed on the rental or sale market. It may even help a motivated seller move on with his or her life. Beware: *It can also cost you money.*

Possession dates should be negotiated with instruction from your lawyer. That way, your lawyer can redo the calculations. A new assumption date, for example, may mean you are now responsible for an additional mortgage payment. The interest portion of that payment will increase your costs and that impacts your business plan.

What do you need to do?

Check the dates

Check your contract and mortgage payment date before agreeing to any changes in possession. Have your lawyer rework the mortgage payment, tax and any other applicable adjustments.

NOTES:_____

_____

_____

_____

_____

_____

_____

_____

_____

_____

_____

_____

_____

_____

TIP #83: USE CLOSING DATES STRATEGICALLY TO MAXIMIZE YOUR CASH FLOW.

Maximize your cash flow and minimize your vacancies when you strategically choose the appropriate closing dates.

This tip builds on the previous two tips. It also demonstrates how sophisticated investors put in an extra 10% of effort to maximize their profit potential. Here, the investor must acknowledge how closing dates impact their cash flow—and then use that information to give their own portfolio a welcome cash infusion!

WHAT DO YOU NEED TO DO?

Understand that the strategy differs if the property is currently tenanted or is/will be vacant when you take possession

Currently Tenanted Properties
Pick the fifth day of the month for your closing date. This gives current owners time to collect the entire rent for the month. It also means you receive the pro-rated rent for that month as a discount on your final cash-to-close statement from your closing agent (typically your real estate lawyer).

The timeline for a currently tenanted property, using November (30 days in the month) as an example, looks like this:

- Offer accepted Friday, September 23.
- Conditions removed Friday, October 7 (14 days after accepted offer).
- Closing date Saturday, November 5 (29 days for closing).
- Monthly rent $800, collected on the first of November by current owner.
- You receive a credit on your cash-to-close statement for 25 of the 30 days of rent ($666.67).

If you want to boost your cash flow:

- Choose November 5 as the closing date.
- The first full mortgage payment will be due one month after closing (December 5).

- Phone the bank that holds your mortgage and ask to move your payments to the first of the next month (January 1).
- The bank will either add the interest portion for the month to the principal balance, or require you to make an interest-only payment for the first 26 days (Dec. 5–Dec. 31).
- The net effect is that you collect almost three months' rent before you have to make your first full mortgage payment.

November: receive a rent credit for 25 days	$666.67
December: collect full rent	$800.00
January: collect full rent	$800.00
Total	$2,267.67

Pay your first full mortgage payment on January 1, and collect almost three months' rent before you make your first full mortgage payment.

🌑 KEY INSIGHT

This approach equals a reduction in the cash-to-close funds that come out of your pocket. The approach also standardizes all mortgage payments to the same day (1ˢᵗ of the month) and lets you collect almost three months' rent before paying your first full mortgage payment.

Vacant Properties

Here, you want to choose the last Thursday of the month, four to six weeks after your condition removal date. The key with this strategy is to negotiate right-of-access prior to closing, after all conditions are removed. This can be as simple as including the following condition on your offer: "The seller to allow access to buyer upon condition removal and 24 hours' notice to show prospective tenants and/or contractors."

Once you get acceptance of this condition on your offer and after you have removed all conditions, you or your property manager can start marketing this property to your potential tenants. You will have four to six weeks to find an equity-building tenant or tenants!

Renters typically move in the last weekend of the month. If you take possession on the last Thursday of the month, your new tenants will move in almost as soon as you take possession. This eliminates any vacancy issues!

Here's how the strategy looks:

- Offer accepted Friday, October 7
- Conditions removed Friday, October 21 (14 days after accepted offer)
- Closing date Thursday, November 24 (last Thursday of month, almost five weeks after condition removal).

Now factor in the advantage of moving your mortgage payment date:

- If your closing date is November 24, your first full mortgage payment would be December 24.
- Ask the bank that holds the mortgage to move your first full mortgage payment till January 1.

Summary:

December rent	$800
January rent	$800
Total	$1,600

Pay your first full mortgage payment on January 1. Collect two months' rent before making your first full mortgage payment.

 **KEY INSIGHT**

Sophisticated investors use information to make money. This strategy gives you five weeks to market vacant (or soon-to-be-vacant) property to find equity-building tenants. These tenants move in almost as soon as you take possession—and a change in mortgage dates means you put two months' rent into the bank before you make your first full mortgage payment.

NOTES:_____

_____

_____

_____

_____

_____

_____

TIP #84: GUARD AGAINST FRAUD AND IDENTITY THEFT.

Title insurance helps deals close—and close faster.

When a lawyer acts for you on a purchase transaction, he searches title, checks the government records at the registry office and does off-title-type searches to make sure you have a marketable title to the property at every level.

But you know what they say: Mistakes happen.

Title insurance is a tool your lawyer can use to make sure you have a marketable title after a deal closes on a property with fewer than three units. It should never replace the basic due diligence of title searches. Once it's on your title, however, you won't have to worry about details your lawyer may have missed or fret about errors made by the municipality. Because it's faster to get than title-search data, title insurance also speeds up the process of closing a deal.

WHAT DO YOU NEED TO DO?

Ask your lawyer for title insurance

Title insurance is becoming more prevalent in today's real estate markets—and it's cheap insurance for investors. Investors and their lawyers like it because it's faster than municipal searches and comes with added protections against mistakes or zoning issues. Even though it's pretty standard practice, depending on your jurisdiction you may have to ask for it.

Consider the real costs

Title insurance has largely replaced surveys in most regions of the country. Surveys have their place, but a land survey on a single-family home will cost about $1,000. Title insurance will cost you roughly the same as a survey but comes with many added benefits.

Sophisticated investors know most insurers pay out. That means you won't have to hire a lawyer to sue your lawyer for negligence if it turns out your title has a problem. If you have to sue, you will have to *demonstrate* the services you're claiming weren't done and were part of your lawyer's retainer.

Title insurance also covers errors made by the municipality.

Guard against fraud, the new hidden danger in Canada

Title insurance provides some protection from title fraud, whereby people impersonate the title owners and register or transfer a mortgage by using fake identification.

Go retro!

You can keep your bell-bottoms and disco records in the closet for now. When we talk about going retro, we mean you should buy retroactive title insurance on properties you already own.

Ask your lawyer about the benefits of buying retroactive title insurance for properties already in your portfolio. In some cases it might be a waste of time and money. In others, where there are potential issues with the title, zoning or other compliance issues, retroactive title insurance can save the day.

NOTES:_____

_____

_____

_____

_____

_____

_____

_____

_____

_____

_____

_____

_____

_____

_____

_____

_____

_____

_____

_____

PART 8

TENANCY ISSUES:
MAKE DEFENCE YOUR
BEST OFFENCE

TIP #85: GO FOR THE (PROPERTY MANAGEMENT) GOLD.

Quality property management makes—not costs—you money.

What do vacancies, unnecessary repairs, tenants who don't pay the rent and tenants who won't leave all have in common? Inadequate property management. And it only gets worse! Problems with deferred maintenance, calls in the middle of the night, ruined vacations and costly legal bills related to tenancy are all solidly linked to poor property management.

WHAT DO YOU NEED TO DO?

Pay attention

Quality property management is a cornerstone of successful real estate investment. It's also the one item investment-market newcomers are quickest to write off, since they don't get the salient investment point: Efficient property management makes you money!

Buying is easy. Managing is hard work

Think about how long it takes you to buy a property. Even with strict attention to the due diligence of your system, we're talking hours, maybe days. Property management lasts the lifetime of your investment.

🕐 KEY INSIGHT

Poor property management is one of the biggest single causes of real estate investment failure. Quality property management makes life easy, keeps the income rolling in and helps keep you confidently investing in more properties.

Know the financial costs

Poor property management equals decreased revenue, negative cash flow, substandard maintenance, high tenant turnover and increased advertising costs. Oftentimes, hiring a high-quality property management company is well worth the cost (usually running between 4% and 11% of gross rental income).

Your job doesn't end when you hire a quality manager. It's now *your* responsibility to ensure you manage the managers and make sure they are truly doing an amazing job for you. Remember, the bottom-line results are your responsibility, even if you are not actively managing.

Recognize the emotional cost

Properties have two costs. The first is the obvious financial one. The second and much more important cost is emotional. Sometimes a property looks like a good investment. But after you own it for a period of time, you realize it keeps you up worrying at night. This is a sign the emotional cost is not worth the financial reward. Sell the property and move on to a property that has a lower emotional cost.

Poor property management equals higher stress levels, sleepless nights and lost relationships. Visit www.realestateinvestingincanada.com to discover the latest property management and real estate investing systems for Canada.

Hire a first-rate manager first

There is a vast difference in quality among property management companies, and it is not reflected in the prices they charge.

You can contract full-service property management companies that do everything for you, then send you the cheque at the end of the month. This will cost you a monthly percentage of the collected rent. If you wish to do more of the management yourself, you can contract a rent-up service. They find you a quality tenant and usually charge a one-time fee.

No matter what level of management you choose, make sure you complete your due diligence on the company. Ask for references, drive by properties they manage and see for yourself what they offer in terms of quality and attention to detail.

Talk to the tenants in properties they are managing so you can gauge the relationship and their responsiveness to the tenants. Recognize the vast difference between managing a property through times of peak versus low demand. Make sure the company you hire has experience in the good times—and knows what to do when the rental scene gets tougher.

Fellow investors are a good place to get the names of quality management companies. The investing world is not very large and a property management company's poor reputation will spread like wildfire. Even when a company is referred to you, make sure you do your due diligence.

🚫 KEY INSIGHT

Problems with property management will interfere with your system. Contact your local landlord association or a local chapter of the Real Estate Investment Network to ask about courses on proactive landlording. Being a proactive landlord will quickly free up your time, reduce your hassles and show you are an investment realist. You need to think about what to do *when* a problem arises, not *if a* problem arises. Prepare yourself in advance.

NOTES:_____

_____

_____

_____

_____

_____

_____

_____

_____

_____

_____

_____

_____

_____

_____

_____

_____

_____

_____

_____

_____

_____

_____

_____

_____

TIP #86: UNDERSTAND MATTERS SURROUNDING TENANCY RULES.

Keep your regulatory knowledge current.

Every province has its own tenancy regulatory board, which is aligned with the federal Department of Consumer and Corporate Affairs. Their regulations guide landlord and tenant issues. (A list of government websites outlining landlord and tenant laws in each provincial and territorial jurisdiction is provided in the Appendix.)

These rules and regulations are continually changing, and it is the landlord's responsibility to work under the most current legislation. In some provinces, the regulations favour the tenant, while in others the legislation is much fairer. Sadly, the rules are typically designed to control bad tenants and landlords. As a sophisticated investor, you want to do whatever you can to ensure you never have to use the majority of the confrontational rules.

Throughout this part, we will discuss how the tenant and landlord relationship can be mutually supportive instead of confrontational.

The names of the various boards vary. In British Columbia, it is the Residential Tenancy Branch. In Alberta it is the Landlord and Tenant Advisory Board and in Ontario it is the Ontario Rental Housing Tribunal (even the name sounds confrontational, doesn't it!).

WHAT DO YOU NEED TO DO?

Contact your local board

Use the government website to find the name of the regulatory body in your province or territory. Download the complete regulations to keep as a reference. Most provinces also have tip sheets or regulation summaries to help you with the most common issues.

Many of the boards also give you a package containing all the pertinent forms for administering your properties and your tenant relationships.

 RED FLAG

Not knowing the law is never an excuse for breaking it.

Be active: Join a local or national association

In real estate investment, as in life, it is best to surround yourself with people who are doing the same thing as you. This helps you avoid making the same mistakes as others and it gives you great access to key suppliers and potential mentors.

Attend your landlord association's meetings and be an active member, not a passive one. Use its information packages and take its educational programs. It's apt to cost you more time than money, and the information you glean will be worth every second and every penny.

Change your mindset

If you are convinced that tenants are bad and will phone you in the middle of the night to clean out their toilets, get rid of this old myth! It is just not true. A roomful of 600 active real estate investors was recently asked, "How many of you have ever had a middle-of-the-night call from a tenant?" Only two put up their hands and, once we heard their stories, we told them exactly how they could have prevented that call by solving the problem in advance.

A second myth you need to toss aside says that the relationship between a tenant and landlord needs to be confrontational. This is absolutely false. The relationship is only confrontational when the landlord hasn't chosen his tenants well, or hasn't worked to build a more supportive relationship. There are literally millions of wonderful, long-term, hassle-free tenants in every community across the country. These tenants will gladly pay all the expenses of operating your property, including the mortgages and taxes. All you have to do is provide them with appropriate housing!

🕐 KEY INSIGHT

Picture your rental property as if it were a video rental store. There are two other competing rental stores in the area and you need to find out how to attract clients to your store instead of the competition's. You also want to find ways to keep these clients for the long term. Now apply this analogy to rental real estate. You are surrounded by competitive rental units and you must attract the renters, then keep them for the long term. The best way to do that is to provide potential tenants with a clear reason why they should choose your "store" (rental unit) over the competition. If you can't think of a reason right now, you had better start!

Treat real estate like a business

Many beginner landlords seem to believe the real estate business is different from other businesses. As you will quickly learn, this is a huge mistake that could cost you thousands of dollars in poor decisions.

For example, stop thinking of your tenants as tenants and begin thinking of them as paying clients. Your job is then focused on attracting good, long-term, paying clients—not tenants. Why is this important? Simply, it gets you out of the "old world" of real estate advertising (classified ads in the back of a newspaper) and into a whole new world of marketing. You can now look at the marketing strategies used in other industries and transfer them into your business. Always be on the lookout for ways other businesses effectively attract their clients. Then ask yourself, "Can I adopt this strategy in my real estate business?"

Remember, the clients you are trying to attract will be paying you thousands of dollars per year (in rent). An $800 per month renter is not an $800 client—they are a $9,600 client.

Once you understand the importance of this change of mindset, you will start to look at the market from a competitive point of view. Rather than blindly purchasing an investment property because it fits your system, make sure you are doing an analysis of competing properties in the region. Look at what they have that you don't, and vice versa. Highlight these differences when they make your property look better than the competition's.

🏴 RED FLAG

Being a lazy investor is a great way to bankruptcy. Step out of the box with your thinking and you'll leave the problems behind in the dust!

NOTES:_____

_____

_____

_____

_____

_____

_____

_____

_____

TIP #87: BE CREATIVE IN YOUR ADVERTISING STRATEGIES.

Learn the key to maximizing your cash flow.

As in every business, advertising plays a critical part in building cash flow. Advertising is especially critical in the real estate business, because your whole goal is to attract quality tenants who pay top market rents.

With this in mind, we will discuss strategies to make you stand out in both a hot market and a cold market. The key is *not* to follow old beliefs or old strategies. The following details are from a comprehensive 10-year study of sophisticated investors.

WHAT DO YOU NEED TO DO?

Determine what source of advertising is most cost effective in your market

There are many creative ways to attract tenants in any market. Here are some, both creative and mainstream. Tap into as many as you can to attract the perfect tenant in the least amount of time.

🛈 KEY INSIGHT

Classified ads in newspapers will provide you with the least cost-effective way to attract tenants. In some cases, it is still worth the effort and expense. However, you may wish to note that most sophisticated investors attract the best long-term tenants by being proactive with their marketing. They don't just rely on classified ads.

Here are some proven cost-effective strategies to attracting quality tenants:

1. Put "For Rent" signs in the window and on the lawn. Potential tenants will either see the sign or hear about the rental through word of mouth.
2. Get referrals from current tenants. Ask your good tenants for referrals, and give them incentives for doing so.
3. Share names with your fellow real estate investors. This is another critical reason for surrounding yourself with like-minded real estate investors.

Key Insight continues

Once their suite is filled, they'll often have a few quality prospects left over from their advertising. Tap into that resource.

4. Use on-line ads.
5. Post ads at local military bases.
6. Post ads at large construction sites.
7. Contact the human resource departments of major employers.
8. Contact the local police service, especially one that transfers its members from town to town.
9. Post ads in university or college newspapers, or on-line. Contact housing directories at schools.
10. Put flyers on vehicles in nearby office buildings.

Be creative

It is important to be creative as you work through this list. Consider where your "target market" would see your advertising. Be different; don't be afraid to stand out. Your job is to attract the type of prospect you want. Remember, the volume of calls is nowhere near as important as the quality of calls.

Have a marketing strategy

Having a marketing strategy is critical to your business, whether you are in real estate or auto repair. Without an effective marketing plan you will continually feel as if you are behind the eight ball. Marketing includes writing ads that will attract positive attention to your suites, from how they look to how they smell.

🔑 KEY INSIGHT

As a landlord, attracting and keeping the right tenants — cost effectively — will be the single most important action you take. Advertising represents a small portion of your overall marketing plan. But once you master advertising, it will lead to higher rents, fewer vacancies, longer tenancies and higher sales prices.

NOTES:_____

_____

_____

_____

_____

Tip #88: Make the Most of On-Line Advertising.

Jason Leonard, co-founder and president of Landlord Web Solutions Inc., delivers the latest on how to make the most of your virtual ad campaign.

The Internet has reached "fixture" status in the contemporary rental industry. Once dismissed as a gimmicky medium, the virtual marketplace has proven its value on two fronts.

1. Technology. The Internet boasts an extremely large user base, has no physical limitations and is highly searchable, making it very popular with renters; and
2. Cost. It is way cheaper than print advertising. Whether you're targeting students or trying to rent in a particular geographic area, on-line advertising can work for you because it will let you find your target audience with minimal cost.

Who uses the Internet?

Landlords who think their clientele "doesn't use the Internet" are completely wrong! People from every walk of life now make their way on-line. They access the Internet at home, work or school and at libraries, cafes, seniors' centres and community centres. The Internet does not care about one's economic status, age or ethnicity. It is a huge mistake to assume your target market is not using the Internet, since very few people in society now lack access.

What do you need to do?

Narrow your target

Are you working in a national or regional market? If it's national, advertising on a national listing site like Gottarent.com is a great place to start. It features listings in most Canadian cities and has a proven record of success at creating high-quality leads for landlords.

If you only have properties in one province or one city, add a smaller, niche-market advertising website to your marketing mix. For instance, landlords in Toronto often use ViewIt.ca, which has a strong Toronto market presence. Likewise, provincially based websites like RentBC.com and

Rentfaster.ca, which covers Alberta, are also quite successful at providing landlords with quality leads from specific geographic areas.

Tap into social networks

Social-networking websites also provide marketing-savvy landlords with some unique advertising opportunities. Websites such as Facebook.com allow you to target your ads to a narrowly defined audience.

For landlords trying to reach students, Facebook is especially powerful. You can easily narrow your audience to target the students of a particular college or university! The possibilities are endless. You can control who sees your ads and how often they see them.

Free sites work, too

Landlords should also consider advertising on free listing websites like Craigslist.com and Kijiji.com . These websites may require more time and effort in terms of updating the advertisements, but they are genuinely effective in generating rental leads.

⚑ RED FLAG

Free listing sites are notorious for spam so you may want to meet potential renters before taking any money from them.

Ⓢ SOPHISTICATED INVESTOR STRATEGIES

Pay attention to the advantages of on-line ads:

- There are no restrictions on how much you can say about the property, since on-line ads are not typically sold by the word or character.
- The ability to show floor plans, photos, virtual tours and even videos of the property. This is especially helpful for those moving to your city from a distance.
- An interactive map to the property can give driving directions.
- You can track how many people viewed your listing.
- You can calculate your cost per lead which will help you decide on future advertising expenditures.
- On-line advertising offers an extremely wide reach. You gain a competitive advantage by finding renters who are moving to your city before they move there.
- You can discontinue your advertising as soon as you've found a tenant, thus eliminating any further calls.

TIP #89: OPTIMIZE FOR SEARCH ENGINES.

Does your webpage do its job? Jason Leonard zeros in on what might be wrong.

Most people agree that Google is the first place most people turn to these days when they're looking for information. So ask yourself: If someone is on Google looking for a place to rent in your community, will they find your website?

For most Canadian landlords who already have a website, the answer is no. That's because landlords generally contract web designers who can design pretty websites, but don't offer a service called search engine optimization (SEO).

WHAT DOES SEO DO?

SEO optimizes your virtual visibility. With traditional advertising, you pay a fee in exchange for an ad that makes your phone ring. When the ad expires, your phone stops ringing and your vacancies stop getting filled. To counter that, you renew your ad and your marketing budget takes another hit! Google renders that cycle obsolete—but only after you optimize your web visibility.

To be as visible as possible, you want your ad to show on as many sites as possible and to be on the sites that pop up on the first page results of Google. Take a look at the websites that consistently make that list. Check for the keywords and phrases they have in common. These are the sites where you want your potential renters to find you. If you're not advertising on those sites, you're missing out on the *majority* of potential renters in the marketplace.

Now imagine for a moment that your website is ranked highly on Google and is generating 500, 1,000 or maybe even 5,000 potential renter visits a month to your website. Yes, first page results for multiple keywords and phrases can generate that kind of traffic for rental websites in many Canadian cities.

WHAT DO YOU NEED TO DO?

Invest in SEO

SEO is the process of improving the visibility of a website by using key words and phrases that will make that site pop up on the first page of a

Google search. If you already have a website or you're thinking of building one, investing in SEO can be one of the single greatest investments you make in your overall marketing. Once you secure your place in the search engines, you'll be amazed at how fast you can trim traditional advertising expenses.

If you already have a website, hire someone to optimize it for you. If you don't yet have a website, make sure future sites includes an SEO plan. And don't make SEO an after-the-fact detail. Well-designed websites are built with SEO in mind from day one. It should be a core part of your website plan.

 **KEY INSIGHT**

Once you pay for SEO, every prospective renter who visits your website because of the position you earned in Google is free.

For more on-line marketing ideas, tips and solutions, visit www.landlordweb solutions.com .

NOTES:_____
_____
_____
_____
_____
_____
_____
_____
_____
_____
_____
_____
_____
_____
_____
_____
_____

TIP #90: PROPERLY SCREEN PROSPECTIVE TENANTS.

Real estate investment is a business. Make sure your due diligence extends to tenant selection.

Did you think your due diligence was complete after you bought the property? For some unfortunate or unthinking investors, this is true. However, as a sophisticated investor you will quickly learn that doing the extra 10% of due diligence on a potential tenant makes all the difference in the world.

A robust residential real estate market typically spells some trouble for the rental industry. When more people are buying homes, fewer are renting. As a matter of fact, many unsophisticated investors use a region's higher vacancy rate as an excuse *not* to have fully tenanted properties. Once again, they allow outside influences to affect how they run their businesses!

🕐 KEY INSIGHT

In every real estate market, hot, cold and in between, there are renters—lots of them. It does not matter what the vacancy rate is. Your job as a "business owner" is to ensure you attract as many "clients" for your business as you can, with no excuses. Some investors slow down their marketing efforts when they hear vacancy rates are going up. This is the *exact opposite* of what you should do. When others slow down, you ramp up. This is how you make sure the smaller number of renters available keeps coming to *you* instead of to the competition.

Another terrible mistake unsophisticated investors make is to become impatient because their suite has been vacant for two months. In frustration, they rent to anyone who responds to their ad. This is a *huge* mistake and it will ultimately cost the landlord substantially more in time and money. Never (never!) think you have to rent your property to the first person who looks like he has the cash to move in.

Sophisticated investors use due diligence to support a tenant-search mantra that goes something like this: Quality property. Quality tenant. Quality property. Quality tenant.

What do you need to do?

Pre-screen tenants

Before you show a property, conduct a telephone screening to make sure the next step in the screening process is worth your time. There is no need to show the property to everyone who calls and is interested. Remember, you're looking for a long-term "client" for this property.

Use a formal question checklist to guide the conversation

You are choosing the tenant, not the other way around. Make sure you take control of the conversation early. During the initial telephone call, ask key questions such as:

- "When are you looking to move to a new place?" You'd be surprised at how many callers are just "thinking about moving." Just take their name and number and move on. Don't waste your time if they want a suite far in the future and you need to rent now.
- "How long do you plan to rent?" This question is critical. They may only need your place for three months while their new house is under construction. If you want a long-term tenant and you don't ask this question, you may be sorely disappointed when they move out after a few months.
- "How many people will be living in the unit?" You want to know if this is a good match or not. If you are renting a one-bedroom suite and your prospect is a family of four, this is probably not a good match for the long term.
- "Do you have any pets or plan on getting any?" Keep this question open-ended. By stating "pets" instead of naming specific animals (dogs or cats) you will get a much clearer answer.
- "How long have you rented your current residence?" You are trying to filter out short-term "hoppers." If they say less than a year, ask them about the length of time at the previous place to see if there is a trend.
- "Where did you hear about this place?" As a business owner, you will want to know what marketing is working and what is not.
- "What kind of work do you do?" Many beginning landlords ask, "Do you have a job?" That isn't the right question, since most people will say

yes even if they work only six hours per week at the local coffee shop. You want someone who can afford to pay your rent over a long period of time.

- "How long have you been at this job?" Look for stability.
- "Have you given your current landlord proper notice?" This helps identify the potential for future problems. Some tenants don't follow rules well, and if they say no to this one, then you might want to continue your search—no matter what their backstory is.

Spend your time showing the property only to prospective tenants who make it through this telephone interview.

 **KEY INSIGHT**

Many tenants believe only one security deposit exists and you will hear about current landlords who won't release security deposits until the middle of the month. Never agree to wait. *Never* let a tenant change your rules. And never give possession of a property until you have cash (not a cheque) for the full first month's rent and the security deposit (or last month's rent, depending on your local laws).

Conduct a background check

Once you complete the telephone interview and show your property, you may think you know whether you want to rent to this tenant. This is wrong. You have just begun your due diligence!

Ask prospective tenants to complete a formal application to lease. This covers the information you already collected over the phone, but includes contact names and numbers for follow-up checks.

Make sure the application the prospective tenant signs gives you permission to do a complete credit and criminal background check. When you become a member of your local landlord association or the Real Estate Investment Network, you can get template application forms that work for your jurisdiction. In order to do a complete check, the prospective tenant needs to provide you with complete and accurate information. Tell them clearly that you won't be processing their application until you have all the information.

RED FLAG

Don't waste your time with prospective tenants who do not complete the form (no matter what their excuse). If they don't have the time or inclination to fill out a form regarding something as important as a place to live, you can imagine what other excuses may arise once they become tenants.

Always phone current and previous employers and build some rapport. Tell them you are a business owner (manager). Mention that you realize they are sick and tired of employees who don't live up to their resumes, just like you are tired of prospective tenants who aren't totally honest on their rental application. Ask them how the prospective tenant treats company assets and other employees. Ask if they would rent a property to this individual. Ask about their prospects for long-term employment.

KEY INSIGHT

When talking with an employer, ask them if they are confident that the prospect will be responsible. If they say yes, ask them if they are confident enough, in theory, to co-sign the rental agreement, thus guaranteeing the rent will be paid. You are not asking them to do this. You are looking to see how confident they are in this prospect.

Always call the prospect's most recent landlord, but take a sophisticated-investor approach to the call. You want to find out the prospect's real rental history and if the prospect is telling the truth on the application. As you get your answers, remember that a current landlord may not tell the whole truth if she is looking to rid herself of a problem tenant.

Build confidence in your information by talking to at least two previous landlords.

SOPHISTICATED INVESTOR ACTION STEP

Some prospective tenants who lack a sound rental history will often ask their friends or relatives to "play the part" of the previous landlord. They prepare this relative with what to say when you call. The one thing they don't know is that you are a sophisticated landlord and you understand

Sophisticated Investor Action Step continues

that this might go on. You can circumvent this by calling the "landlord" and saying, "I understand that you have a suite for rent." There are two possible answers to this question. First, they say they're full, or second, they ask what you're talking about and say you've got the wrong number! This is a quick way to discover the difference between a real landlord and a set-up.

Conduct a complete background check

There are a few services that provide landlords with the ability to do complete background checks on potential renters. This complete background check includes

- **Credit history.** Look for solid credit, but don't expect it to be perfect. You're simply looking for potential financial reasons why they won't make your rent payment.
- **Criminal background.** You want to know whom you are renting to. Many landlords have absolutely no issues with renting to people with a criminal history. Still, it's in your best interests to know the facts.
- **Rental history.** There are some services that keep a database of tenants, using information provided by your fellow landlords. The database will tell you the history of the tenant's rental behaviour and allow you insights into issues that could arise with this tenant. You must have written permission from the tenant to access any of this information, and the wording must be very specific on your rental application form.

🔑 KEY INSIGHT

It is critical that you do complete due diligence on your prospective tenant. A gut-feeling decision can lead to a real pain in the gut over the long term. If this due diligence sounds too daunting, there are companies that will do the majority of the screening and due diligence for you. However, as the owner of the property, you may still wish to provide the final approval. Remember, you are ultimately responsible for who they put in there. It affects your bottom line, not theirs! Sophisticated investors won't risk their investment on a "gut feeling" that everything is going to be all right.

TIP #91: DO A MOVE-IN INSPECTION AND KEEP MAINTENANCE UP-TO-DATE.

Your due diligence continues before, during and after your tenants move in.

A full pre-move-in, walk-through inspection with the tenant is an absolute must for any landlord. You can use this walk-through for three important points:

1. To inspect the condition of the property before any of the tenant's property is moved in.
2. To help you set the stage for your expectations of the tenant. This can cover what day their rent is due (and the penalties for not hitting that day), as well as what they are responsible for as far as maintenance and yard work.
3. To solidify the relationship between you and the tenant. Use the time to build some rapport, discuss their likes and dislikes and show them this is not going to be a confrontational relationship. Since most tenants are used to confrontation with their landlord, it's your job in this walk-through to be very clear that you will always be fair and you expect the same from them.

WHAT DO YOU NEED TO DO?

Conduct a move-in inspection

Never ever let a tenant move anything into a property unless you and the tenant have done a complete room-by-room inspection and have both agreed to the conditions. Use a "Move-in Inspection Form" that addresses each and every room. Keep detailed notes on the current condition and have the tenant agree to and sign this form as confirmation of their agreement. Each province has different laws outlining what must be stated on the inspection report; check with your local authority.

Make sure that *all* tenants sign this inspection. Make this a specific policy and you will avoid being forced to take responsibility for problems related to the property's condition when your tenants move on.

🅑 KEY INSIGHT

As you do the walk-through with the tenant, take many digital pictures. Make sure your camera has the date function turned on so you can verify the date. As an added protection, have the tenants in a few of the pictures. Burn these photos onto a disc and then save this in your property file. This serves two purposes. First, the act of taking the pictures in front of the tenant tells them you are serious about the condition of the property. Second, if there is ever a dispute about condition, you will have verifiable proof.

Keep property maintenance up to date

Respect your tenants and build mutual loyalty by keeping the "quality property" component of your real estate investment. Your goal is simple: Make your property the kind of place quality people will want to rent.

Annual inspections are critical for all sophisticated investors. Do a complete walk-through at least once a year to confirm there aren't any maintenance issues you haven't been aware of. While you're there, change the furnace filter and check that the smoke detectors are working. Actions like this demonstrate your commitment to maintaining a quality property.

NOTES:_____

_____

_____

_____

_____

_____

_____

_____

_____

_____

_____

_____

_____

_____

Tip #92: Be Proactive When the Rent Isn't Paid.

Don't let the hassle of dealing with a tenant in rental arrears become an eviction horror story.

"Take immediate action" is the underlying mantra of the sophisticated investor's approach to tenant issues. Waiting or hoping that a problem will go away will only bring pain and heartache. As a business owner, you need to make sure you are being paid a fair market price for your "product" (rental property) and not allowing people to "shoplift" from your store.

That's how sophisticated investors think of the process. Living in your property is the product and rent is the payment for it. If rent is not paid, it is just the same as if they walk into your video store and take $800 of videos without paying. If this happened in your video store, you would take immediate action. The same principle needs to apply here.

All landlords should have an arrears policy in place before the first tenant moves in. This system must work within the local landlord and tenant laws. If you consistently have people who don't pay their rent on time, it is a direct reflection upon you, your business systems and those you choose to put in your suites. In other words, it is your responsibility.

That being said, there are many proactive ways to eliminate or dramatically reduce rental arrears. For instance:

- Put into place up-front penalties renters will incur if they do not pay their rent on time. These penalties should be written into their lease document—which, of course, they must sign.
- Clearly define these penalties in a follow-up letter sent a couple of months after they move in (not immediately as it will get lost in the move). Use a pleasant tone in the letter. Use words such as, "I know you aren't the type of person who would not live up to their legal obligations by missing a rent payment; that's why I chose you for this property. However, it is part of my system of clear communications to make you aware of what was in your lease:
  - Rent is due on or before noon on the 1st of the month.
  - If rent is late, there is an immediate penalty of $xx.
  - For each day the rent is late, a penalty of $xx is added."

- Reiterate: "Once again, I know you're not the type of person who wants to waste your money on penalties, so I'm sure these don't pertain to you. This is a place you will be proud to call home for years to come. If you ever have any maintenance issues, please don't hesitate to call me at (555) 555–1212."
- If a renter is late in paying rent, you live by your rules. Of course, you have complete discretion as to which of your rules you want to enforce. Take the emotions out of it; this is a legal business transaction. *Your goal is to make rent matter. You want your tenants to know you are serious about collecting rent—and that there are penalties for those who do not pay.*

WHAT DO YOU NEED TO DO?

Get first month's rent and a security deposit (or last month's rent) up front

It sounds a little harsh, but you are a landlord, not a bank. Make sure you get the security deposit (or last month's rent) up front with the first month's rent. (Make sure you know your local tenancy laws and use the details to protect your investment.)

Get the deposit and first month's rent in cash, certified cheque, money order, or by on-line or direct deposit. Never, ever accept an exception to this rule. This sets the tone that you are serious about the payments you are expecting. As any good landlord will tell you, it is much easier to get nicer than it is to get harsher as the relationship progresses.

 RED FLAG

If the cash, certified cheque, money order or on-line deposit is not in your hand or your bank account, your tenants don't move in. Period.

Include penalties for late payment

Wherever legally possible, build penalties for late fees and NSF cheques into your lease. To make tenants understand that you are serious about arrears, make these fees substantial. Sophisticated investors make the choice easy for the tenants who think they can choose between paying or not, by making it financially painful if they choose the latter option.

Get postdated cheques

In most provinces, you can ask for postdated cheques for rent payments. Your time is money and you do not want to make rent collection part of your monthly agenda. If you do, you will pay for missed appointments, return trips and a wagonload of excuses!

Accept cash only as a last resort. It's a security risk and there is no paper trail. *Always* provide a signed receipt (with duplicated copy) for the rent paid.

Always think ahead: If you accept cash as a partial payment, how will you prove rent arrears? The practice opens up a lot of grey areas.

 **KEY INSIGHT**

> Some sophisticated investors have arranged to have credit card, debit card or on-line/direct deposit payment options for their renters as a convenience. Renters have really gravitated towards this approach. It is easier for them and there is a paper trail.

Always follow your own arrears policy

When you meet a tenant to sign a lease, go over your rental arrears policy. Make sure it says exactly what will happen if a cheque fails to clear. *For example: If the cheque does not clear, I will issue 14 days' notice to vacate.*

If the tenant pays in full, including applicable penalties, the vacate notice may be dropped. If it is not paid, the notice to vacate remains in force, the landlord retains the security deposit for unpaid rent and gets the property back.

Learn the law

Rest assured the law is on your side, as long you make sure your actions are in step with the law.

All landlords should join a local landlord association. It will provide educational opportunities regarding the local residential tenancies act. It is also good to get a quality advocate or bailiff on your side as it's their job to deal with any uncomfortable tenant situations. In almost all cases, you will never need them. Still, it is good to know who to call.

 **KEY INSIGHT**

> The landlord/tenant relationship is governed by law. Write a tenant lease based on that law and be prepared to take immediate action if a cheque fails to clear. Be strong, yet fair and always keep the relationship as open as possible. Because you don't own thousands of suites, your close relationship with your tenant is one advantage you have over the big guys!

TIP #93: CONFIRM THE EXISTING TENANT DETAILS.

The place you want to buy is being marketed with "existing tenants." Make sure those two words aren't investment-speak for "assumable headaches."

Rental properties may be sold with tenants' agreements in place. Some vendors may even promote those tenants as an added asset to the deal. After all, even new investors know that the advertising and due diligence involved with acquiring tenants costs real time and money. Who wouldn't see existing tenants as money in the bank?

That's not how the sophisticated investor thinks. *Experience shows that existing tenants demand the same due diligence as new ones. Since you didn't negotiate any of the terms of their tenancy, you must assume you know nothing about those terms.*

Sophisticated investors want to have as much information as possible on the current tenants and their terms of tenancy. This way they can make a very clear decision as to whether they wish to take the property as tenanted or vacant.

To get these details you should use a tenant confirmation form (an example is provided at the end of this tip). This form, which confirms all of the terms of their tenancy, is to be completed and signed by each tenant. Since a landlord and tenant's recollection of the tenancy terms often differ, it is best to get these straightened out long in advance. It helps you determine whether the rental income statements given to you by the vendor are accurate. If you are in a jurisdiction where security or last month's rent is in the landlord's hands, this form will clearly outline what amounts are to be credited to you at closing. Being clear keeps everyone honest.

 RED FLAG

Make sure the tenant confirmation form is signed and dated by all tenants.

WHAT DO YOU NEED TO DO?

Review the status quo and make sure you have all the details

Do not accept anyone's "word" on tenancy terms. Meet your new tenants face to face. Ask how they feel about the property and their plans to stay or go. Only good outcomes can be realized by being completely honest with your questions. This should be a part of your due diligence.

Review their lease agreement and make sure you can live with its terms. Poor leases are not uncommon, but you don't have to get stuck with one!

If a tenant doesn't have a formal lease, clearly explain to the tenant that a lease will be put in place that outlines your rules. If the tenant will not accept this, you may wish to move on to another property.

🔵 SOPHISTICATED INVESTOR TIP

If you don't want to rent to any of the current tenants or plan to undertake extensive renovations, you can always request vacant possession as part of your offer to purchase.

🚩 RED FLAG

Read a copy of each lease that is in place. Look for situations that may not be appropriate for you. The need for caution is especially strong if the existing tenancy isn't based on a formal lease agreement! When the current tenants' leases expire, make sure you get them to agree to your new lease, with all of your rules and regulations.

💡 KEY INSIGHT

Bad surprises are a natural consequence of due diligence that falls short of its mark. That's why you are studying a real estate investment system that stresses property score cards, analyzer forms and checklists for everything from vendor motivation to prospective tenants! Apply your due diligence strategy to *every* tenant relationship and every property you own and you'll start to see why sophisticated investors can talk about "quality tenants and quality property" as an investment strategy.

NOTES:_____

_____

_____

_____

_____

_____

_____

Tenant Confirmation Form

Date_____
    (Day)   (Month)   (Year)

My name is _____
            (First)   (Middle)   (Last)

I currently rent suite # _____ at _____

_____   _____
            (Address)   (City)

DETAILS of my tenancy are as follows:

1. Current rent: $ _____ /month

2. Security deposit: $_____

3. Date I moved in: _____
                    (Day)   (Month)   (Year)

4. I have a written lease with my landlord: YES   NO

4a. If NO, please describe tenancy arrangement: _____

5. Date my current lease expires: _____
                                  (Day)   (Month)   (Year)

6. I am currently up to date with my rent payment: YES   NO

6a. If NO, I currently owe: $ _____

7. There are no side deals, prepaid rent or rent-discount (i.e., free-rent) arrangements between my landlord and me, other than that I am a tenant as set out above.

Dated this _____ day of _____, 20____.

Tenant name _____   Witness name _____

Signature _____   Witness signature _____

Tenant name _____   Witness name _____

Signature _____   Witness signature _____

Other comments: _____

PART 9

LEGAL INSIGHTS AND TAX TIPS: WHAT YOU'VE GOT TO KNOW (SO IT WON'T HURT YOU)

TIP #94: HONESTY IS THE ONLY POLICY.

Swim in the grey waters and you will eventually be bitten by the sharks.

One of the great things about the Canadian real estate market is that it gives investors a chance to create long-term wealth if they follow a system and have patience. Many people, though, equate making a fast buck with success. Late-night TV and huge "get rich" ads have programmed Canadians to have very little patience in any wealth-creation strategy. In reality, "get rich quick" is a marketing hook, not real life. The saddest part of this equation is that those who chase the fast dollar often have to wade into what is politely called "grey water." This is where all of the real estate sharks hang out—and wait for their next prey.

How do you avoid the grey water? It's easy. All you have to do is be completely honest and above board with all your transactions.

Novice real estate investors get to meet a lot of people while assembling the team they'll work with en route to achieving their personal goals. The team will include real estate agents, bankers, mortgage brokers, lawyers, accountants and other investors. However, novice investors are also often prey to the grey-water sharks that teach or advocate strategies that, when looked at in the bright light of day, are either outright fraud or will rapidly lead them to bankruptcy.

You need to quickly spot the difference between the ones who are "selling you" and the ones who are supporting you. This can be complicated, because the "grey-area sharks" are amazing sales people and have mastered the "I'm here to help you" speech. This makes them difficult to pick out. The bottom line is you need to steer clear of anyone who even hints of the illegal or grey-water deal.

This warning is not made lightly, nor should it be ignored. The rules are pretty simple.

WARNING: GREY WATER AHEAD

1. Be wary of those who try to teach *and* sell you real estate. The potential for a conflict of interest is just too high.
2. If you are instructed to sign a document that contains a false claim, because you need to get a mortgage or close a deal, recognize that you're already swimming with the sharks and it is time to get out of the water.

3. If you are not able to get a second legal opinion on a deal, no matter how small, see this as a *huge* red flag.

4. If you are being told not to declare every aspect of your real estate transaction to every party involved (i.e., withholding information from a banker, lawyer or purchaser), then you have just jumped into grey waters. Be prepared to be bitten.

5. If someone recommends a particular course of action (e.g., structuring your corporations, buying in a certain town, arranging for a bunch of new credit cards), make sure you check to see if they have a personal interest (usually financial) for that advice. For instance, arranging to set up three corporations before you buy your first property may not be a great strategy for the novice investor. It is, however, a great strategy for lawyers and accountants who make fees every year from these corporations—whether you own property or not.

6. If your "gut" tells you something isn't right, dig deeper before you are pushed into grey waters. In other words, always "look behind the curtain!"

First, always remember that the difference between a below-average investor and an over-achieving investor amounts to a mere 10% increase in effort. In other words: You don't need to cheat to win.

Second, as you get your system in place, keep these two general business rules front and centre:

I will only make commitments I have every intention of fulfilling.
I will never sign a document that isn't really true.

WHAT DO YOU NEED TO DO?

Learn to recognize fraud

You may, for example, encounter a mortgage broker who says you have to sign a document stating that you're going to move into the property you're purchasing as a primary residence, even though you plan to use it as investment property. They'll tell you that "other people are doing it," or "it's not illegal unless you get caught."

They'll tell you this is necessary to:

- secure a good interest rate or,
- secure good mortgage terms.

They are wrong. This is fraud and it's illegal.

An expert mortgage broker has the ear of the top players in the lending world and the expert can get you competitive terms and interest rates without ever asking you to sign a false document. If your mortgage broker or banker tells you differently, get a new mortgage broker who actually understands how it all works.

Take a step back

The arrangement described above, because it's not based on fact, borders on bank fraud. If the lender decides you have committed a fraud, the bank goes after you—not the broker. If the deal is worth enough, the police will also get involved. Good-bye free world after that!

It's wrong to think mortgage fraud only hurts the bank. Fraud can be used to manipulate housing prices in particular neighbourhoods. It can also give organized crime access to property that can be used to grow or manufacture street drugs.

Fraud can cost you your business

Major mortgage insurers such as Canada Mortgage and Housing Corporation (CMHC) and Genworth Financial Canada have substantially increased their investigations into homeowner loans. They're looking for people who say they're moving into a property as a primary residence and who obtained a loan on that basis, even though these borrowers really purchased the property as an investment.

The cost of getting caught runs high

In Edmonton, in 2004, 55 people were caught in just one small investigation. They're losing their property and their credit rating, and they're being sued for damages. In November 2005, four more were jailed for transactions like this and 2010 saw Canadian banks and police launch legal action against dozens of investors who appear to have signed mortgage documents that were not true. Known as "straw buyers," these people are alleged to have signed mortgage-application documents for a fee of several thousand dollars, even though they were not the ultimate buyers of the houses involved.

Be honest. Ask yourself, "Is this something I can tell my mortgage company about?" If the answer is no, don't do it.

Avoid dishonest people

Stay away from mortgage brokers who suggest dishonesty as a good policy. You don't need fraudsters on your team.

Avoid lawyers or accountants who seem to be creating overly complex structures and transactions if you are just starting out. Get a second legal or accounting opinion *before* you sign on.

There are professional and ethical brokers, lawyers and accountants out there who will work hard and find you the right deal—without ever thinking about putting you in harm's way.

🚩 RED FLAG

Once exposed, a fraudulent deal can trash the only reputation you have. If it's the same reputation you plan to use to access financing, build a team of professionals and attract joint venture partners, then you don't want to take the risk!

💡 KEY INSIGHT

Honesty is always the best policy. In fact, sophisticated investors will tell you it's the *only* policy. New investors, especially if they have a little nest egg ready to work with, may attract the interest of some less-than-honest businesspeople. Here, as in life in general, if a deal sounds too good to be true, it probably is.

🚩 RED FLAG

Never become a "straw buyer." One of the ways people are attracted to "fast money" in real estate is through the opportunity to be a "straw buyer." A straw buyer is someone who uses his name, credit history and signature to arrange for a mortgage on a property. The fraud artist then pays the down payment, assumes payments on the mortgage and pays the straw buyer a fee for his services. It sounds like a no-risk deal to the straw buyer, but it's fraud, pure and simple. Many of these cases end with the fraud artist not making payments on the property. The straw buyer then assumes the debt—and has to explain why he signed a false document. *Never ever* give up your name or credit for quick cash (unless you only want to see your friends during visiting hours!).

🚩 RED FLAG

Steer clear of anyone who tells you a "negative cash flow" property will save you money on taxes! Nicknamed "alligator," because they eat you alive, negative-cash-flow properties take money from you each and every month. They also take you farther and farther away from financial freedom. Still not convinced? Ask yourself this question: How many negative-cash-flow properties can you afford to own before you end up broke?

TIP #95: TITLE LAWS DIFFER REGIONALLY.

Keep your titles clean. Real estate laws differ from province to province. Author Barry McGuire of Edmonton and lawyer Mark Warkentin, a managing partner with Linley Welwood LLP in B.C., look at how that applies to caveats.

The legal implications of having a caveat registered against a property you own underscores the need for real estate investors to make sure they understand basic real estate legal terms relative to the province in which they're doing business.

In Alberta, for example, a *mortgage* gets registered on its own as a mortgage and a *caveat* is the device by which the land titles office registers certain documents alongside a mortgage. In B.C., caveats are used to correct errors. As such, they are used only rarely and only appear temporarily on a title.

In both provinces, an *assignment of rents* is a legal document that is sometimes registered alongside a mortgage. It assigns all rents and income from a property to the mortgagee. If the buyer stops making payments, the mortgagee may have the right to assume management of the property and collect rents to get their money.

In B.C., assignments or options are registered on title. In Alberta, an assignment of rents and an *option or a right of first refusal* are examples of how others with an interest in property held by someone else can register a caveat against a land title as a way to protect their interest in the property.

🄠 KEY INSIGHT

The legal issues relative to titles are different in Ontario. Lawyer Steve Cohen of Steve Cohen Law, Toronto, says the terminology in Ontario differs. Rather than caveats, Ontario has "cautions." Investors can refer to ss. 71 and 128 of the *Land titles Act* and *Bulletin 2000–2* from the Ontario Land Registry division which provides for "self-cleansing" on title in certain circumstances.

In Alberta, a caveat against a title matters because a caveat is a charge against a property. Let's say you are an investor who sells a property by way of an *agreement for sale*. That means the title stays in the name of the person selling, but the buyer registers a caveat against the title. That caveat essentially says, "I'm buying this property by way of an agreement for sale and I have a buyer's interest in the property."

This kind of caveat protects the buyer from the seller being able to sell the property out from under him or her.

Now, that's the easy part. The critical piece comes if a caveat against a title in Alberta is not acted upon. In this case, the "agreement for sale" buyer doesn't end up closing on the property. If that is the case, the vendor takes back the property and looks to sell it to someone else. And here's where the situation gets interesting. In provinces like B.C., other charges registered on title (mortgage, assignment of rents, agreement for sale, right to purchase, etc.) are discharged by the party who registers them. For example, the bank that registered the mortgage has to discharge it. This usually happens in due course, but it is still a good idea for an owner to pay attention to timely discharges, especially for charges registered in favour of private parties who are less sophisticated or knowledgeable about the need to discharge these items. In Alberta, however, the situation is different. There is no one forcing the caveator to discharge his caveat. *Unless the vendor remembers to get the old "agreement for sale" caveat discharged in that province, it will be listed on the title and could become a major legal problem in the future!*

Here's the process. Ask the caveator to remove his caveat. If they are slow or don't want to get a lawyer to do it for them, tell them they have a legal obligation and, if you have to take them to court, a judge will penalize them. Alternatively, consider getting your lawyer to prepare the discharge of caveat, then get it signed. It will cost you a little bit of money but your title will be clear.

🚩 RED FLAG

In Alberta, a caveat may be registered against your property by a prospective buyer. If that deal falls through, you must have the caveat discharged. Until that happens, no one will buy your property. As long as that caveat is there, it says you're not the only person with an interest in that property. Every time a caveat or even a lien is placed on your property's title, the lien or caveat will continue to stay on the title until you request that it be physically removed by a discharge document signed by the caveator (the person who placed the caveat). Keep your titles clean.

WHAT DO YOU NEED TO DO?

Always assume a caveat has been registered

If you are selling a property in Alberta by way of an agreement for sale and your buyer files a caveat, you have to understand that that is what buyers do. It protects them from you changing your mind. It also protects them from you using their offer as a way to sweeten the price pot and sell the property to someone else!

Clean up the title

If that buyer backs out of the deal in Alberta or fails to close, you need to let him or her move on—as soon as they formally sign a "discharge of the caveat." Make sure the discharge papers are handy. Make sure you register the discharge so you are ready to sell to someone else.

🕐 KEY INSIGHT

No one wants to see a sale go bad because the buyer can't get his financing together or backs out of a deal. But it does happen and you need to be ready when it does. In Alberta, discharging a prospective buyer's caveat is not a sign of defeat. It's a sophisticated investment move that ensures the property is caveat-free before the next buyer comes along.

NOTES:_____

_____

_____

_____

_____

_____

_____

_____

_____

_____

_____

_____

_____

TIP #96: FORECLOSURES EQUAL INVESTMENT OPPORTUNITY.

These deals can be a win-win for both sides.

The best thing about foreclosures and pre-foreclosures is that buyers can sometimes get properties at a good price and motivated sellers can get out from under their debt before it is too late. Investors will often find that pre-foreclosure situations provide some pretty unique opportunities to present creative offers, a fact of life that makes these deals a kind of Holy Grail for some investors. However, the information on foreclosures is much more difficult to find in Canada than in the United States.

A pre-foreclosure property has not yet gone through all the legal steps of a full foreclosure. This means vendors are extra motivated to get out from under a debt they can't afford and you can solve their problem and get yourself a good deal at the same time.

The good deals aside, investors interested in the foreclosure and pre-foreclosure market should educate themselves about how these deals work in the real world, since it's not like it's taught on late-night TV! There is not, for instance, a "foreclosures list" to check and it can be difficult to get solid information or conduct quality due diligence on a property that is in the foreclosures process. There are many legal implications that surround these deals in Canada, and they get even more complex if they are a part of a bankruptcy.

🏴 RED FLAG

Much of the hype and misconception around "great deals" on foreclosed properties comes from the United States, where rules and laws are substantially different from our Canadian laws. Be aware that most foreclosures in this country get sold at market price or only slightly below. It is not like you hit the lottery jackpot when you buy a Canadian foreclosure.

WHAT DO YOU NEED TO DO?

Understand the basics

Often in foreclosures you find vendors who are close to bankruptcy or in bankruptcy. If they are in bankruptcy, there will be a *bankruptcy trustee*. The trustee is in control of the bankrupt person's affairs. The bankruptcy trustee must be involved in any negotiations regarding the bankrupt's property. Their job is to protect creditors by getting as close to market value as possible.

Follow the process

In many provinces you are allowed to be in the court and to stand up and speak to the issue regarding your intent to buy a foreclosed property. Be clear and to the point when your time comes. Make sure you take good notes regarding the judge's instructions. These will be re-written by the bank's foreclosure lawyer and be sent to your lawyer. Good notes regarding the judge's specific instructions will be a major help if there's a discrepancy.

RED FLAG

If you don't believe the order accurately reflects what the judge said, you can order a court transcript and use it to argue for a new order. This is an expensive document and good notes can help avoid this step.

KEY INSIGHT

The bankruptcy trustee represents the creditors of the seller, usually parties other than the lender. The trustee is not there to protect the bankrupt seller. If you want to buy foreclosed properties, you will need to work with bankruptcy trustees. They want the deal to be done quickly and fairly. Prove to them that you're not there to steal the property; you're there to get a fair deal. This approach may lead them to call you first regarding future properties. If the property is not formally in the foreclosure process and you are doing anything other than a straight purchase from a homeowner in trouble (like a lease-back option to the homeowner), make sure the homeowner gets independent legal advice.

NOTES:_____

_____

_____

_____

_____

_____

TIP #97: CONDOMINIUM DEALS DEMAND SPECIAL SCRUTINY.

Condominiums are not all the same. Read the ABCs of the data you need to know.

CONDO TIP A: ALL CONDOMINIUMS ARE NOT THE SAME (OR, MY BIKE CAN'T GO THERE—AND MY PARKING SPACE HAS A TITLE?)

Condominium plans are complicated. So go slow—and get help.

The word "condominium" refers to a type of real estate ownership. In some provinces, these types of real estate ownership are called "strata titles" or "strata corporations." Regardless of the name or whether the property looks like a high-rise apartment-style building, a townhouse development, a side-by-side duplex or a single-family home, owners will have title to a specific unit, and shared interest in common areas.

You can even have condominiums that comprise a number of single-family homes all sharing title to the common-area lands that surround it. Never assume when you hear the word condominium that it refers to an apartment in a big building.

Because each condo is run by a different condominium association, the rules change from condo corporation to condo corporation, and from province to province. All owners will pay maintenance fees (assessments) to the condominium association, with those fees paying to maintain, repair or improve the common areas.

Before you buy a condo to place on the rental market, there are a lot of things you need to know. The most important is whether the provincial laws or condominium bylaws allow rentals in the building. If so, how many are allowed and how many are currently in the building? Many novice investors have regrettably purchased properties in buildings where the rental allotment was already filled, so they had to keep their property vacant or resell it. Some investors regrettably purchased condominium property where provincial laws or condominium bylaws permit the condominium to restrict rentals in the future. That could cripple an investor's business plan, meaning this is information you need to have before you buy!

You also need to know about special assessments required, contemplated or unpaid. These are upcoming major payments, over and above the monthly condo fees, that each owner must pay to the condominium corporation for maintenance of the common areas.

Other details of condo bylaws are just plain quirky. Tenants may not be able to park their bicycles on the balcony, a fact that could negatively impact a prospective tenant if the target tenant demographic for a funky high-rise includes tenants who want to bike a few blocks to work or school.

Others may restrict all home-based businesses. That could be a problem for a target tenant who may want to rent your townhouse and set up a home-based service like a daycare or hair salon.

Some condo bylaws even assign titles to parking spaces, a potential landmine when there may be twice as many unit titles as parking spaces! Others may require condo directors (instead of the management company) to sign legal documents on behalf of the condo corporation. Imagine how that complicates a closing date if even one director isn't available when the buyer or seller needs him to be!

 RED FLAG

You'll only know all these critical things if you have read the condominium bylaws and condominium board minutes. Successful condo investments depend on knowing exactly what the condo bylaws say you are responsible for and what you can and can't do as an owner.

WHAT DO YOU NEED TO DO?

Call in the experts

Sophisticated investors ask, "What's behind the curtain?" When it comes to condo purchases, that can mean looking behind several curtains (or the same curtain, several times!). Review financial statements, the condo reserve fund study, the condo reserve fund plan and the minutes of the most recent AGM, plus one year of board meeting minutes. Have your lawyer review legal documents, including the condo plan, to ascertain if there are any legal actions against the condominium corporation generally, or against the unit you are buying. Sophisticated investors will go a step further and have these documents vetted by a company that specializes in reviewing condo documentation.

Ask specifically about titled parking spaces. The only way to know for sure is to review a copy of the condominium plan. That plan will also detail what else owners have agreed to.

Get specific information

If someone acting for the corporation tells you there are no special assessments required, contemplated or unpaid and there is no deferred maintenance, get it in writing. (See Condo Tip B.)

Knock on doors

Knock on the doors of other owners and talk to them about the condominium. Get their perspective on how it works and whether residents are happy.

Always complete the full condo due diligence checklist

See the Appendix for a detailed condo due diligence checklist that every investor should complete before removing final offer conditions on a condominium purchase.

CONDO TIP B: STUDY THE CONDO'S DEFERRED RESERVE PLAN

You need to find out how the condominium association manages its owners' money.

Condominium owners hold title to their units and share ownership on some property in common. This has the potential to be good or bad, depending on how the condominium board is being run. When everything's working right, it's a pretty "worry free" approach to owning your own home. But condo owners, including investors who manage the units as rental properties or buy individual units for short- or long-term investment, need to ask some tough questions about what happens when things aren't working so well.

Condominium associations set up a **reserve fund** as part of their initial organization. Individual owners pay into the reserve, creating a pool of funds to be used for basic maintenance, repairs and upgrades. Later, after the initial set-up (two years), the condo board (using an Alberta example) must carry out a "deferred reserve study" (DRS) by a qualified person. The board must next prepare a "deferred reserve plan" (DRP), which is used to implement the findings of the study.

There can be a big difference between the DRS carried out by a "qualified" person (i.e., an engineer) and the DRP, which is implemented by the condo board. A DRS is often an extremely conservative bum-covering document which, if implemented, would raise fees excessively. Boards often cut back on the DRS in the DRP.

If maintenance gets behind, the condo association may levy a **special assessment** to deal with problems. If these assessments aren't paid, the work may still not get done! In the end, that's **deferred maintenance**—and deferred maintenance costs money.

What do you need to do?

Ask for the DRS and DRP

In most provinces, condominium corporations are required to have an outside company produce a financial study (often called the condo reserve fund study) that clearly outlines the current condition of the common areas, the predicted future replacement timeline of major common components and the costs for doing so over the coming years. This is in addition to the annual budget plan the condominium board sets out.

Match the documents

Now review the plan and study together. Is the condominium board doing what the study says it should be doing for maintenance and building a reserve fund? The condo board does not have to do everything the study suggests. But if they are not building an adequate reserve fund to cover obvious major future expenses as set out in the condo reserve fund study, then you can expect to receive a hefty bill in the future.

Cover thyself

If the deferred reserve study isn't complete (perhaps it's in the process), you need to talk to your lawyer about an addition to your contract. Include something like this: "Seller warrants there are no special assessments required, contemplated or unpaid." If you want to have the vendor clearly state their knowledge on the condominium's financial and structural situation, you can get them to sign a statutory declaration. See the Appendix for a sample you and your lawyer can use as a template.

Condo Tip C: take another look at that condo deal

Make sure your "great investment" doesn't lead to your great downfall.

Condominiums that haven't yet been built can look like pretty good investments. Before you sign the developer's contract, however, you better be darn sure you can assign your interest in the unit, or sell it to another investor, without the developer's permission.

You also want to be very clear that the builder has the money and talents to actually bring the building to completion. Too often, you will see investors' money disappear because the builder disappears. Make sure you do your due diligence on the builder.

 RED FLAG

Never ever pay future value for a property. In other words, in the case of a property not yet built, make sure you are paying what it would be worth on today's market, not what it is projected to be worth when it is completed. Be smart and don't let greed grab hold of you.

What do you need to do?

Read the contract

You have to go over the contract in detail. Remember, it was written by the builder's lawyers so you know who it is written to protect. Have *your* lawyer read through it carefully and explain any potential landmines she may uncover.

You must be sure of the price. You have to know if you can expect a GST/HST rebate (and you can, as long as you are the owner/occupier). The GST/HST rebate rule is not the same for investors as for owner-occupiers. (If you're buying more than one condo, it's going to be tough to convince the Canada Revenue Agency you're an owner-occupier!)

You have to know whether you can assign your interest in the unit or sell to someone else without permission. Never assume this is possible.

Involve your lawyer

Condominiums purchased as investment properties demand additional due diligence. Basic contract forms may be a good start, but you don't want to sign them until you've had legal advice, since you're apt to need changes. At the very least, you need to be sure you understand what you've agreed to do.

Assemble your buyers

If one condo looks good, 10 must be better. Right? Wrong. If you don't have your buyers lined up for re-sale when the deal's about to close, your financing could be at risk. And don't expect the developer to give you any extensions on the deal. He's busy building and selling. Besides that, he's got your deposit cheques, which he keeps if the deals don't close.

🛈 KEY INSIGHT

Fast money is a great motivator. It also tends to mask the real truth about fast-money deals. Namely, they are speculative and financially risky. Keep perspective at all times when investing. For instance, if you are buying a pre-built condominium hoping to sell it for a quick profit or rent it when the property is finished, make sure you remember you are not the only one with this plan. As the building gets close to completion, the dozens and dozens of investors who bought alongside you will also be planning to cash in. This means you will have a ton of competition to sell your property, or a ton of competition to rent it out. The basic rules of economics state that if there is a fixed demand and a high supply, prices must come down. Sophisticated real estate investors go into investments that are *not* speculative. They look for opportunities where others aren't lining up right beside them. A good deal is only good if it fits your long-term wealth system. Make sure you are being honest with yourself. Always ask, "Is the property I am looking at a speculation or a real-life investment?"

NOTES:_____

_____

_____

_____

_____

BONUS TIP #98: UNDERSTAND GST/HST ON NON-RESIDENTIAL REAL ESTATE.

Real estate accountants George Dube, CA, and Joseph Martins, CGA, of Dube & Associates (www.georgedube.com) discuss who must pay for the GST/HST on purchases and note a few other points to consider.

GST/HST is like tax law generally: complicated.

Canada's Goods and Services Tax (GST) and Harmonized Sales Tax (HST) are not generally payable on the purchase of real estate where the property is a used residential complex. Commercial (in our context "commercial" means non-residential) real estate is a different matter.

Commercial real estate is GST/HST payable and any rent collected in a commercial building also has a GST/HST component. You also need to know the following.

1. The purchaser often pays.

Where GST/HST is payable, it is the purchaser who generally must pay the GST/HST directly to the Receiver General. This is an exception to the general rule of having the vendor pay the GST/HST. There are critical conditions that determine whether the purchaser or vendor must pay/remit the taxes, and you will need to ensure you know who must pay. If GST/HST is not remitted to the Canada Revenue Agency (CRA), the CRA can pursue the seller or buyer, depending on the situation.

The *Excise Tax Act* provides that where the purchaser was to remit the tax, even if you have receipts that show you paid the GST/HST to the vendor, the purchaser can still be held responsible for paying the GST/HST. You would be surprised at how often this situation occurs and the purchaser ends up paying the GST/HST amount twice. The purchaser will typically use their normal GST/HST return to report the transaction. However, they may need to use form GST60 GST/HST Return for Acquisition of Real Property where, for example, you will use the property 50% or less in your commercial activities or you are a non-registrant.

🚩 RED FLAG

Never pay the GST/HST to the vendor and rely on the vendor to pay it to the CRA. Verify through Subsection 221(2) of the *Excise Tax Act* who must remit the tax.

2. **You need to check that GST/HST number if you are the vendor.**
   If GST/HST is payable but the purchaser is registered for GST/HST, the vendor can rely on what is now Subsection 221(2) of the Excise Tax Act and not collect GST/HST from the purchaser provided that all conditions have been met.

 RED FLAG

> Check the GST/HST number to make sure it's valid. Subsection 221(2) of the Excise Tax Act says the vendor does not have to charge and collect GST/HST if among other requirements the purchaser is registered for GST/HST. If, however, the vendor relies on a *misrepresentation* of information regarding proper registration, the vendor is responsible for its collection and payment!

What do you need to do?

Determine whether the purchaser or the vendor must remit the GST/HST

If as the vendor you are relying on the exemption to remit due to the buyer's GST/HST status, you can refer to the CRA's Web Registry (www.cra-arc. gc.ca/esrvc-srvce/tx/bsnss/gsthstrgstry/menu-eng.html).

Alternatively, you can call the CRA Business Window (1-800-959-5525) and provide the purchaser's name and GST/HST Registration Number to ensure that it is valid. The CRA official will confirm registration status over the phone. You can also ask for official, written confirmation of that status.

NOTES:_____

_____

_____

_____

_____

_____

_____

_____

_____

BONUS TIP #99: FIND OUT ABOUT THE GST/HST REBATE FOR INVESTORS.

George Dube, CA, and Joseph Martins, CGA, describe how investors may be eligible for GST/HST rebates plus transitional tax relief when purchasing new residential real estate.

Investors investing in a new residential building will be pleased to learn that they may qualify for a GST/HST rebate. While the details about the specific rates of savings depend on the province where the investment is located and the timing of the investment, this is another area where quality tax advice can save you money.

REBATES AND TRANSITIONAL SAVINGS

Qualifying investors may receive a full rebate of 36% of the GST paid where the price of the building or unit is less than $350,000. Alternatively, the GST rebate is phased out where the building or unit cost is between $350,000 and $450,000, leaving no claim after $450,000. Depending on the province, different rates and thresholds exist for the provincial component of the HST rebate. Further, transitional rebates may be available from the provinces where HST is being implemented, for example, most recently in British Columbia and Ontario.

Caution must be exercised when acquiring properties from builders to ascertain whether the price quoted considers that the builder will be assigned the purchaser's GST rebate as part of the payment. While it is quite typical for the rebate to be assigned, we have seen cases where the purchaser assigns the rebate to the builder and the builder "double dips" by additionally asking the purchaser to pay the GST rebate at the time of closing. Carefully go over your statement of adjustments to ensure you have received credit for the rebate where applicable.

We have seen statements where the adjustments are so confusing that by the time the pluses and minuses are done, the lawyer has ultimately managed to eliminate the GST rebate or even have the purchaser pay the rebate twice out of their own pocket. Hence, using an experienced real estate lawyer is a must.

To qualify for the rebate, some of the key requirements include the following:

- Investors must provide "long-term" residential accommodation, which is considered to be a period of at least a year and which may be under one lease or a series of leases. If the building has 10 or more units, the CRA will allow the entire building to qualify where at least 90% of the units will meet the one-year test.
- Non-residential components of a building (such as space for commercial stores or offices on the main floor of a mixed-use building) would be excluded from the calculation using a "reasonable" formula to allocate the GST/HST applicable to the different units of the building.
- Generally, the unit the investor buys must be a "self-contained residence" and have private kitchen facilities, a private bath and a private living area. It can also be a suite or room in a residence for the disabled or seniors, or in a hotel, motel, inn or boarding house.
- Going back to the one-year test, the first tenant is "reasonably expected" to occupy the unit as their primary residence for at least one year. To decrease the possibility of future disagreements with the CRA regarding this expectation, sophisticated investors will require a written lease that states a minimum one-year term, versus a month-to-month arrangement.
- Investors must also repay the rebate if they sell the unit during the first full calendar year after closing. That is not required if the purchaser acquires the unit as his primary place of residence, or that of a relation. This exception means the GST investor rebate actually has two separate one-year qualification rules. You can own the property for one year and rent it for one year.

Investors who want to claim the GST investor rebate must file a prescribed form, GST 524 GST/HST New Residential Rental Property Rebate Application, and possibly GST 525, Supplement to the New Residential Rental Property Application – Co-op and Multiple Units. You will also have to submit the purchase agreement, statement of adjustments and lease with the first tenant(s).

Generally speaking, investors have two years after the end of the month of closing to apply for the rebate. With the new electronic filing requirements for GST/HST for fiscal periods ending after June 30, 2010, the documentation is to be filed by the time you file your GST/HST return electronically. In filing the forms, reference to the CRA's guide RC4231 GST/HST New Residential Rental Property Rebate will be required. That guide also serves as an excellent summary of the rules and details the various provincial and transitional measures available to investors.

More information is available from the CRA website: www.cra-arc.gc.ca .

(George Dube is co-author of *81 Financial and Tax Tips for Canadian Real Estate Investors.*)

NOTES:_____

Bonus Tip #100: RRSP Mortgages Demand Extra Attention to Detail.

Another look at secondary financing, this time with an RRSP twist.

There are two things you need to know about registered retirement savings plan (RRSP) mortgages. First, if you lend money from an RRSP, the Canada Revenue Agency (CRA) says it can only be to an **arm's length party.** This means that *lending to direct relatives is not possible.* The mortgage must also be administered the way a third-party mortgage would be administered, including market interest rates and collection procedures.

Second, it has to be **commercially reasonable** to make it a qualified investment in your RRSP. Commercially reasonable means that if the RRSP mortgage loan is audited by the CRA, the CRA is going to look at all aspects of the mortgage loan to see that it fits within the market guidelines.

In other words, the CRA wants to be sure you haven't given a sweetheart deal to someone as a favour and you are keeping the collections up on the monthly payments.

What do you need to do?

Set it up right

The first thing the CRA auditors will look at is a certified appraisal of the property. That's how they will establish the value of the property and assess whether it is commercially reasonable. Make sure you have one on file.

Factor the loan-to-value (LTV) ratio

Lending rules don't allow a bank to lend more than 75% of the value of the property because those loans are deemed too risky. If you get above the 75% mark, and it is not insured by CMHC or another mortgage insurance provider, you will need to go to a secondary lender where the interest rate will be higher. If your RRSP mortgage sits in the 75% to 95% area, CRA will be satisfied with a higher interest rate. If the loan doesn't meet the "commercially reasonable" criteria, it won't pass a CRA audit.

Keep a paper trail

You need paperwork that justifies the loan. The more paperwork in your file when you put the RRSP loan together, the better. Make sure you have done all background checks as if you were the bank. Conduct credit checks, employment checks, etc. The CRA will look for proof that you followed these commercially acceptable steps. They will also look for a certified appraisal, some comparisons of interest rates and some comment on why the LTV is higher or lower than what is normally commercially given.

 RED FLAG

The higher the LTV, the more risk you have. Make sure you are very clear as to the risk level you are willing to take in your RRSP and that you are getting paid an appropriate amount of interest for the risk level. Before you lend out of your RRSP, make sure you know *all* the rules. This is a complex investment strategy and if done incorrectly it can lead to major tax implications. Some great information is available in the "RRSP in Real Estate" section at www.realestateinvestingincanada.com .

Be fastidious

Conventional lenders approve loans after a detailed application process. Apply the same level of scrutiny to your RRSP loans. Most importantly, always remember you are the lender. You are making the lending decisions—and you are financially responsible. Do not let emotions get in the way of making the right decision. Play the role of the banker and protect yourself with quality due diligence on the borrower and the property.

NOTES:_____

_____

_____

_____

_____

_____

_____

_____

_____

_____

_____

BONUS TIP #101: INVESTORS DRIVE RRSP MORTGAGES.

If you want access to RRSP mortgage financing, it is YOU who MUST drive the details.

With registered retirement savings plans (RRSPs) getting less-than-stellar returns, a growing number of investors are turning to investing in mortgages within their RRSP. This can give a sophisticated investor a consistent rate of return backed by a quality piece of real estate. In the right cases, the risks can be very low, the volatility next to zero and the return on investment substantial.

These RRSP mortgages don't just help the RRSP holder, they also help the real estate investor who can now access these mortgage funds to further their investments. These are serious and sophisticated investments, from both the RRSP holder and real estate investor's points of view.

The RRSP holder *must* complete at least as much due diligence as a bank would, making sure the lender and the property provide enough security for their RRSP. It is highly recommended the RRSP holder *never, ever* lend over 90% loan to value, even if it is someone you know and trust. Even at 90%, make sure you get the full market interest rate or are legally participating in the equity appreciation. In fact, you should do as much due diligence on the property as you would if you were going to buy it yourself. You need to know what you are getting yourself into.

If you are a real estate investor who is borrowing these funds, always remember you are not dealing with a bank that can afford a loss or missed payment. You are dealing with a family's retirement money and you must never miss a payment or fail to fulfil any other obligations under the contract. Pay full market interest rate, make all the payments on time and help these RRSP holders achieve their retirement goal. That should be your only focus.

Real estate investors need to recognize two things.

1. RRSP mortgages are complicated and you must get a second mortgage lawyer's advice to complete the package of forms required by the borrower and lender. One slip of the pen and the deal can trigger substantial tax consequences. Never let this process be run by someone without extensive experience; it is too financially dangerous.

2. If you, as the sophisticated investor, wish to be a borrower from a self-directed RRSP, you must become the driver of the process. That means it will take quite a bit of your personal time to get the deal done. You will be walking the deal from start to finish and your lawyer will be by your side, but you must stickhandle through all the red tape and communicate with the various parties involved.

WHAT DO YOU NEED TO DO?

Negotiate the loan

When an RRSP plan holder gets together with a borrower, they need to negotiate the formal terms of the loan. This agreement, which includes the dollar amount, interest rate, length of loan, payment structure, lawyer contact information and property address (legal and municipal), must also outline the current mortgaging in place. The agreement must be in writing and be signed by both parties.

The borrower (real estate investor) and lender (RRSP holder) then need to complete the package of forms required by the RRSP trustee. Make sure these are reviewed in detail by a legal expert familiar with the RRSP second mortgage process before they are submitted to the trustee.

 **KEY INSIGHT**

RRSP mortgages are not to be considered real estate investments. These are financial transactions that have a real estate security behind them. If you are using your RRSPs to invest this way, make sure you know all your exit options. Get the key questions answered:

1. How do I collect my money if the borrower stops making payments?
2. Can I sell my mortgage to another party if I require the cash?
3. What occurs upon the expiry of the term on the mortgage? Is there instant renewal or am I paid off?

See a lawyer

Have your lawyer prepare the mortgage and other documentation so as to match the signed agreement. The lender and borrower should have separate legal representation. This ensures each party is clear on what they are signing and the commitments they are making, and avoids the potential for a conflict of interest.

Instruct your lawyer

A lot of investors forget the simple act of instructing their lawyers about what they want them to do with a file. This is important in a basic real estate transaction as well as more complex transactions such as an RRSP mortgage. The RRSP lender needs to check that his lawyer is adept at RRSP mortgage transactions. If not, find someone who is. The RRSP lender's lawyer will then be instructed to act for the lender and prepare the mortgage document and any transfer documents required by the trustee.

As the sophisticated investor looking to borrow from the RRSP lender, it is important for you to understand all the steps this process will take and to be prepared for it with proper documentation. A good start would be for the borrower to instruct her lawyer (who should also be familiar with sophisticated real estate investment, including RRSP mortgages) to develop a template letter the RRSP lender can use to instruct his own lawyer. The letter should include specific instructions for the RRSP lender's lawyer. The RRSP lender fills it out and gives it to his lawyer along with the trustee package of forms and the signed mortgage agreement from step #1 above.

🛈 KEY INSIGHT

RRSP financing is quite a different process from a regular mortgage. There are many additional steps and much more explanation required. It is the full responsibility of the borrower to make sure all steps are followed by all parties and all documentation is completed to get the deal done in a timely manner. This process can lead to the borrower speaking directly to the lender's lawyer or their RRSP trustee. The RRSP lender, on the other hand, often sits back, silently relying on the borrower to handle the deal. The lender is simply looking for improved results in his RRSP.

🚩 RED FLAG

If you plan to borrow from an RRSP or lend money out of your RRSP, it is critically important that you understand all the intricate details and legal ramifications of the process. To learn more about how it works and the opportunities it holds for both parties, visit www.realestateinvestingincanada.com and click on the RRSP Strategies link. This is a complete program written by Canada's own "Mr. RRSP," Valden Palm.

BONUS TIP #102: JOINT VENTURES: GET IT IN WRITING.

Make sure your joint venture is worth more than the paper it's written on.

Joint ventures (JV) are a great way to share the financial risk of an investment. These are formal relationships where two or more parties decide to work together on a specific real estate project pooling money and expertise. This can be a venture that combines companies, people or other joint ventures. These relationships must be taken seriously and the legal documentation must be in order. Although complex in nature, joint ventures can be the quickest and least risky way to enter into real estate deals.

But things can (and will!) go wrong if every aspect of the JV isn't treated as a formal business relationship. Indeed, the fastest way to derail a JV is to make the error of confusing friendship and business partnerships.

In brief: Friendship evolves with time. Joint-venture relationships evolve according to the details of a written document. Joint ventures are serious business and emotions can't get in the way of solid business decisions. In fact, getting into a joint-venture relationship with a close friend can prove disastrous to the friendship if the legal documentation is not clear on rules and responsibilities.

Partners can, for example, opt against the "hassle" of financial reports that are properly prepared and routinely filed, because they trust each other. However, what do you do when your lender wants documentation of your investment success? And what if there is a financial dispute on the operations of the property? Where will the hard and fast numbers be?

A second problem is often lethal if the relationship is not formalized in writing. This occurs when partners modify their business plan or agreement on a handshake, with the changes to the initial JV agreement never formally made in writing. That's great until someone "can't remember" the amendment—which will occur more often than not.

Still not convinced *your* JV needs to be this formal? Then ask yourself the tough questions.

What happens if your JV partner moves, needs cash, gets divorced, dies—or simply changes his mind? If you don't have these contingencies in writing, you can find yourself in a very difficult situation—emotionally and financially.

What will you do when the estate of a deceased JV partner decides it doesn't like the way the business operates and is not prepared to support your management decisions? This could leave you in a joint venture with a hostile party that can bring your business creation crashing down around you—all because you didn't get these contingencies in writing at the beginning.

⑤ SOPHISTICATED INVESTOR TIP

No matter how large or small the relationship, and no matter how well you know the person, it is paramount that you make your agreement in writing, signed by both parties. Always design the "divorce" in advance, as it is much easier to agree to those critical steps early in the relationship—before there is conflict.

❶ KEY INSIGHT

A joint venture is only as good as the parties involved. The parties must bring different strengths to the relationship in order for it to be successful over the long term. A typical successful joint venture would include a real estate expert and a silent financial partner. A classic mistake of novice investors is to enter into a joint venture with someone who is in the same position (knowledge or financial) as they are. For instance: Two beginning investors with no cash get together to try to buy a piece of property—a big mistake. This is a relationship that is doomed to struggle. Only enter into relationships that become stronger when the parties are combined as a team.

WHAT DO YOU NEED TO DO?

Keep your JV firmly on track

Write a formal joint-venture agreement and operate the JV according to that document. Make sure the contract stipulates proper financial reporting be made to each party. If the JV needs to be modified, negotiate any changes and amend the formal agreement in writing.

❶ KEY INSIGHT

Joint-venture relationships are an amazing way to build your property portfolio by pooling money and expertise to buy more properties. Novice investors can use JVs to learn how the investment business works if they complete a joint venture with a veteran and trusted investor. Think of it as a win-win mentoring relationship, whereby you exchange investment cash for financial gain and knowledge.

⚑ RED FLAG

Novice investors should know that there are veteran sharks in the waters and they're looking for rookies to take advantage of. Make sure you have done complete due diligence on the potential partner, including criminal background checks, securities violations and past projects. Don't just jump in because they have a high profile and you think you like them. Dig deep and dig hard. Many of these sharks have mastered the "trust me" sales pitch. Be careful if they aren't being very open about past dealings or they don't want you to use your own lawyer for independent advice. There are even "seminar leaders" or "experts" who set up business to take advantage of rookie investors. These people are motivated by self-interest and may direct vulnerable clients into dangerous deals that are slanted to favour the seminar leader. The deals they offer may even sell property to seminar clients without disclosing key financial components of the deal. These relationships are especially dangerous and require an extra level of due diligence on the novice investor's part. Make sure the deal is fair for both parties, that the joint-venture relationship is clearly laid out in writing and that you have an independent lawyer review the agreement. Don't let blind trust and enthusiasm replace the all-important due diligence.

NOTES:_____
_____
_____
_____
_____
_____
_____
_____
_____
_____
_____
_____
_____
_____
_____
_____
_____

BONUS TIP #103: GET THE REAL GOODS ON CAPITAL GAINS.

Property rollovers are more than a new trick for an old dog!

Many real estate investors get into the business hoping that profits made on their investments will qualify as capital gains, meaning they will be taxed in a much more favourable manner. This is quite true in many cases, especially for those who are holding properties to build long-term wealth. However, there are many cases where capital gains tax deductions are not applicable. These cases can cost you thousands of dollars on each transaction.

 RED FLAG

Not all real estate transactions are treated as capital gains. Many novice investors miss the key rules around capital gains tax and end up paying full business or personal income tax on their real estate transactions. It is *critical* that you have a quality real estate-specific tax accountant on your team. For instance, if you buy a property and do few or no renovations, hold it for a short period of time (less than two years) and sell it into the market at a higher price, Canada Revenue Agency (CRA) may deem those profits as business or personal income rather than a capital gain. Suddenly, your tax bill skyrockets and your profits disappear.

Get full accounting advice but remember a typical calculation for capital gains says you are taxed on only 50% of the gain. Business or personal income means you are taxed on the full amount! It's a huge difference, so know your rules.

Some people also blindly use the strategy of buying a property in their personal name and then transferring it to a corporation they own a short time later. It sounds like a simple strategy, yet this transaction can trigger personal income tax issues if not done correctly.

Things get a little trickier when you try to use a capital gains tax-saving strategy that involves rolling a property over into a spouse's name. Similar complications can arise when you transfer a property title after a significant amount of time has passed since the initial purchase. (There may even be some issues about who owns the property to start with!)

Section 73.1 of the *Income Tax Act* is one of the sections most commonly applied to real estate investment. It allows the "rollover" of property to a spouse at no capital gain.

That's the good news. On the flip side of the ledger, capital property transferred between spouses, even if a rollover under Section 73.1 applies, could still be subject to the rules in *other* sections of the *Income Tax Act*.

Say we have a husband who wants to roll a property over to his wife. Sections 74.1 and 74.2, for example, require that both the capital gain and the rent earned after transfer be "attributed" to the transferor (in this case, the husband). Under these provisions, the transferor will have to calculate the capital gain and the rent earned after the transfer into his own income. (These "attribution rules" are discussed in more detail in Canada Revenue Agency's *Interpretation Bulletin IPT-511*.)

The attribution rules do not apply if fair market value is paid by the wife and the husband elects to not have Section 73.1 pertaining to the rollover apply. Other rules may apply if you're transferring property to a corporation, especially if the property's rolling over at a different value than when you bought it.

Clear as mud? That's why sophisticated investors make tax decisions on the advice of their tax professionals. Before you sell or transfer any properties whatsoever, make sure you have the opinion of tax professionals who completely understand real estate transactions. Many believe they do, but only a select few have the experience and knowledge of the intricate details.

WHAT DO YOU NEED TO DO?

Get professional tax-planning advice

The *Income Tax Act* is a whopping 1,500 pages long and its application is complicated.

There are many ways to operate your real estate business in a tax-friendly rather than a tax-heavy environment. That's why there are large law firms and large chartered accountant firms where everybody is a tax expert. Find a tax expert who has extensive investment real estate experience.

Meet regularly with your expert team

Work with your professional to deem what your best strategies are based on what you want to achieve. Each year, sit down and sign your annual returns—and plan the coming year as far as acquisitions and sales go.

Be proactive

Look for tax-advantaged ways in which to operate. It is much easier to make the adjustments up front rather than after the transaction takes place. Sadly, many investors wait until they see their tax bill before they decide to make changes. These retroactive changes, although possible in some cases, come with major costs that could have been avoided if a plan had been in place.

RED FLAG

It's tough to undo a business transaction that impacts your tax bill. Make tax planning part of your investment business—or pay the state piper!

SOPHISTICATED INVESTOR ACTION STEP

Don't allow yourself to get caught up in the way the masses think about paying taxes! Paying a lot of tax is a good thing: It means you are making a lot of money. *The key is to have strategies in place where you are paying the least amount of tax legally allowed.* Remember, never swim in the grey waters and always have a good plan to deal with your purchases, your operations and your sales. If you do this, you can simply smile when you write your tax cheque—because you'll know without question that you have created additional long-term wealth for you and your family and haven't wasted money on needless expenses and taxes.

NOTES:_____
_____
_____
_____
_____
_____
_____
_____
_____
_____
_____
_____
_____

BONUS TIP #104: REGISTER YOUR BOOK.

Be sure to register your book at www.realestateinvestingincanada.com to receive valuable updates and information from the real estate investing experts at the Real Estate Investment Network, including a free CD covering the latest market changes.

NOTES:_____

BONUS TIP #105: KNOW THAT YOU'RE HELPING BUILD HOMES FOR FAMILIES.

Part of the royalties to the authors will be donated to Habitat for Humanity, a cause supported at large by the members of the Real Estate Investing Network.

NOTES:_____

APPENDIX

- Property Goldmine Score Card
- All Properties Due Diligence Checklist
- Condominium Purchase Due Diligence Checklist
- Statutory Declaration
- REIN Property Analyzer Form
- Support Tools and Key Contacts

REAL ESTATE
INVESTMENT
NETWORK™

#1018, 105 – 150 Crowfoot Cres. NW, Calgary, Alberta T3G 3T2
phone (403) 208-2722 fax (403) 241-6685 www.reincanada.com

PROPERTY GOLDMINE SCORE CARD

Property Address: _____

Town: _____ Prov: _____

Source: _____ Tel: _____

Property Specific Questions

❑ Can you **change the use** of the property?

❑ Can you buy it <u>substantially</u> **below retail market value?**

❑ Can you <u>substantially</u> **increase the current rents?**

❑ Can you do small **renovations** to <u>substantially</u> increase the value?

Area's Economic Influences

❑ Is there an **overall increase in demand** in the area?

❑ Are there currently **sales over list price** in the area?

❑ Is there a noted **increase in labour and materials cost** in the area?

❑ Is there a lot of **speculative investment** in the area?

❑ Is it **an area in transition**—moving upwards in quality?

❑ Is there a major **transportation improvement** occurring nearby?

❑ Is it in an area that is going to benefit from the **Ripple Effect?**

❑ Is the property's area in **"Real Estate Spring or Summer?"**

❑ Has the **political leadership** created a "growth atmosphere?"

❑ Is the area's **average income increasing** faster than the provincial average?

❑ Is it an area that is attractive to **baby boomers?**

❑ Is the area **growing faster** than the provincial average?

❑ Are **interest rates** at historic lows and/or moving downward?

_____ = Total √s

Does This Property Fit Your System?   ❑ yes ❑ no

Does It Take You Closer to Your Goal?   ❑ yes ❑ no

© 2004 www.reincanada.com

ALL PROPERTIES
DUE DILIGENCE CHECKLIST

Due diligence is critical for ANY property you are considering investing in. Whether you are a silent partner or the actual person finding and investigating a property, you must do your own independent due diligence. This checklist will provide you a foundation from which to work, and will assist you in asking the critical questions. Remember, it does all come down to the accuracy of numbers. DO NOT SKIP ANY STEPS! (If you are purchasing a condo, use this form PLUS the Condo Due Diligence Checklist together.)

Location:

❑ How many checkmarks does the area get using the **Property Goldmine Score Card**? *(6 checks or more is best)*

❑ What is the nature of the local economy?
Diverse _____ or Single Industry _____

❑ In what area of town is the property located?
Older _____ Newer _____ Transitional _____

❑ What is the type and quality of the surrounding properties?
Type: _____
Quality vs. Rest of Neighbourhood: _____

❑ What amenities and services are nearby?
Transit _____ Shopping _____ Schools _____
University/College _____ Major Employer _____

Building:

❑ What is the overall curb appeal? (scale 1 to 10) _____

❑ What is the overall interior appeal? (scale 1 to 10) _____

❑ How well has the property been maintained? (scale 1 to 10) _____

❑ Are there any deferred maintenance repairs required in the next 12 months? YES / NO
If YES, list them: _____
If YES, estimate cost of repairs: $ _____

❑ Are there any appliances you need to purchase? YES / NO

❑ Has a complete professional inspection been completed? YES / NO
If NO, when are you scheduling it for? _____

❑ Is a Real Estate Property Report (site survey certificate) available from the vendor?   YES / NO

    If YES, is it acceptable to your lawyer for closing?   YES / NO

Financial:

❑ Have you completed a **Property Analyzer Form?**   YES / NO
(You must complete the form for EVERY property before you make your offer.)

❑ Do the results of the **Property Analyzer Form** fit your investment system?   YES / NO

❑ If currently a rental—are financial statements available for the property?   YES / NO
    (If NO, look for a different property)
    What is the expense-to-income ratio?
    (35–45% is workable)   _____
    Are the numbers believable?
    Do they fit market norms?   YES / NO

❑ What is the current rent on the property?
    (If not currently rented, what should it rent for according to your analysis of the market?) $ _____

❑ What are rents for similar properties in the area? $ _____

❑ What is the vacancy-rate history of the property?   _____%
    When vacant, does it seem difficult to re-rent?   YES / NO
    What is the vacancy-rate history for the area?   _____%
    How does that compare with the property's history?   _____%

Additional Critical Due Diligence:

Check the following items to ensure you're not buying unknown trouble:

❑ Confirm taxes and other charges are current (city hall).

❑ Confirm no outstanding work orders or compliance orders (city hall, health department).

❑ Open or past complaints registered to the address. Known as a problem property (police).

❑ Who will be managing the property? _____
    If YOU—is there a reliable company when you get tired of managing?   YES / NO

❑ What banker/broker has a program to assist you with the financing on this property? —————————————————

❑ What is the vendor's REAL motivation level? (0 = none, 10 = extremely) —————————————————

❑ Do you plan on keeping the current tenant— do they fit YOUR tenant profile? YES / NO

❑ Do you need vacant possession to make it fit your system? YES / NO

CONDOMINIUM PURCHASE
DUE DILIGENCE CHECKLIST

In addition to completing your Property Analysis Form, when purchasing a condo or group of condos you need to take a very close look at the following:

1. Building:

❏ How many units in the building? (*25+ is best*) _____
❏ What is the ratio of owner-occupied to rentals? _____
   (*looking for potential "anti-renter" situation*)
❏ What is the age of the building?
   (*age is important for financing; condition of buildings; maintenance is important for costs*)
❏ Are there any deferred maintenance issues pending? _____
   (*see Condo Reserve Fund Study & last 24 months of condo board minutes*)
   If YES, review and estimate total cost of:
   (*remember that each unit will be responsible for its portion of these costs*)
   A. Roof replacement or repair $_____
   B. Mechanical
      (*does it need engineer inspection report?*) $_____
   C. Interior or exterior refurbishment $_____
   D. Post-tension deterioration $_____
   E. Parking lot resurfacing $_____
   F. Intercom system repair/replace $_____
   G. Other $_____
❏ Is the parking area of adequate size?
   (*important to your tenants and your exit strategy*)   YES / NO
   A. What is the ratio of stalls to suites?   _____ / _____
   (*a minimum of 1 stall per unit is advised*)
   B. Can you rent additional stalls?   YES / NO
   C. Is there adequate on-site visitor parking?   YES / NO
❏ What is the typical rent for the property? $_____
❏ Does the opportunity to increase the rent exist?   YES / NO
   If YES by how much? $_____
❏ What is the building's previous year's vacancy rate?   _____%
   How does that compare to area average?   _____%

❑ What is the typical renter profile in building?
(e.g., age 25–40, M/F) _____
❑ Does this fit your desired renter profile?   YES / NO

2. Legal:

❑ Is there pending litigation against the condominium
corporation?   YES / NO
(the Condo Board must reveal this to you—also check board minutes)
❑ Is there a recent Phase 1 Environmental Study available?   YES / NO
❑ Is the property approved for CMHC financing?   YES / NO

3. Condominium Corporation:

❑ Talk with representatives of the condo board to get a feel for
the atmosphere.
❑ Review two years of condo board meeting minutes for potential
problems.
❑ Review the annual condo budget.
A. Compare last year's budget for accuracy with actual operating
costs.
B. Review the upcoming year's budget to see if appropriate
adjustments have been made.
❑ Review the condominium's bylaws.
A. Do they hold any penalties towards renter units?
(e.g., renter restrictions, large damage deposit to condo corp.)
B. Define whether there is an easy grievance arbitration procedure.
❑ What are the monthly condo fees
and what do they include? $_____
A. If they seem high, do they include heat and/or power?   YES / NO
B. If they seem low, is there an adequate amount allocated to the
reserve fund for future repairs, or will a condo fee increase be
needed?   YES / NO
❑ Read the rental management contract *(and rental pool agreement if
in place)*.
A. Are the contracts coming due for negotiations?   YES / NO
B. Are management costs slated to increase in the near future?   YES / NO
C. Speak with management company representative
AND on-site manager to get a feel for their thoughts on
the building.

- ❏ Is there a rental pool in place?
  - A. What is the unit factor for distribution of pooled rents? _____
  - B. Who manages the pool? What is their fee? _____%
  - C. Read the guidelines—can you participate? YES / NO
- ❏ Is the building insurance policy adequate? YES / NO
- ❏ Review the condominium's financial statements for an adequate reserve fund vs. upcoming required repairs.
- ❏ Are there any pending or current cash calls to be paid by the owners? YES / NO
- ❏ Ensure you complete a **Property Analyzer Form** with accurate market numbers.

STATUTORY DECLARATION

CANADA

PROVINCE OF____

IN THE MATTER OF TITLE TO:

Legal Description: _____

_____

_____

AND THE SALE THEREOF FROM:

Vendor: _____

Vendor: _____

TO:

Purchaser: _____

Purchaser: _____

TO WIT:

WE / I _____

of the City of _____, in the Province of _____,

DO SOLEMNLY DECLARE THAT:

1. To the best of my/our knowledge, information and belief there are no special assessments contemplated by the Condominium Corporation, that voting rights have been assigned and that there are no legal actions pending or contemplated by or against the Condominium Corporation.

2. I/we have not received a notice convening a special or general meeting of the unit owners of the Condominium Corporation respecting any of the following matters:

   (a) the termination of the government of the condominium property;

   (b) any substantial alteration in or substantial addition to the common elements or the renovation thereof; OR

   (c) any substantial change in the assets or liabilities of the Condominium Corporation.

3. I/we have not received any notice or communication whatsoever from the Condominium Corporation or its agents requiring me/us to carry out any repairs to or restoration of the subject unit and/or the common elements, including that portion of the common elements designated in the declaration as being for the exclusive use of the vendor of the subject unit.

4. I/we have not made application to the Condominium Corporation for its approval of any structural change, additions, improvement to or renovation of the unit in accordance with the registered declaration and bylaws of the Corporation; nor have I/we or any other owner or owners collectively, to the best of my/our knowledge, information and belief, made application to the Condominium Corporation for the approval of any alteration, addition, improvement to the common elements whether substantial or not, and in this regard I/we have not received a notice or other communication of any meeting of the membership held or to be held by the Condominium Corporation for the purpose of considering any alteration, addition, improvement to or renovation of the common elements. Similarly, I/we are not aware of any change or proposed change in the assets of the Condominium Corporation as reflected in its most recent and audited financial statements, save as follows:

_____

_____

_____

_____

_____

_____

_____

_____

_____

_____

_____

_____

_____

_____

_____

_____

5. Neither I/we nor to the best of my/our knowledge, information and belief, my/our predecessors on title have made any unauthorized change, addition, improvement to or renovation of the unit or the common elements contrary to the registered declaration and bylaws of the Condominium Corporation.

6. There have been no claims or demands whatsoever during my/our period of ownership by the Condominium Corporation or in any way related to my/our ownership and occupation of the subject unit and the common elements.

AND I/WE MAKE THIS DECLARATION CONSCIENTIOUSLY BELIEVING IT TO BE TRUE, AND KNOWING THAT IT IS OF THE SAME FORCE AND EFFECT AS IF MADE UNDER OATH.

SEVERALLY SWORN before
me at the City of _____
in the Province of _____

this _____ day of _____ Vendor: _____
20____

Vendor: _____

A COMMISSIONER ETC.

REIN™ PROPERTY ANALYZER

Property Data:

Address: _____   City/Area: _____   Date Viewed: _____

Asking Price: _____   Size (sq. ft.): _____   Age: _____

Major Repairs: _____   Est. Repair Cost $ _____

Owner: _____   Tel: _____   Fax: _____

Source: _____   Tel: _____   Fax: _____

Overall Condition: 1   2   3   4   5

Income & Inspection:

Suite # or Desc.	# of Bedrooms	Current Rent	Projected Rent	Increase Date	Inspection Comments

Total Monthly Rent $ _____ $ _____

Total Annual Rent $ _____ $ _____

Expenses:

	Current Annual	Current Monthly	Projected Monthly	Comments
Heat (gas, oil, electricity, hot water, other _____)				Paid by Tenant/Landlord
Electricity				Paid By Tenant/Landlord
Water/Sewer				Paid by Tenant/Landlord/Condo
Taxes				Included in Mortgage Payment?
Condo Fee				Last Increase Date:
Insurance				(for analysis only—actual cost factored in on page 2)
Property Management	%			Current Management Rating 1 2 3 4 5
Vacancy Allowance	%			Current Vacancy _____ %
Rental Pool Mgmt.	%			
Repairs & Maintenance	%			Overall Condition 1 2 3 4 5
Resident Manager				Current On-site Impression 1 2 3 4 5
Other:				

TOTAL MONTHLY $ _____ $ _____

TOTAL MONTHLY INCOME less TOTAL MONTHLY EXPENSES (Before Debt Service) =

Current: $ _____   Projected: $ _____

TOTAL PROJECTED INCOME $_____

(from bottom of page 1)

Mortgaging/Debt Service:

	Balance	Interest Rate	Expiry Date	Monthly Payment
1st Mortgage		%		P I T
2nd Mortgage		%		P I T
Vendor Take-Back		%		P I T
Other		%		P I T

TOTAL DEBT SERVICE $_____

NET CASH FLOW $_____

Purchase Details:

PROJECTED PURCHASE PRICE $_____

1st Mortgage Funding ($_____)
2nd Mortgage Funding ($_____)
Vendor Take-Back ($_____)
Other Funding ($_____)

TOTAL DEBT FUNDING ($_____)
DOWN PAYMENT REQUIRED $_____)

Purchase Costs:

Professional Inspection $_____
Value Appraisal $_____
Real Property Report (Survey) $_____
Mortgage Broker Fees $_____
Legal Costs (incl. disbursements) $_____
Staying Power (Reserve) Fund $_____
Immediate Repairs & Supplies $_____
Immediate Renovations $_____
Land Transfer Taxes $_____
Title Insurance $_____
Property Insurance $_____
Other _____ $_____

TOTAL PURCHASE COSTS $_____

TOTAL CASH REQUIRED TO CLOSE (Down payment + Purchase Costs) $_____

1. Does this property take me closer to my goal or farther away? ❑ Closer ❑ Farther
2. Does this property fit my system? ❑ Yes ❑ No
3. At what price would i have to buy the property for it to cash flow? $_____
4. Will this property be impeccably property managed? ❑ Yes ❑ No
5. Who will manage the property? _____

SUPPORT TOOLS AND KEY CONTACTS

Real estate is a team game and the strength of your team will help determine how quickly you achieve success. In addition, keeping on top of key economic trends as well as changes to laws that affect real estate investors is absolutely critical.

With this in mind, here are some additional support tools, websites and education materials that can greatly assist you.

Landlord and tenant government websites

The following is a list of government websites that outline landlord and tenant laws. Many of them provide shortened versions of their acts in plain English. It is important for you to review information for your areas.

British Columbia www.rto.gov.bc.ca

Alberta www.landlordandtenant.org

Saskatchewan www.justice.gov.sk.ca/Landlord-and-Tenant-Act

Manitoba www.gov.mb.ca/fs/cca/rtb/index.html

Ontario www.ltb.gov.on.ca/en/index.htm

Quebec www.rdl.gouv.qc.ca

New Brunswick www.snb.ca/irent

Nova Scotia www.gov.ns.ca/snsmr/access/land/residential-tenancies/default.asp

Prince Edward Island www.gov.pe.ca/law/statutes/pdf/l-04.pdf

Newfoundland and Labrador www.gs.gov.nl.ca/faq/landlord_faq.html

Northwest Territories www.justice.gov.nt.ca/RentalOffice/index.shtml

Yukon www.community.gov.yk.ca/consumer/landtact.html

Nunavut www.gov.nu.ca/

REAL ESTATE INVESTMENT NETWORK—REIN™

The Real Estate Investment Network™ (REIN™) is a group, led by best-selling author Don R. Campbell, dedicated to providing real estate investors with unbiased research and strategies for the Canadian marketplace. Members of REIN meet monthly in select cities across the country. Some of its members live outside Canada. Now entering its 18th year of operation, REIN has assisted members in riding the upward swings in the market while avoiding the downturns. Members have safely and securely purchased over $3.3 billion of residential real estate. REIN's members focus on long-term wealth as opposed to get-rich-quick schemes. Their success comes from focusing on real-life economic fundamentals and putting the ACRE system into action. This system takes the hype out of the marketplace so you can focus on what works right in your backyard.

REIN is an exclusive paid-membership program of more than 3,000 members across the country, which is dedicated to educating its members about how, where and when to buy Canadian real estate. From networking with other active investors to providing direct access to leading-edge experts, it is the most complete program of its kind anywhere in North America. You will never have to buy from, invest with or put money into any real estate deal with anyone in, or associated with, REIN. In a nutshell, REIN offers a program dedicated to showing Canadians how to create long-term sustainable wealth.

REIN's single objective is to help you become an experienced, confident and wealthy real estate investor. There are no huge upfront fees; REIN believes that money is best spent investing in real estate—not on seminars.

To receive a FREE CD and report on the benefits of being a member of Canada's most successful real estate investment program, with over $3.3 billion purchased and 18 years of market experience, call 1-888-824-7346 today or e-mail your mailing address and telephone number to Don R. Campbell's office at info@reincanada.com or visit www.realestateinvestingincanada.com and click on the REIN button. We look forward to helping you achieve your own "Personal Belize."

ABOUT THE AUTHORS

Don R. Campbell is the author of the Canadian bestseller *Real Estate Investing in Canada*, a book that all real estate investors should have as an action tool and reference. Don is president of the Real Estate Investment Network (REIN), whose membership exceeds 3,000 successful Canadian investors and whose investment in Canadian residential real estate tops $3.3 billion.

In his real estate seminars, Don shares his years of hands-on experience as he teaches strategies in live workshops across the country (www.reincanada.com) that he has personally tested in the real world. He has helped investors achieve their dreams and he and REIN members have raised more than $630,000 for charities such as Habitat for Humanity. To tap into Don's experience and learn more about his workshops, visit www.donrcampbell.com .

Peter Kinch is the founder of the Peter Kinch Mortgage Team and the PK-Approved Dominion Lending Centres network of brokers across Canada. Those brokers are trained to deal with investors. In 2009, he was recognized as the #1-volume-producing mortgage broker in Canada by CMP magazine. Peter's mortgage career has focused almost exclusively on real estate investors. He provides mortgage education on financing and real estate portfolio development through educational seminars, workshops and presentations. He's channeled that niche market expertise into work as a lobbyist for the investor community with many chartered banks and trust companies.

Peter is a regularly featured mortgage guest on various radio and television programs across the country. An accomplished author, his works include *The Mortgage Minute*™ Vblog and *The Canadian Real Estate Action Plan*. The *Plan* walks investors through the process of creating a business-plan approach to buying real estate.

For more information, please visit www.peterkinch.com .

Barry McGuire had his first opportunity to invest in real estate while still at law school. He had a friend who seemed to be buying every house near the University of Alberta, renting it out and building a real estate empire. Barry was a student and needed a place to stay while going to law school, so he used his student loan for the down payment on his own property and quickly found five other students who also needed a place to stay. The positive cash flow was tremendous and replaced the missing student loan. Better yet, three years later, the property had tripled in value!

This early lesson was not forgotten, and Barry continues to enjoy a diversified real estate-investment portfolio. Thirty-five years later, Barry's legal practice is focused exclusively on real estate.

In his daily legal practice at Ritchie Mill Law Office in Edmonton, Alberta, Barry loves to assist clients with the planning and consulting issues that help ensure successful real estate purchases. He believes that a sound education in real estate fundamentals is one of the best tools in any real estate investor's toolbox.

Over the years, Barry has had extensive involvement with the Alberta Real Estate Association in preparing and teaching credit courses for real estate agents. He has also taught these courses for the Real Estate Training Institute, an independent trainer of real estate professionals. His Focus Workshops train investors to jump-start their real estate careers, understand joint ventures and write creative real estate deals. Check Barry's website, www.barrymcguire.ca, and e-mail him at info@barrymcguire.ca.

Russell Westcott is a veteran real estate investor, researcher and educator and is the Joint Venture expert of the Real Estate Investment Network, Canada's leading real estate education program. An accomplished, passionate and entertaining presenter and expert on many trends in real estate, Russell is recognized for his creative buying strategies, which range from forming joint-venture partnerships to turning one property purchase into three or four through leverage financing. He has consistently continued to build his portfolio ever since he started to invest, and he shares his expertise with REIN members at workshops across Canada.

Russell lives his life around four principles: 1) health, happiness and enjoyment of life, 2) family and relationships, 3) contribution and growth and 4) abundance and gratitude. He lives by his credo: "You can have anything in your life if you provide massive value that significantly improves people's lives."

INDEX OF TIPS

Habitat for Humanity®